Salute the
EAGLE

Published in 2017 by Footprints Press

website: www.hiltonbarber.co.za

Cover design and page layout by Anthony Cuerden
Email: ant@flyingant.co.za

Printed by Pinetown Printers (Pty) Ltd; Pinetown, KwaZulu-Natal

ISBN 978-0-620-73483-7

Warning - This book contains some graphic imagery and language that some might find offensive.

Salute the
EAGLE

One year of my life in
the Angolan bush war

Kevin Vos

Foreword

To all of the men who I was privileged to have fought alongside and to have led into battle: I had over the years since we had gone our separate ways always wondered what it would be like to see you all again, how would we have changed and what would we be like.

I have read countless non-fiction books on war and the relationships that the men have built up in the times of war and I had an inkling of what they were writing about. But as I grew older and as the opportunity presented itself to make connections with some of you over the years, I slowly started seeing and feeling a bond of ... something.

I remember bumping into Andy Prew at PMB University and having a pie at the Union with him. My boet was with me and Andy Prew said, 'Mark, you saved our lives when you brought us back through that minefield.' I noticed my boet look at me and just nod. Seeing Deon on another occasion in PMB and seeing how easy it was to just trust, that there was no pretence around the greeting of each other.

Then Aubrey, the platoon sarge, whom I trusted completely and knew, had my back in all situations.

Taking the decision to start putting a reunion together was for my own good, as I had to see what had happened to all of you whom I had shared hardship with and trusted you with my life.

I've spoken to other Bats and platoon commanders and to date have yet to come across a platoon that was close as we were. I am also aware that Platoon 2 got split up and added to during the war, but ultimately it was still the core of the unit. I think of Andre van Zyl and his section that got left in Novo Redondo - van Aardt, du Toit etc. .

In essence, what it boils down to is that we had something that others did not; others who had also done *diensplig* (and I am not negating their own experiences), it's just not often, if at all, that you see a group of men who know that what we went through, it changed our lives and made us who we are today.

My wish is that Kev's book be published and become a best seller as this has SO MUCH personal stuff in the writing that it needs to be told. The characters of the members of that platoon is the gel that makes us appreciate each other in the latter part of our lives; everyone had their piece of that history and the interaction of the personalities is what makes it so important. The absurd shit we got up to is what makes the part of our time together so readable.

I also believe it is our duty to tell our sons and maybe daughters about what we went through so as they can appreciate why we are like we are today. And, I know from experience it is far easier for them to hear it from a third party than from the horse's mouth as it is lost through their own vision of their father.

Take care all of you
Mark[1]

---

1. Lt Mark Coetzee, a National Service Lieutenant showed incredible leadership. He cared a lot about his people where ever he went. During training he wasn't there to stuff us around and he got great respect from all of us.

Introduction

Operation Savannah was the first large scale cross-border operation into Angola by the SADF (South African Defence Force) during the bush war.

It was a covert operation with a small SADF component supporting FNLA (National Front for the Liberation of Angola) and UNITA (National Union for the Total Independence of Angola) soldiers in their fight against FAPLA the military wing of the communist MPLA (Popular Movement for the Liberation of Angola) backed by Cuban forces and Russian Advisors. The SADF personnel posed as mercenaries and wore non-South African uniforms, having limited access to the usual resources such as artillery and combat aircraft. Initially, this small component signed secrecy documents, effectively relinquishing their rights to the Geneva Convention. The SAAF, however, provided logistical support to the operation by transporting supplies as well as, when required, medical evacuation.

The number of SADF troops grew rapidly until the operation became the largest deployment of South African troops since the Second World War. The operation was also supported, albeit not openly, by the USA through the CIA and surprisingly also by a number of prominent African leaders at the time.

Ops Savannah started in earnest during October 1975 and officially ended in March 1976. The South African soldiers who were initially deployed were mostly 18/19 year old conscripted National Servicemen with elements who had volunteered for specialist units like the Parabats and the Recces. Most of them had no idea of what the operation was all about and simply followed orders from day to day. As the war progressed more and more servicemen in conventional units were deployed, with standard infantry and specialist units like artillery and armour, playing decisive roles in the campaign.

Ops Savannah was initially fought on two fronts namely The Coastal Front (Task Force Zulu) and the Central Front (Foxbat). During the war this approach and the battle groups changed on an ongoing basis and at one time, there were three attacking fronts, along the coast, the central front and eastern side of Angola.

The campaign was a combination of clandestine, unconventional warfare and there were notable conventional battles fought during this time;

- Lt Col Jan Breytenbach leading battle group Zulu, earned the reputation as the Rommel of Angola by covering 3000km in 33 days, engaged in running battles up the western part of Angola.

- The defeat of the SADF/UNITA force at Ebo, in which an Eland 90 column and UNITA Infantry were ambushed by a combined Cuban/Fapla force, six or seven Eland armoured cars were lost and nearly 100 UNITA troops killed. Muddy conditions hampered the mobility of the armour. The South African politicians and SADF leadership kept this defeat secret from the South African population, and the truth only came out years later through reports and writings by those involved in the battle.

- The defeat of the Cuban/MPLA forces at the Battle of Bridge 14 towards the end of the campaign. This battle is regarded by the SADF and the politicians of the time as a decisive and heroic battle. Many articles and stories were written about the Battle of Bridge 14, and the SABC with SADF help, even made a short re-enactment film about the battle after the campaign.

- The capturing of the town of Luso (now called Luena) on the eastern front, where a FAPLA armoured bulldozer was encountered by the SADF.

By mid-December the South African Government had to deal with increasing international press criticism and a change in US policy. The withdrawal of the SADF forces was therefore based on political reasons much to the frustration of military leaders in the field who believed that Luanda was within their reach. That being said, by the time the campaign had reached this stage thousands of Cuban forces backed by Soviet weaponry and advisors were firmly entrenched in Angola, so a bloodbath had been avoided...

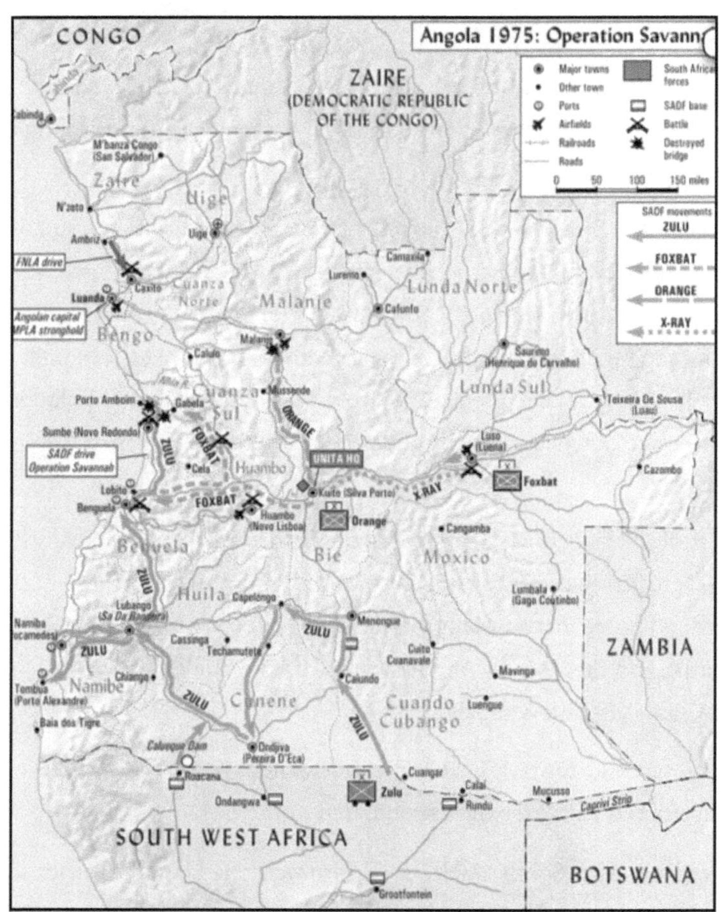

Map showing the extent of Operation Savannah

Table of contents

Prologue — 10

Chapter One: **Flashback** — 13

Chapter Two: **Call-up** — 21

Chapter Three: **I'm no damn officer thank you!** — 28

Chapter Four: **Welcome to 1 Parachute Battalion** — 38

Chapter Five: **Attrition** — 46

Chapter Six: **Time to find your feet, young man** — 56

Chapter Seven: **Hey Junior!** — 66

Chapter Eight: **The training ground** — 72

Chapter Nine: **No pain, no gain** — 78

Chapter Ten: **Jumping out of perfectly good aeroplanes** — 85

Chapter Eleven: **The Okapi knife** — 90

Chapter Twelve: **Mercenaries** — 98

Chapter Thirteen: **The Okapi avenged** — 105

Chapter Fourteen: **The little battle group** — 112

Chapter Fifteen: **Pineapple beer, ponchos and a dead cow** — 116

Chapter Sixteen: **Christmas Day** — 126

Chapter Seventeen: **Tolkien's rock** — 128

Chapter Eighteen: **The rocket man** — 147

Chapter Nineteen: **Sneaking around on foot** — 159

Chapter Twenty: **White vision mind fuck** — 190

Chapter Twenty One: **Tantrums and depression ended** — 195

Chapter Twenty Two: **Boys, we're going home!** — 210

Chapter Twenty Three: **Betrayal** — 220

Chapter Twenty Four: **Bye, bye soldier** — 228

Epilogue — 231

Appendix — 234

Prologue

The dark sky was just starting to show a glimmer of light when he began to move.
The bush was soaked from the night's rains and soon it wasn't long before his clothes
were drenched from brushing up against the vegetation. He held the small boy over
his shoulder, draped like a sack of potatoes. He could smell the smoke from the kraal
fire on the boy, the smell of countless African huts. He bore his burden with ease, his
thin frame belying the strength he had, his muscles like cords under his dirty jacket.
The small boy was a dead weight and he slipped once on his way down to the river,
dropping the boy on to the wet ground, picking him up with ease and making his way
cautiously down to the river bank.

By the time he reached the river's edge the sky was starting to turn grey and he could
see the water, grey like the dawn, flowing like treacle, sluggish, as if the river was
resisting waking to the new day.

He placed the boy gently on the ground and as he placed the child's lantern on the boy's
chest, disjointed random thoughts crossed his mind, images of burial rituals, tombs
and artefacts. The lantern was a work of art hand-made out of old Coca Cola cans and
clear plastic. Within the frame was contained a small stump of a candle, Long cold,
its wick as black as ink. Like a child launching a toy boat, he pushed the boy gently
into the river and as the current took hold, the body rolled over onto his its side, the
lantern falling into the river with a soft plop. On an impulse he grabbed the lantern and
tried to put it back on the boy's chest, but the child body had already drifted out of his
reach. The boy's eyes stared at him, lifeless, accusingly, and the thin man regretted not
having at least remembered to brush them closed when he could. Water poured into
the boy's mouth as the river accepted her bounty; the man turned, placing the lantern
in the branches of a small tree; for no real reason, he just placed it there. He stood and
watched the dawn, his face taking on a haggard aspect which belied his eighteen years.

He thought of the boy's eyes as the river took him; and the man wept.

"What difference does it make to the dead, the orphans **and** the homeless, whether the mad destruction is wrought under the name of totalitarianism or in the holy name of liberty or democracy?"

Mahatma Gandhi

This book is dedicated to Denis, who died so young.

And to my wife Nicky, my friend and soul-mate.

To my brothers in arms and to all the young men

who fought and died in wars.

Warriors all!

I salute you!

Chapter One: **Flashback**

It was a rainy Cape morning, the wind blowing straight over Robben Island and bringing the rain with it. The alarm kept up its irritating jingle and Kevin shut it off with a clumsy slap of his hand. Another day in sunny South Africa, he thought with disgust, heaving himself out of bed. Nicky had left; he could feel that her side of the bed was cold already; he hadn't even heard her go. Must have been the damn beers last night, he thought as he staggered to the shower. He let the hot water sting him into wakefulness, shedding the shit feeling and the shit taste in his mouth. Getting dressed he made his way to the kitchen,

'Hoi!' he shouted. 'Where are you all?'

'They've gone shopping,' yelled his son Warwick from the lounge.

'With what?' Kevin retorted, 'the bloody bank is dry! Jeez, what the hell,' he thought. He made some toast, smeared a bit of marmite onto it and washed it down with a cup of crappy, "no name brand" instant coffee. He wandered off to his garage workshop to keep himself busy and to put his financial shit on the back burner. The place looked like hell, a mess. Maybe today was a good day for a bit of spring-cleaning, he told himself looking round. Right, he decided, I'll start with all of this old army crap stored for over thirty years, gathering dust and wasting all of this space. A time to clean the soul; thought Kevin loads of history up there in all those boxes, memories some good, many bad. Setting up the step ladder he began to pull the stuff down; boxes, kit bags, even an old emergency parachute. What hell possessed me to pinch that thing, he thought, as he watched the chute bounce off the dusty heap lying on the floor? He climbed down and started sorting through the boxes, boots, army browns ...To try and put that shirt on would be like squeezing your dick into an undersized condom, he thought with a wry smile, subconsciously rubbing his belly. Those were the days he thought, super fit, strong and truly believing you were indestructible. How wrong it all was what a fucking waste! As he went through it all he made a mental note, light a fire and burn the lot, sacrilege to have some bum walking around in his old army kit. He turned out the last kit bag and remembered what they called it the army, a "ballsak" or translated a "ball bag." It brought a smile to his face, remembering all of the old army chirps. An image sprang to mind, a red-faced, Permanent Force corporal yelling at him, hoarse of voice and red in the face. 'You troop, look at me like that again and I'll rip your head off and shit down your throat. What the fuck are you smiling at? Do I look like your sister the whore?' The language, Kevin remembered how he struggled to come to terms with it back then. He shook the kit bag hard and then he heard it, a small clink, clink, clink followed by a rolling sound, a glimpse of something rolling under the workbench, a blue glint as it disappeared. Bloody hell! It can't be, Kevin thought as he descended the ladder in two quick bounds. Getting to his knees he looked under the workbench and could faintly see it lying there in the sawdust as if flipping him the bird. Picking up a scrap piece of wood he scraped it out and picked it up, rolling it between his fingers in wonder, not noticing the bits of sawdust stuck to his fingers.

Kevin rolled it between his fingers, not noticing the bits of earth stuck to his fingers. The size of an apricot, it glinted faint hints of blue light; he could see the pink colours of the dawn refracted through its centre.

'Hey Prewsky,' Kevin whispered to Andy, 'I think I found a diamond!'

'Let's check?' whispered Andy softly. Kevin tossed it over to Andy Prew who caught it deftly with his left hand. He rolled it over a few times in his fingers, flipping it from hand to hand as if testing its weight.

'Crap, KD, it's just a shiny rock,' responded Andy and then in typical, irritating Prew fashion, he flicked it down the side of the hill.

'You know what Prew, you're a real cunt!' Kevin responded as he carefully crawled down to retrieve it. 'Hey, you two,' called the Loot in a hoarse whisper, 'you are going to get the lot of us shot and if we are compromised because of your kak I'll be the first to double tap you, so shut the fuck up!'

Kevin didn't respond as he crawled silently back into position, flipping the bird at Andy who gave him a really shitty smirk in response. He slipped the stone into his webbing and with the rest of them watched the sun begin its battle with the mist.

Kevin could never get over the beauty of Angola. The fog lay dense on the lower ground in the bottom of the valleys like a thick, grey snake, an old African puff adder. The hills and mountain tops were pink in the early morning, rolling away into the distance towards Luanda. The men lay silently, the fog deadening sound as if they were in a world enveloped in cotton wool. The five of them had walked for eight days, anti-tracking as they had been taught, removing all traces of their progress until they had reached the hill and climbed three quarters up to the peak. There they had silently built their hides and for nearly a week had been waiting for Cuban movement and had seen nothing.

'Prew,' Kevin whispered, 'I'm getting gatvol of this mountain.'

'Me too,' responded Andy. 'I'm sick of this hill and of you as well.'

'Thanks boy, I fucking love you too,' Kevin replied. 'We're wasting our bloody time. The intelligence is crap as usual. All those boys do is sit in a comfortable office in HQ and stuff up the information blokes like us give them, turning good stuff into shit!' 'Only one more day and we can get the hell out of here, get back to Cela[2] eat some real food and ballasbak, I'm fed up with rat-packs!'

They lapsed into silence. Sitting on a hill like a bunch of baboons, Kevin thought. It seemed only yesterday that he and Andy had volunteered for paratrooper training. Both did their basics in the same infantry unit and both had volunteered on the same day. They had soon after become as thick as thieves and it remained so ever since. And so the day dragged on, each man taking the watch in turn, scanning the road and the trees below; the binoculars leaving red rings under their eyes. Another shit day in Africa and one to forget, thought Kevin.

That night they again heard the deep boom of artillery in the distance, like thunder in the night sky. Glad we are not on the receiving end of that, thought Kevin; every night the rain, mosquitoes and some poor bastards getting revved, almost always in that order.

The next morning arrived, watching the dawn and bringing with it the same routine; just this time there was an upbeat feel about the day ahead. The word had gone out that the boys were moving out; until the Lieutenant put a stinking lid on it. 'SITREP boys,' he whispered, 'shit news. We have to stay longer. I just got the order now; another three days at least!' He looked at the four of them and for once he didn't have anything cute to add. He simply crawled back to his hide.

'I think he is as pissed off as we are,' remarked Andy.

'No smart-arse comment from him this time.' 'Check the two Dutchies; they are also the hell in,' remarked Kevin, referring to Lappies and Jan, the two Afrikaans boys with them on the hill. 'We're screwed, Prew, there just about no rats left. I'm going to starve to death on this bloody hill,' he moaned. 'We'll eat lizards and berries. We are the cream of the army, KD, trained to live off the land,' stated Andy, playing the windup artist as usual. 'Well, like cream, shit also floats on water and in any case you'll be OK, Prew, you're a fat little fuck with lots of storage to live off. I'm the skinny one, boet, I'm going to die first,' Kevin whined.

'That's OK,' replied Prew, 'When you're dead I'll eat your calf muscles first. I read that if you have to eat a person to survive then eat the parts like calf leg muscles, biceps and so on.'

---

2. The Cuban forces were driven out of Cela by a combined UNITA and FNLA operation. It became the only position north of the river Cuvo under the control of the invading forces. Had that not been the case, the bridge over the river would have been destroyed, thus denying the invaders to cross over. (Angola the Failure of Operation Savannah 1975, Miguel Junior)

'I've got a better plan, let's shoot the Loot and we rather graze him,' chirped Kevin.

'That fucker will taste like shit!' was the instant response from Andy. Kevin chuckled and so the conversation went on, typical of all young men beset by boredom; the difference being that these were jaded young men at war, seeking diversion, escapism and making light of the bad times.

The rations ran out two days later and soon the mood began to change.

Luckily the rain was frequent; every late afternoon and early evening the rain poured down in buckets, and soaked everything. It was demoralizing. The nights were long and wet. Miserable and drenched to the bone, they lay shivering in their bivvies (bivouacs).

After a while the wind came up from the east and began to chase the clouds across the night sky; and it was not too long before the clouds gave up the fight, leaving the sky clear and the stars bright enough to light up the ground.

'Check next to Orion's belt, Prew, those three stars.'

'Looks like a bully beef can, brother, with its lid half open.' observed Kevin.

'You're right KD, but now you've made me hungry,' groaned Andy.

'That's the last damn thing I needed to hear. Shit man, my guts are touching my spine. If we don't move out tomorrow we're going starve to death up here!' Both men dropped off to sleep, wet and miserable, it was a fitful night. The next morning arrived, bringing the same routine. Then an hour later the Loot simply said in true Para parlance 'That's it, we're out of here. Stand up, hook up! They've pissed me off, expecting us to sit up here like bloody baboons on a hill until we starve to death. Prew, Vos, decide which of you are on point!' he ordered. Kevin almost blured out 'Why us and not the others', but surpressed his objection and instead looked Andy in the eye.

'Ching, chong, cha! Rock, paper, scissors, best out of three,' he whispered. Andy braced himself and the two of them, fists behind their backs, set about settling it democratically. Ching, chong, cha, Andy paper, Kevin rock, Andy one up. Ching, chong, cha, Kevin paper, Andy scissors.

'Shit Prew, you've won!' Kevin groaned as he hoisted his kit onto his back. Checking that his rifle had one up the spout and that the safety was on due to the rough terrain, Kevin began to move down the hill silently. He scrabbled from rock to scrub to rock, his eyes scanning left to right, his eyes moving in arcs, looking into the bush and scrub, not at them but into them so that you could see anyone hiding within. Regularly he cast his eyes down on, sweeping the ground to ensure no earth had been disturbed, watching carefully for loose earth, footprints, anything which could spell danger, looking for evidence to indicate the presence of anti-personnel mines.

The men were silent; none of the banter and bullshitting of the last few days. This was the real thing, where lives could lie in the balance. As they moved downwards the last two men set about anti-tracking, trying their best to minimise any obvious traces of their passing. Soon they reached the base of the hill and lay down for a short rest of fifteen minutes, rifle safeties off, fingers across the trigger-guards, listening.

The Loot gave the signal to move out and they began to move advancing silently through the bush and scrub, in a line abreast, spread out within eyesight. Soon the vegetation became thicker and they moved to single file, walking silently, not talking, using hand signals only, going down at regular intervals, resting while the Loot took their bearings with a compass. The African sun beat down relentlessly, sucking up the water from the water-drenched earth until the air was heavy with moisture. The muggy air and heat was oppressive, sucking the moisture out of them and draining their already depleted energy reserves. By late afternoon the men were exhausted having rested for longer than fifteen minutes only once, at midday for an hour when the heat was at its most intense. This, as to move in the heat would have been stupid.

The hunger became all-consuming and they were weak with it. They came to a road and began to walk alongside it until it forked, the left track dipping down and away, the right one rising steeply upwards. The dirt road was rutted and eroded by the rain, its surface crumbling, not having been maintained since the Portuguese had left Angola.

'We are sleeping here tonight. There is no point in going any further,' the Loot announced. 'With a bit of luck a vehicle will pick us up here tomorrow morning. I'll try and radio our position and situation through in a few minutes. We can't travel much more without food.'
He began to ramble a bit.

'If we commandeer anything we will give our presence away.'

He split them up, Andrew and Kevin positioned at the fork in the bush covering the way they had come and with a clear view of the road up the hill; Lappies, Jan and the Loot opposite them covering the left fork and the same approach as Andy and Kevin. They spent a fitful night in the bush, hungry and being pounded by mosquitoes.

No one slept. The distant sound of artillery could be heard, muffled by distance and the mountains like the rolling thunder of a far-off storm. At last the morning arrived, the sun pushing the night away until only remnants of it were left skulking in the shadows.

Kevin had a splitting headache from hunger and realized that there was little chance that they would be able to travel much that day. He noticed that there was no movement from the guys from across the road. So they simply lay there, waiting in silence for the Loot to come up with some plan.

They were too exhausted and hungry to even talk and they lay in the bush for about an hour before Andy heard the sound first.

'KD, KD, wake up!' he whispered. 'Can you hear that? It sounds like metal scraping sand or something.'

Kevin rolled over and could now hear the sound as well. He lay there in silence, listening intently. It was coming from the top of the hill and suddenly they could see the source of the noise. A small black boy, running and pushing a bicycle rim along, propelling it with a metal rod while expertly slowing it and guiding its progress; preventing it from running away down the hill; his bare feet slapping on the hard earth, face gleaming with snot all shiny and happy. The boy reached a point in line with Lappies and Jan where he stopped and tilted his head as if listening to the bush; he took a tentative step towards the bush when suddenly a great hairy arm lunged out. Attached to the hairy arm was a meaty, ham-sized hand which gripped the boy on the top of his head and whipped him into the undergrowth. All Kevin heard was a faint squeak followed by total silence.

'Fuck me, the Dutchmen are going to eat him!' exclaimed Andy, looking at the bush in alarm. Kevin began to chuckle, his face creased with mirth.

'It's not funny KD, those guys are starving, and you know what these boertjies are like; they're capable of anything!' Andy's round face was filled with genuine alarm.

'Piss off Prew,' Kevin retorted, grinning, 'I have a Dutch surname. We're of the same stock and the only difference is I speak English. I would never chomp a kid, bloody hell, you dumb Welshman!'

'I'm not a fucking Welshman, KD, I'm bloody French,' snarled Andrew, giving Kevin a murderous look. Kevin smiled, he loved winding his buddy up.

They watched the bush intently, when suddenly the boy was ejected onto the road and began to run pell-mell up the hill, his legs pumping in panicked urgency.

'Now we're screwed, totally bloody compromised,' groaned Kevin, 'Every damned darkie within a thousand kliks knows we're here.'

'Fuck it, fuck it, fuck it!' yelled Andy in frustrated anger, and gesturing towards Lappies. 'Are you bloody, fucking stupid, now half the bloody planet knows where we are!' He paused before continuing.

'KD, best we get ready to spark, boet, if the shit hits the fan you and I are heading down towards the river. These dumfucks can sort themselves out!'
'Calm down, *Soutie*,' called Lappies from across the road. 'He's going to fetch us some food. I told him it's that or we are going to burn down his village.'

Kevin could here Jan sniggering as Lappies finished his sentence. 'Why do they always have to pull the *Soutie* chirp?' bitched Andy.

'It's as old as the hills, old news, stale, shit; one leg in England and one leg in Africa and your cock in the sea, *soutie*...salty.'

'Piss off, Dutchies!' yelled Andy, his face red with irritation. 'SHARRRRRUPPPP!' yelled the Lieutenant.

Silence returned to the bush ... a rather sullen silence.

'That Loot is an idiot. He's going to get us killed, Andrew,' said Kevin. Using his friend's name Andrew in full meant he was serious. He continued. 'On the last OP he stood up on the side of the hill and shook out his sleeping bag, right there in the open for the whole damn world to see. I pointed it out to him and he got all arrogant, told me there were no people in the area and it was safe.

'Fucking moron!' he ranted on, 'I bet he told Lappies to grab that kid!' Andy didn't bother responding and so the rant died a quiet death.

They lay there in silence, waiting.

About an hour later they saw a group of women and children coming down the hill. There was neither laughter nor banter as was the custom of Africans. Unusually the children, about twenty of them, walked closely to their mothers, not daring to run around as children do. One of the women had a large pot on her head, balanced with apparent ease, her gait made graceful by the weight of it. They walked to where the others were hidden and placed the pot carefully on the ground and waited. The children stood silently a few drifting back the way they had come, ready to sprint away at the drop of a hat. The three men from across the road emerged from the bush and walked to the woman.

The Lieutenant spoke to them for a few minutes, handed over a few Escudos which didn't seem to please the woman too much. She said something to the group with her and they turned back the way they had come, the children taking off laughing and squealing, the mood totally changed.

By the time the pot's lid was removed Kevin and Andy were standing next to the others, hunger driving caution to the wind. They ate the maize-meal porridge straight out of the pot, using their hands African style, shoulder to shoulder, jostling each other. There was no salt in it; bland porridge had never tasted as good as this, thought Kevin, as he stuffed his face.

Even the Loot who always affected a superior attitude, was stuffing it in, a small lump of porridge stuck to the tip of his nose. He didn't notice it, too preoccupied with filling his guts. One day you're going to kill us all, Kevin thought.

The grinding sounds of diesel engines woke them the next morning the sound rising and falling with the dips in the road. They had spent another wet night the rain poured for hours and the world was drenched.

'We might be hungry but we sure as hell won't die of thirst in this shithole', muttered Kevin under his breath.

The first Noddy car came over the hill, it's 90mm gun pointing menacingly forward like a terrier looking for a fight, it's Browning machine gun manned by a scruffy gunner, a Cuban cap pointed jauntily on his head. A military Unimog followed looking for all the world like it was about to topple over, rolling from side to side as it crested the hill closely followed by a second Noddy car.

The scruffy looking convoy did a U-turn and ground to a halt at the fork. Soon they were all aboard, grinding their way up the hill, the lot of them pissed off and grumpy like old men.

'The least these wankers could have done was to bring us some chow', complained Lappies in his thick Afrikaans accent. There were a few grunts of agreement as the Unimog pitched and lurched through the eroded ruts in the road.

'Fuck me, but one day's one day this thing is going to bliksem over and kill us all,' grunted Andy, looking decidedly miserable. 'I feel like a tick on a dog's backside sitting on top of this thing.'

'They should put armour plating around its sides, and then at least I'll feel a bit safer,' added Kevin.

'You *Souties* are fokken stupid, because then this blerry thing really will moer over,' added Lappies, with a smug expression on his face.

Oh, for fucksakes, what a pearl of wisdom, thought Kevin, trying to make the most of the situation, trying desperately to prevent his arse from bouncing painfully on the wooden bench. What possessed me to volunteer to join this lot, he thought woefully.

What indeed?

Chapter Two: **Call-up**

If your time to you
Is worth savin'
Then you better start swimmin'
Or you'll sink like a stone
For the times they are a-changin'

Bob Dylan

'Hey Dad', called Kevin, brandishing an official looking sheet of paper, 'I've got my call-up papers, I'm going to a unit called 11 Commando, in Kimberley.'

'That's pretty all right,' said Denis as he took his sixteen year old son's call-up papers and began to scrutinise them.

'Kimberley hey, commandos, interesting, better unit than where I was, where must I sign?' And that was the upshot of it; legal guardian's signature, hand the paper in at the headmaster's office the next morning and you were on your way in becoming the property of the state. The government used the schools to issue and receive call-ups, so once in the system there was no way out of it, stuffed like a trussed up chicken!

A year later, in January 1975, Kevin found himself standing at the Rand Easter Show grounds in Johannesburg, saying goodbye to the family. Tears seen everywhere as young men bade their families farewell; brave young faces, many of them standing with their long hair blowing in the wind, still innocent; some apprehensive, some not, most sad to say goodbye but what the hell! We all have to do this don't we? It's the law of the land. You get called up and you go to serve your country. To fight communism, to defend the free world!

A fresh faced corporal walked up to them, looking smart in his pressed, crisp browns, his green beret mashed onto his head at jaunty angle over his right ear; a glinting springbok head proudly mounted on the beret.

'Right people!' he stated matter of factly, 'time to say bye-bye!' he turned around smartly and walked off.

'What a friendly young man,' said Kevin's mom as she kissed him on the lips,

'looks like you're going to be in good hands my boy.'

Kevin said goodbye to his sisters and brother; kisses and hugs all round. His sister Gianne was crying and soon all of the girls were crying their eyes out. Even his oldest sister, who generally made no bones about her dislike for him, had a few tears running down her cheeks. Blood is thicker than water, thought Kevin as he hugged her goodbye. His brother Darrel stood there stoically and shook Kevin's hand. Not a tear in sight.

'Bye son', said Kevin's dad, firmly shaking his hand with just a hint of a tear in his eyes but nothing obvious. 'You be good and do what you're told. Keep your head above the water, keep it low and you'll be fine,' was his last bit of advice.

It was good advice, Kevin would soon discover, the head being kept low bit!

The train pulled out of the show grounds; young men waving, long hair blowing, the mood in the train surprisingly upbeat, almost jovial. A sense of adventure mixed with youthful exuberance, a heady combination. Kevin saw the smart looking, friendly corporal walking slowly up the carriage aisle, Kevin smiled and waved at him, the corporal looked straight through him and Kevin felt almost hurt. Naive Kevin.

He looked around; there were five other young men in the compartment, all shapes and sizes; English boys, Afrikaans boys and one Portuguese youngster. The Porra was not happy and sat glumly in a corner near the window. A Portuguese national, he was as pissed off as hell, as his father had "volunteered" him into the army. He was a troubled kid and had been causing considerable shit as far as his father was concerned. So let the army turn him into a man was the logic.

'I'm going to get basics over and then I'm going to volunteer for the Recces,' announced a spotty fellow with greasy long hair. His name was Peter and he was a Jeppe boy.

'Who are the Recces?' asked a fat boy called Roger, his round pink cheeks framed by a shock of red hair. He looked like Roger the Dodger thought Kevin, straight out of a comic book.

'Special forces, boet, special forces, they go behind enemy lines and blow up shit and cut throats,' answered Peter, his eyes burning.

'And you Kevin, what are you going to do' someone asked?'
Kevin thought for a second and responded,

'I'm going to spend a quiet year in Kimberly, minding my own damn business and I'll try to get this shit over as soon as possible!'

'Well that's not being very patriotic,' said Jan, an Afrikaans boy from Boksburg.

'You're going into the army to do the thing, man, you know, do it, you unit!'

His voice lifted in patriotic fervour. Kevin began to felt a knot developing in his stomach. It wasn't going to be easy living with wankers like this. One of the guys opened a bag with mommy's packed food and it wasn't long before the whole bunch were munching away merrily, swapping food and talking crap; conversations, a little larger than life, compensating for their insecurities.

A skinny fellow from Germiston hauled out a guitar and the Porra, who later introduced himself as Manuel, hauled out two bottles of sour, home-made wine and the party soon started to hot up. Mixed with coke, the "katembas" had a glorious effect on Kevin and any vestiges of homesickness were soon forgotten.

Some bright spark decided that Manuel was a shit name and before long everyone was calling Manuel "Automatic", a name which stuck for the rest of the train journey.

The jovial mood changed later to something more sombre, no extra alcohol was to be had so it was not too late before most of the train was asleep. Apart from the corporals, walking the carriages, not saying much but exuding a sense of suppressed aggression, as if they couldn't wait for tomorrow.

The Porra snored all night like a bastard!

The yelling started about an hour out of Kimberley, voices screaming as the "friendly" corporal and his mates set to work. The voices quickly became hoarse from yelling and screaming as they herded the luckless conscripts onto the station platform.

'Don't smile at me, you useless cunt, do I look like a whore or your fucking girlfriend?'screamed a lance jack at a shell-shocked trooper.

Formed into ragged lines, they were marched to waiting trucks outside the station, trudging in a straggled, out of step, line, a collection of civilians, their eyes wide and befuddled. Kevin kept in the middle of the group, trying to be inconspicuous; he could hear his father's voice, 'keep your head down son, keep your head down.'

'Put your kit on the ground and don't forget where you put it', roared a bull of a man, a castle badge on each sleeve and the name Calitz sewn onto his chest.

'If any of you homosexual, arse-fuckers lose the flea-ridden, infested shit you brought with you, then don't come crying on my shoulder, because if you do I will fuck you up!' he bellowed, veins standing out on his neck.

'We are going to treat you to a delicious breakfast prepared by the loving hands of our excellent cooks here in Eleven Commando,' he yelled.

'Enjoy it, don't complain because you are getting it for nothing, fokkol, mahala, anything for free is a bonus. So eat up you are going to need it!'

And with that he did a smart about turn and marched off.

The queue into the mess hall was long and as they shuffled along, Kevin looked at a pile of steel trays, with compartments pressed into them. A rough hand pushed him back, '*Gaan haal jou fokken varkpan, jou dom troep!*' (Go fetch your fucking pig-pan you dumb troop!') screamed a skinny lance corporal, adolescent acne splattered across his face like a birdshot wound.

Each pig-pan compartment was designed to hold a different food type. No chance of that happening though! Before he could react, the cooks had heaped porridge, toast, sugar, egg, milk and bacon, in that order on a steaming heap in the middle of his *varkpan*. He could see the spiteful malice in their eyes as they did so. Kevin, feeling thoroughly disheartened, didn't react; he simply walked dumbly to a vacant chair and sat down next to Peter.

'Army cooks love blue, everything in this place is blue,' said Manuel the Porra, in his thick Portuguese accent. He pronounced 'place' as 'plaish'.

'Look,' continued Manuel, 'the walls are blue, the tables are blue, even the floors are blue and check this out, even the eggs are blue,' he indicated the wobbly, yellowy-blue pile in his plate.

'Except the ceiling, it's white like us!'

'You're not white,' piped up Pete, the Recce wannabe.

'You're a Porra, a fucking sea-kaffir, all you Porras came over from Madeira.

You're all as bad as the local kaffirs, man!'

Manuel gave Peter a murderous look, his dark eyes going black.

'You really are a pain in the arse, you racist shit, Peter. That wasn't called for, really!' Kevin interjected quickly, before the shit hit the fan. Manuel, ignoring Peter and Kevin, lifted his metal mug up and looked into it, saying,

'Look, even the coffee is blue; check, look.'

They all looked and the coffee certainly had a tinge of blue in it. Looks strange, thought Kevin.

'It's Bluestone,' said Roger. 'My boet was in the army. He told me about it. They put it in the coffee to stop you from getting horny. It stops you from getting a cock-stand. Watch, you'll see. None of us will have a hard-on for the next six weeks of basics, you'll see I'm not bull-shitting you guys!'

'Why stop you from getting a hard-on?' asked Manuel.

'So you don't roger old Roger!' piped up Pete.

This triggered a ripple of laughter, albeit rather subdued by the depressing state of affairs.

The eggs were blue; the porridge was glue and the rest tasted like shit.

But nonetheless Kevin ate as much as he could before a gaggle of corporals walked in and began to blow whistles.

'*Moer uit, moer uit*, get out, get out!' they screamed, wash your *varkpan* in the first drum, rinse it in the second and if you don't do it properly we'll chase you till you puke!' Kevin didn't need to be chased; he wanted to puke in any case. He began to feel all the more depressed.

From then on Kevin, like the rest of them, made it his mission to monitor his cock's physical state every morning, without fail. He also noticed, that the damn corporals made sure that every single man drank his coffee each morning, it was bloody compulsory. Perhaps Roger was onto something, he thought.

'You all look like a bunch of long haired moffies, homos, mommy's girls and we are going to change that!' snarled the skinny corporal, his acne looking like was about to rupture in a flow of yellow custard.

'You are all going to be neatened up, army style, so look at your moffie mates standing next to you closely, because by lunchtime you won't even recognise yourselves, never mind your fucking buddy,' he added, a smug smile on his face.

'Squaaad will turn to the left in threes, leeeeft tuuurrn', he screamed. Everybody shuffled to the left excepting one sad looking man who turned to the right. An expression of absolute joy diluted by distaste bloomed across corporal pimple-face's face.

'Now look at this,' he said, his face millimetres from the luckless boy who was quite possibly dyslexic.

'Can you read and write, boetie, huh, do you know your blerry left from your blerry right?' asked spotty dog, a name which Kevin coined for him in that instant.

Spotty dog turned, looked at the motley bunch standing, frozen before him and pointing into the distance, said,

'Well now, because your little buddy is so stupidly fast asleep, you are going to have to run through that piece of veld, up that little rise there, run around that tree there and run back again here, just to help your buddy wake up.

Now move!' he finished with a snarl.

And so began an hour of running around the tree, going back to say sorry for disturbing its sleep, going back again to fetch a leaf and back again to put the leaf back. Until a third of the squad had deposited the cooks' "delicious" breakfast onto the ground, in random steaming piles across the veld.

They were at last marched to the barber shop, stinking, sweating and in disarray. 'Fall out!' yelled Spotty Dog and the squad rushed to a tap and drank until their thirst was satisfied. They fell into the shade of a tree bordering the parade ground.

'I'm fucked,' said "Automatic", his dark complexion enhanced by the sweat on his face. 'When I get back I'm going to cut off my father's *galo*, merda!' he exclaimed.

Kevin burst out laughing. He always enjoyed the Porras back home, good people with one hell of a work ethic.

'Ah fuck it, Manual; you're going to be OK. You Porras are survivors,' he said, patting him on the shoulder reassuringly. Manuel just shook his head, muttering under his breath.

With that they looked across and watched the convicts emerging from the barbershop.

'*Donder*, but those blokes look like shit!' exclaimed Peter, the Recce wannabee. 'Check it out, looks like they're fresh out of Auschwitz or something,'

'They're too fat for that,' observed one of the squad. 'Check that bloke there near the stairs, looks like a misshapen fucking beach ball, been kicked all over the place he has.'

The group had a good chuckle at that one...

'Better still, boys, have you seen what we look like. Looks like we were dragged behind a pickup for about a hundred miles,' commented someone.

They took stock of themselves and realized that they did indeed look like crap. Their civilian clothes were a wreck, covered in dust and torn from the bushes they had to run through; they were all filthy and covered in sweat.

'That spotty corporal is a cunt, a real fat, sloppy pile of pimply pus,' snarled Jan in his thick Afrikaans accent.

'We were the only ones who were chased around, I hope like hell he doesn't become our section leader, or bungalow boss or whatever the hell you call it,' he complained.

'Hey you lot, stop talking shit and get in line here,' indicated a short stocky corporal.

They complied and while standing there they all watched long-haired civilians walk in and come out transformed, bald and unrecognisable.

'You guys better identify yourselves when you come out of there,' remarked Pete, 'because I won't know who the hell you are.'

Kevin considered this and thought that perhaps this wasn't such a bad thing, especially the prospect of shedding the likes of Recce wannabee Pete.

When they came out of the barbershop they got together under the tree again, except Jan who had hooked up with an old school buddy. None of them would have recognized him anyway. The next stop was the quartermaster's store where they were issued with kit, and a steel chest or trommel. Like army stores all over the world they were shunted from one place to another, with a good proportion of them getting the wrong sized boots.

'Swop with your girlfriends!' snarled the sergeant quartermaster when Kevin pointed out that, while he wore a size 11 boot, he had been issued a size 9. Luckily he managed to swop fairly easily with an equally desperate recruit. They were marched to their allotted barracks, large hangars with rows of beds, housing up to 280 men in a hanger.

'What a cock-up, what a shithole, why the hell is this happening, why the hell am I here?' lamented Kevin despondently. This time it was Manuel's turn to pat him on his shoulder reassuringly.

He had never been spoken to in such a disparaging manner in his life before, by so many people; constantly screaming, always the foul language. Homesickness began to weigh him down and when he thought of home he felt a lump rising in his throat.

Looking around he could see men looking as despondent as he felt; strangely he found this to be comforting.

Chapter Three: **I'm no damn officer thank you!**

I said that time may change me, But I can't trace time.
- David Bowie

And so basics began, inspections, beds lined up with precision, toothpaste tubes had to be squared off, boots and floors polished to a mirror-like finish. Three weeks had gone by in a flash. Roger was right about the bloody coffee, thought Kevin, looking despondently down at his limp member. Not even a hint of a bloody morning glory in three weeks!

'Hey manne, check this out, 'yelled Pete one morning, brandishing his erect member. 'Looks like they've stopped the bluestone'! There was a roar of laughter form the rows of beds. The next day Kevin was relieved to feel a distantly familiar, early morning stirring in his nether regions. He looked under the blankets to observe a splendid morning-glory and he was relieved; at last things were on the up and up!

And oddly, Kevin excelled in basics. Inspections were perfect and as they progressed, his fitness levels rose above the rest of them. He had been a long distance runner at school so he had a good basic condition. Running the 2.4 km route run he consistently finished first or second out of the entire company. It was easy and so were the evaluation tests, he walked them. He forgot his father's advice about 'keeping your head down' and so he was noticed, noticed by the wrong people...the officer corps.

'Left right, left right', corporal Andrews chanted as he marched Kevin and a select group to the administration block. One by one they were called into the commandant's office, Kevin's turn, 'left right, left right, halt!' he called. And Kevin crashed to halt.

'Stand easy troop, I've got some good news for you,' the commandant announced. Kevin slammed his left leg into the rest position, a lot harder than necessary resulting in the wooden floor vibrating beautifully. The Commandant blinked; a hint of irritation showing on his face and Kevin liked it.

'You've been selected to go to officers' school in Oudtshoorn,' the Commandant announced in a friendly voice which was rather odd for a career soldier, the friendly tone being alien to the natural order of things.

'You've done well, Vos, so it's off to Oudtshoorn for you,' he said, beaming, his florid face shining with enthusiasm. He waited for Kevin's reaction, expecting the skinny young man to be happy, joyful or even ecstatic. The Commandant looked at him, waiting, and the pause began to get pregnant pretty quickly.

'So, Vos what do you have to say?' he asked, a puzzled expression starting to creep in along his face.

Kevin though for second, knowing full well that it would be ill-advised to incur the wrath of the camp commander.

'Commandant, what effect will this have on my length of service?' he asked. 'Two years and your national service is over, a walk in the park, just a blip in your life,' he paused. 'Think about it Vos,' he continued. 'An officer, a leader of men, you have shown promise and you are excellent Permanent Force material.'

He finished with a hint of fervour in his voice.

Kevin blanched at the thought, Permanent – Bloody – Force; no bloody way, he thought. Drawing on some inner resolve he responded.

'Commandant, I respectfully decline, I don't want to go to officers' school.' There was a stunned silence, Kevin saw corporal Andrews turn toward him, a puzzled expression on his face. He started to open his mouth and then snapped it shut like a mousetrap as the commandant raised his hand sharply.

"*Nee, kak, jy is 'n fokken gemors van wit vel*; (no, shit, you are a fucking waste of white skin.) You are *naafi*, do you know what *naafi* is troep, you spell it N-A-A-F-I, it means no ambition and fuck-all interest!' screamed the commandant rising from his chair, his ample belly scraping the front of his desk.

'You are typical of all soutpiele. And what makes it worse is you have an Afrikaans surname, Vos, Vos, and you speak and act like a bloody salty. Your grandfather was probably a traitor in the Boer war!' he roared, his chest heaving vibrating and his red jowls flapping.

'The only way you are getting out of this is to get out of my unit before the time comes to go to officers' school, because whether you like it or not, you are going to be an officer, do you understand you stupid arse, *verstaan jy*?'

'Yes Commandant, I understand, Commandant,' Kevin responded in a state of fearful shock.

The Commandant, now on a roll continued, 'The only way you get out of this Vos, is to join the Recces or the Parabats, no other way, understand?' He paused, catching his breath. 'Get this piece of shit out of my office, corporal!' he snarled in closing, plonking himself down behind his desk.

'Aboooouuut turn, forward march, left right, left right,' screamed the corporal in double quick time as he marched Kevin back to the bungalows. Strangely Kevin was dismissed without any further army-style harassment; the corporal simply giving him a foul look and walking off.

'So Kev, what happened? Are you going to Oudtshoorn?' was the first question flung at him as he flopped down onto his bed that evening.

'No ways, boys, there is no bloody way I'm spending an extra year in the army. The commandant is so pissed off at me I'd better keep a low profile,' responded Kevin.

'Although this place is so damn big he probably won't ever bump into me again.

Hey Pete, I'm joining the Recces with you,' he added.

'Well that means four years' service, brother,' responded Pete. 'So you're stuffed boet, going to do extra time no matter which way you look at it!'

Kevin felt a bit put out by Pete's rather depressing response.

'Aw shit, then Parabats it is!' Kevin paused before continuing, 'Who are the Parabats in any case?'

'*Bliksem rooinek*, (shit Englishman,) you don't know who the bats are?

They're Paratroopers, man, tough bastards and a lot of their leader group are Recces too. Good chance you're going to end up being a Recce anyway,' said Jan, a smug look on his face.

'Screw all of you, I'm going for a shit,' said Kevin as he walked out.

The next morning they awoke, not to the sounds of whistles but to howls of pain coming from the shower block. They rushed across to be treated to the sight of a group of men holding down one man and scrubbing him with washing powder and scrubbing brushes. The man on the ground was writhing in pain; the coarse floor-brush bristles had already drawn blood. There were roars laughter coming from the watching men.

'Check, its stinky Watson from Zambia,' chirped a voice from the front, the cunt hasn't bathed in four weeks, his mates are gatvol, have had a guts-full; he stinks like a mineworker from Mozambique!'

'Hey, scrub his balls and don't forget to wash the cheese off his cock,' called another voice.

The scrubbing men suddenly drew back, leaving the shivering lanky 1.8m form of Watson, curled up on the floor in the foetal position. The watching men began to drift off and Kevin could hear the man on the floor sobbing, his body shivering with cold. Kevin felt a pang of pity for him; the army is not a soft place and non-conformance elicited quick justice, jungle justice.

Kevin walked over to Watson, stretched out his hand and helped him up, as he did so he sensed someone near him and turned to see corporal Andrews watching. He looked at Kevin, gave a small nod, turned away and walked out.

Watson was a strange fish, very tall and skinny. He wore thick glasses with frames that would make Clark Kent envious. Too sensitive to be in the army and an abnormally shy boy, he had a phobia about being naked or semi-naked in front of the other soldiers in the unit. So he had simply stopped bathing and as a result began to stink to high heaven. What possessed the idiot to volunteer for military service puzzled Kevin. And many of the other conscripted young men told him how stupid he was, very clearly and vociferously, driving poor Watson to the edge.

He took to showering late at night when the whole barracks were asleep and it wasn't long before the dreaded words, 'queer, homo, moffie, queen' began to be thrown at him. Kevin tried to befriend him, but Watson was a closed book and kept to himself; he cut a lonely figure. Kevin felt sorry for him. But in the army the strongest survived, or rather, the stronger collective survived and people like Watson were simply cannon fodder.

The stress and daily fucked-up grind of basic training; push ups, sit ups, running, drilling, inspections, rifle inspections guard duty and exhaustion, coupled to his own little dose of homesickness and depression, helped Kevin to reach a decision. Watson was simply going to be a waste of energy, so he cut him loose and left him alone.

Sunday mornings were a happy time, they did not have to wake up early and there were no inspections, the only requirements being breakfast and having to attend compulsory church parade. There were no exceptions and irrespective of denomination or faith, all had to fall in for church parade. The Calvinist Nationalist Government demanded it; don't ever neglect church and country, the black majority yes, but not church parade!

So it was only at 07h00 on a beautiful Highveld morning, in February of 1975, that someone found the cold, stiff Watson hanging from the roof beams in the shower block. He was fully clothed in full uniform, as if he wanted to look dignified, presentable and most of all not being naked before his peers; even in death. But he was not dignified; his eyes looked as if they were going to explode, the thick glasses magnifying them grotesquely, his face bloated and purple in colour.

His bowels had voided and the stinking mess had run down his legs, collecting around his ankles and in his boots; as if mocking his last attempt at dignity. Kevin turned away, shocked, his stomach heaving. It was the first dead person he had seen and it would definitely and horribly not be the last!

That morning at church parade the chaplain spoke of home and loved ones and it all became too much for him. Kevin cried and when he looked up, expecting some mockery or reproach it was not to be. There were other boys, not yet men, standing there and they too were crying.

The chaplain spoke passionately of life, salvation and of suicide being a sin condemning the "suicidee" to eternal suffering in hell; a clumsy, insensitive attempt at preventing a repeat of the morning's event. Kevin felt a deep anger towards the chaplain and the government-backed Calvinist religion he stood for.

But young men are resilient and it wasn't long before Watson was mostly forgotten. His kit and bed were removed and his squad remained at nine men until basics were over.

'Hey Vossie, come here,' called Corporal Andrews. 'It's your big day, you slab of misery. The bats are here and I hear that you can't wait to volunteer, you useless waste of white skin! God should have covered you in black skin, more fitting of a lazy chunk of shit like you, lui kaffir, lazy kaffir!' he finished in a scream, the spit hitting Kevin in the face. Kevin felt the heat rise in him, the aggression and racist vitriol were having their effect; the corporal saw it in his eyes and smiled.

'That's right why don't you hit me?' he grinned as he said it, a hard glint in his eyes.

'Here, right on the fucking button,' he said touching his nose.

Kevin didn't respond.

'Ja I thought so, fucking geelgat, yellow belly! Go join those other glory boys over there next to the Land Rover,' he growled, indicating a motley looking bunch waiting next to the Landie.

'But first go and fetch your steel helmet, webbing and rifle, go… fuck off!'

Kevin ran into the barracks collected his gear and departed amongst a few calls of encouragement from his mates. He had long given up convincing any of them to join him, not that you could blame them he thought, they just had to sit out the year in 11 Commando, no shit choices for them, the lucky bastards.

He jogged past the scowling corporal Andrews, slowing to a walk to brace the higher rank and ran the last few paces to the waiting group. It wasn't long before they were on the *garrie* grinding its way towards the far end of the base.

Twenty minutes later they arrived at the rugby fields. Another group of men was waiting there, taking the number to about sixty men. They were told to sit and wait and like any other soldier anywhere, they found a comfortable spot to pass the time. There was an air of expectancy about the group, and it wasn't long before the banter and shit-talk took over.

Kevin wasn't at all excited by the whole damn concept. After all, he had been forced into making a choice and he had taken the lesser of the evils as far as he was concerned.

His thoughts were cut short when they saw the Land Rover returning; the driver had handed the vehicle over to two men who stopped it on the edge of the rugby field in a cloud of dust. They got out of the vehicle and the first thing Kevin noticed was that they had a leanness about them. They were older men, career soldiers, proud of who they were and it showed. Each placing a maroon beret on their heads, they casually walked towards the men. There was no frenetic crap about them, Kevin thought as they got closer; just an air of business.

The corporal in charge screamed, 'Fall in, fall in,' and once the men had arranged themselves into a squad he called,

'Aaaateenshunn!'

He snapped a salute at the two paratroopers, a major and a sergeant. 'Let them stand at ease and let them sit down,' the major said softly and the corporal obliged.

'Gentlemen, so I believe that you want to become paratroopers?' asked the major.

'Yes Major!' The group chorused.

'That gentlemen, was a rhetorical question,' he responded. 'You would not be here if you didn't want to be a paratrooper, not so? So if any of you have any doubts about being committed, then please leave now.'

Kevin was stunned, "gentlemen", "rhetorical question"….. For fucksakes, terms he hadn't heard from anyone of rank since he arrived in this dump! Bloody hell!

No one left.

The major continued, 'Good. It would appear that you all really want to become paratroopers.' He paused and continued, 'In order to qualify, you will need to pass a medical exam, an aptitude test, an interview, you must have a standard ten certificate; you must have no tattoos on any part of your body and you will need to pass the pre-selection physical evaluation, do you understand?'

'Yes, Major!' The group chorused.

'If any of you feel incapable of satisfying any of the criteria I have mentioned, then leave now and stand next to the flagpole,' he said quietly with a hint of finality in his voice. There was a groan from behind Kevin; six young men stood up and moved to the flagpole.

'Now,' the major continued, 'the first evaluation is to do the 2.4km run carrying helmet, webbing and rifle in under 11 minutes, the standard infantry criteria is 12 minutes, as a paratrooper you will do better. Go to the start point next to the *garrie* and the sergeant will carry on.'

After the run the pre-selection continued, sit-ups, carrying another man one hundred meters with full kit within a certain time, push-ups; each time some men falling off the wagon. From 60 there were 42 left.

Kevin remained in the running with some ease. Perhaps this isn't going to be all that bad, this paratrooper thing, he thought. His self-confidence on the up and up, he passed the aptitude test with flying colours.

Of the 42 there were 29 left.

They were loaded onto a Bedford truck and taken back to the main camp, the horrible beast of a thing stinking of petrol and grinding its way back into history, World War Two transport consigned to serve out the rest of its life in training camps. Always the romantic, Kevin had time to consider the poignancy of it all.

'Strip down to your underpants and stand in a line in front of the door,' instructed the sergeant.

Kevin couldn't help but notice that during the whole process not one voice had been raised. Things were getting better; looks like elite units were a different kettle of fish, he thought. They treat you the way volunteers should be treated, like responsible professional soldiers. As if someone had read his mind one of the parabat wannabees piped up, 'It looks like this is going to be a walk in the park, these people treat you like real people, you know.'

'Not like a heap of shit,' agreed another rangy looking fellow with red hair. 'I'm sick and tired of these arseholes calling me period head, cunt head, sanitary towel dispenser, carrot fucking top, for fuck-sakes I'm feeling better already!'

There was a ripple of laughter amongst the men.

Soon it was Kevin's turn. He walked into the medic's room and encountered a young doctor, fresh from his internship, or university, two pips on his shoulders.

He looked bored.

'Drop you unders please.'

Kevin did so and jerked in reaction to the doctor's cold hand on his testicles. 'Turn your head to the left, cough, turn your head to the right, cough,' instructed the doctor. 'Good, pull your underpants up and turn around.'

Kevin felt the doctor's hands on his shoulders, back and neck, pressing firmly. For a terrifying moment Kevin expected to have something shoved firmly up his bum! He handed a vial over, 'Urinate in there please.' Kevin found it a little disconcerting having to take a piss into a bottle with the good doctor watching.

No way anyone could pull a jippo move here he realized, remembering one man collecting a diabetic's vial during basics so that he could be sent home.

'You can go out and call in the next man,' said the doctor dismissively. Kevin felt like a bloody guinea pig.

'What's with the hand on the balls?' asked a rather ruffled Manuel a little later.

'It's to check if you've got a hernia, if your balls lift when you cough, then you're okay,' said Roger with a knowledgeable note to his voice.

'You and your fucking brother again?' chirped a snide voice from the back.

There was a ripple of laughter amongst the men.

'I hope my balls lifted,' thought Kevin out aloud. The ripple of laughter repeated itself. Half an hour later they were still sitting in the sun in their underpants. Kevin and Manuel got dressed while the rest sat in the sun, catching a tan. Lying in the sun, their white bodies reflecting the sun like a slime of slugs, thought Kevin.

A gaggle of geese and a slime of slugs, wonder if that was accurate he mused.

Just when he was feeling boredom creeping in, Corporal Pus-Face screamed, 'What the fuck are you motherfucking chunks of shit doing lying around bare- arsed like this?

Get the fuck dressed and fall in next to the Bedford!'

Once again they were subjected to the grunting and groaning of the old veteran as it ground its way towards the admin block.

'Strip down to your underpants and stand in a line in front of the door,' yelled corporal Andrews, who was waiting for them; his eyes narrowing as he noticed Kevin amongst the men.

'Oh for fucksakes!' muttered Kevin under his breath, irritated by having to undress again and seeing his favourite corporal at the same time.

'What did you say, VOSSS?' spat Andrews. 'Have you a little complaint that I can sort out for you, huh?'

'No complaint corporal,' responded Kevin, his voice even.

'I am fucking amazed that a waste of white skin like you has actually made it this far,' he snarled, stepping closer his face inches from Kevin's face. Kevin averted his eyes; the last thing he needed was to do something stupid now, knowing that the first thing the corporal wanted was for him to retaliate, to screw it up for himself.

'Corporal, bring them in,' interrupted the paratroop sergeant in a quiet voice.

Corporal Andrews stepped back, giving Kevin a scowl. Kevin was relieved; he knew that the corporal was doing his best to cock it up for him. One by one they stepped in to be interviewed. Kevin walked in and stood rigidly before a panel of three men. It was the first time he saw the third man, his maroon beret on the table, his eyes an intense blue. They were cold eyes. Kevin felt terribly vulnerable, standing there before them in his underpants while the questions were fired at him;

'Why do you want to be a Parabat?'

'What is a Paratrooper?'

'Do you have any tattoos?'

'Turn around, pull your onderbroek down….yes we see, you have no tattoos.'

And so the questions were fired at him while standing at attention, feeling awkward in his underwear and answering as quickly as he can.

When they were all processed they were told to wait next to the Bedford; thankfully they didn't have to wait too long this time. The sergeant came out and they were told to form up. Their names were read out. Kevin heard his name being called, Manuel's name too. They waited in anticipation.

'Congratulations gentleman, you leave for parachute battalion tomorrow morning.

See you there,' stated the sergeant matter of factly as he turned away.

Of the 29 there were 21 left.

The 21 boarded the train from Kimberly at lunch time the next day, but not before some had loaded up with a shitload of booze.

'Hey cocks,' shouted an Afrikaans bloke called Beyers in Afrikaans. 'I've got enough dop here to get half of 11 Commando pissed!'

Kevin smiled, Beyers said the letter rrrr with a pronounced grgrgrgrgr in the back of the throat. Like a light growl it was the classic West coast accent, 'the rgrgrabbit rgran argground the block'.

Most of them got totally pissed that night.

For some inexplicable reason the army had not sent a rank along and so for the first time in six weeks they were unsupervised. And so, but for a handful, it became a binge of enormous proportions. Sadly there were was no pussy on the train, someone had observed loudly, not that Kevin would have partaken of any, with him being a virgin and all.

He had bought a flagon of Sedgwick's old brown sherry.

Manuel showed his "class" by producing a bottle of single malt whiskey, which he proceeded to desecrate by drinking it mixed with Coca-Cola.

A real peasant mix, thought Kevin.

'Fuck, but you Porras are peasants a bunch of crass fuckers,' commented a bloke they had only met yesterday.

He was a faceless individual, thought Kevin - if you looked at his face then looked away you'd have forgotten what he looked like in minutes. He would make a good spy, he mused.

'Come suck my cock, *cabeça de merda*,' retorted Manuel, the whiskey and rising anger colouring his face. In his minds eye Kevin saw a large turd flying through the air in slow motion, heading inexorably towards a very large fan.

'Chill guys, really, the last thing you need to do is cause shit for yourselves before we get there tomorrow,' reasoned Kevin.

'What the fuck has it got to do with you in any case,' snarled Mr Faceless, his eyes clouded with the brandy he had poured down his throat. Kevin backed off, mostly due to common sense but also due to just a touch of fear. Faceless made the mistake of thinking that Kevin's prudence was cowardice, so he stood up to give Kevin a hard shove.

The shove never happened, Manuel hit Faceless hard on the side of the head with a flat, paddle-shaped hand. His fingers were spread and Faceless went down to the sound of a loud, meaty thwack! He hit the floor and started to snore almost immediately. There was a stunned silence in the compartment. Manuel had earned instant respect from all of them.

An equally stunned Kevin was in awe, he had never seen anyone being hit that hard before!

'*Sua mãe é uma prostitute*,' muttered Manuel, looking down at the snoring Faceless and taking a slurp of his peasant mix.

Kevin tried to sleep to the sound of *klackity clack…clickety click, klackity klack, klickety click*, the sound of the train's wheels on the rails. He had heard that if you placed one foot on the ground while your head was spinning it would help lessen the effect… The problem though was that he was on the top bunk so his damn head just kept on spinning.

He had a vague recollection the next day, of someone puking out of the train window, the puke flying back into the compartment like a cluster of soppy leaves blown in by the wind.

What a balls-up!

The next morning the train stopped at Bloemfontein station. The compartment stank of puke and sour arse and Kevin thought that he was going to die.

Fortunately for all of them, the train arrived at four in the morning and was shunted into a siding; otherwise the gods alone would have known when they would have woken up.

Chapter Four: **Welcome to 1 Parachute Battalion**

Wax on, Wax off.
The Karate Kid

Dawn found a miserable, misshapen lot sitting outside of the station looking and feeling like shit. Kevin had taken four aspirins and managed to drink litres of water. Nonetheless, it felt like a large parrot had shat, masturbated and vomited into his mouth and his head felt the size of a melon. Looking around he realized that he was not alone and an irrational sense of relief prevailed.

At six in the morning they were picked up. A lone military truck arrived; a private stepped down from the cab and beckoned to them and so they were delivered to 1 Parachute Battalion in all their glory.

'Good morning, men,' said a tall, thin 2nd Lieutenant, giving them the once over.

'My name is Lieutenant Andy Coetzee and welcome to Parachute Battalion. Please put your kit down on the veranda and let's see if we can get some breakfast for you lads.'

Good grief! And so it carries on, mused Kevin. Nothing like being treated with respect, he thought, as the rangy Loot led them to the mess hall.

'Chef, get these guys well fed, will you please,' ordered the Loot, not commanded, but asked!

'See you gents in an hour,' he said, walking out.

'Good god!' exclaimed one very hung-over recruit as he surveyed the spread before them. Not varkpanne, pig pans. No food dumped randomly in a heap, followed by the dreary trudge to long tables of despondent men, sitting and forcing swill down their collective gullets. No, instead here it was six men to a table, white crockery, two loaves of bread one brown and one white. You had a bloody choice! Honey, butter, jam, toast, coffee and even orange juice; bacon and eggs which were not in the slightest blue.

'Not a fukken hint of blue!' exclaimed one man.

'This is going to be magic,' said Manuel. And for the first time nobody gave him the chirp and certainly nothing clever was heard from Faceless, who now kept his mouth firmly shut. He had a wonderful purple bruise on the side of his head, just a gentle reminder to them all that Manuel had a sting in his tail.

An hour later, the lieutenant found them lounging about next to their kit.

'Right chaps,' he said, adopting a pseudo-British-officer class accent.

'As I said, welcome all. I have been asked by the Commandant to give you a personal tour of the unit. See that building up on the top of the road there?' he pointed to a large building at the top of the road.

'Well that's the packers' building; it's where they pack the parachutes. You have 40 seconds to run up the hill, around the back of the packers building and to get your arses back here, NOW GO!' he roared.

'Do you see that cage there at the bottom of the road, that's called an aviary. Get your arses down there, salute the eagles residing in SAID FUCKING AVIARY and get your arse back here, MOOOOVVVE!'

And so they were given a personal guided tour of the base. And it wasn't long before they had deposited their respective breakfasts in steaming, random piles during the course of the good lieutenant's tour.

'You lot, you are sleeping there in the second bungalow,' indicated a stocky corporal.

'You are part of Alpha Company that is, A Company for those of you dumb fuckers who don't understand what Alpha is. The rest of your little friends are getting fucked up at De Brug[3] and will be back later tonight. So until then stay out of sight, I don't have the time to suck your dicks today so I don't want to hear, smell or see you dumb fuckers for the rest of the day,' he snarled, as he turned and walked away.

'Oh shit, same old same old army,' muttered Kevin, as he flopped down onto his bed.

Shit, shit, fucking shit!

He felt like screaming and kicking the walls down.

Why the fuck am I here?' Bloody hell, why?

They were woken at four the next morning to the sound of whistles blowing, and voices screaming. The previous night they had been left alone, probably because no one knew they were there and those who did know just probably forgot they were there. It was a little chink in the bureaucratic armour which Kevin noted and would learn to put to good use pretty quickly. The army was run like a tight ship, but it did have a few leaks. But they weren't so lucky this time. The bungalow door crashed open to reveal a terrifying sight. A Staff sergeant, in crisp browns, black cloth wings sown on the right side and "Marais" sown on the left. His hair shaved almost to the bone except the very top, which Kevin would later note was bedecked by a clump of hair which looked every

---

3. The airborne force training centre near Bloemfontein.

bit like steel wool. But this time a maroon beret was perched on the top of his head looking as if it were two sizes too small. A small moustache decorated his upper lip, its size fractionally larger than the one once sported by Adolf Hitler. He looked like a fucking Nazi storm trooper and instantly inspired terror and without having to utter a single word. He exuded pure malice. Kevin felt a knot of fear in his gut!

'And who are you?' he asked, his head cocked to the side as if beckoning an answer.

There was a stone silence, every one of the 21 volunteers being too shit scared to answer.

'I asked you lot a simple question, or is it that you are all from the school of the deaf and fucking dumb, you retarded arseholes! Who the fuck ARE YOU?' he screamed.

'We are volunteers from Kimberly, 11 Commando,' replied a short, stocky fellow with a large, bulbous nose. Kevin didn't know the man's name but he had an earnest, friendly expression etched on his face.

'We are volunteers from Kimberly, 11 commando, WHO!' the staff sergeant asked, his face starting to redden.

'Sorry, we are the volunteers from Kimberly, STAFF!' yelled the stocky fellow, smiling.

'What the fuck are you smiling at? Am I your fucking sister or better still, am I your fucking girlfriend, do you want to fuck me?' Asked the staff, his voice laced with sarcasm.

'No, sir.'

'I am not a fucking sir, I am a bloody staff, you don't even call officers, sir in the South African Defence Force, this is not the British army, do you get it you bloody SOUTIE. Get the fuck out of this pigsty NOWWW!' he screamed, his voice hoarse from days of yelling and shouting at the hapless souls who were in his care.

The short bloke left in a blur, the rest stayed standing rooted to the spot, stiffly at attention.

The staff sergeant looked at them, his eyes half-shut, his face turning redder, and oddly a slightly amused look developed on his face.

'And why are you still standing there like a bunch of fucking flower pots, DID YOU HEAR ME, I SAID GET OUT OF THE FUCKING BUNGALOW AND I MEAN NOW, BEFORE I PUNCH YOU IN THE FUCKING FACE!' he screamed, his voice sounding like an old raspy foghorn.

And so it was that they had made their acquaintance with staff, "Sakkie" Marais, from then on referred to as staff Sakkie; always addressed with a great deal of fear and serious respect.

* * *

The Choirmaster

'SING YOU FUCKERS, SING,' screamed the corporal as they marked time,

'A left right, left right a left right hey, a left right hey, huk, huk, huk, huk, huk, huk, hey, forwaaarrrd MARCH, a left right, hey.'

They were wearing full kit and steel helmet; they had not yet been issued with rifles.

Their boots were hitting the ground in unison, crump, crump, crump…

'I SAID SINNNNG!!!!!'

Two things they learnt quickly, never walk in the unit, always run and when you were told to sing paratrooper songs you did so, loudly, and with a great deal of enthusiasm, even if you weren't at all enthusiastic about it.

'We're parabats We're parabats

We're a long way from home

We're highly bedondered so leave us alone

We drink when we're thirsty we drink when we're dry

We drink when we're sober we'll drink till we die.

Cigarettes and whiskey and wild, wild women

We've killed the sergeant major, so try and kill us, us, us!'

Crump, crump, crump went the sound of boots. Kevin didn't feel like singing and nor did most of them, so the rendition was pretty crappy.

'I SAID SING, FUCKERS, SIIIINNNNG!' roared a different voice.

It was staff Sakkie and immediately the volume picked up, this time the good staff acting as the choirmaster.

'Hadi-hay, hadi-oh, what do you say, what do you know,

Widdley, widdley, waddley woe.

When you hear this battle cry, the parabats are passing by.

Hadi-hay, hadi-oh, what do you say, what do you know,

Widdley, widdley, waddley woe.

When you hear the whistle blow, the parabats are on the go.

Hadi-hay, hadi-oh, what do you say, what do you know,

Widdley, widdley, waddley woe.

Take your hat and hold it high, the paratroops are'….

The singing had spluttered and faded to a grinding halt.

'HAAAALT!' roared the staff.

He made the squad right turn and they stood there silently waiting with bated breath for the inevitable to happen.

'I will rip your fukken arms off and beat you to death with the wet end, do you dumb fuckers understand?' he asked, his voice strangely soft.

'NOW FUKKEN SING WHEN I TELL YOU TO FUKKEN SING, YOU OXYGEN THIEVES, YOU DON'T DESERVE THE FUCKING AIR YOU BREATH, YOU USLESS PIECES OF RUNNY HORSESHIT!' he finished with a roar, his face taking an a mottled claret hue which almost matched the colour of his maroon beret.

Kevin could have sworn that his moustache began to bristle like a porcupine's quills. He was bloody terrified and when the command came he began to sing with gusto and massive enthusiasm.

And so it carried on … the boots hitting the ground in unison, crump, crump…

'I SAID SINNNNG!!!!!'

'I walk down the street, I knock on the door, the lady said PARABAT!

You've been here before.

Hallelujah, I'm a Parabat.

Hallelujah, Bats again.

Hallelujah, give us a beer now

And...'

There was a sudden explosion of sound in Kevin's head, like a great, big, bloody church bell as Sakkie hit him on the back of his helmet with the butt of his rifle.

Kevin went down like a sack of shit.

His steel helmet was knocked forward cutting the bridge of his nose open, he could feel the blood running down his nose and dripping onto the ground as he lay there.

'WHEN I TELL YOU TO SING YOU SING, DO YOU COW-CUNTS UNDERSTAND!' roared the good staff.

He bent down, looked at Kevin's nose, grunted something and with a smack to the back of Kevin's head he stood up. At least Sakkie cared, thought Kevin sarcastically. And so it was that the cow-cunts understood to a man and they sang until their voices were hoarse. It wasn't long before the singing took on a different shape. As the weeks wore on the singing began to be part of who they were and what the unit stood for and Kevin came to understand the meaning of "Esprit de Corps".

The hated marble

All morning long the whistle had dictating when they should fall to the ground, when they should stand up, when they should roll and when they should do push-ups. The whistle dictated when they should drink and even when they could take a shit.

In the beginning the whistle reminded Kevin of his school days, the warm sun, the smell of freshly mowed lawn and rugby practice. Rugby matches played amid the cheers of the school supporters, the girls' voices clearly heard singing the school songs, egging their champions on to greater athletic endeavours. Now its harsh burble was just a horrible, fucking prelude to pain; he hated the fucking whistle. Running with Manuel across his shoulders in a fireman's lift, in full kit 100 meters in one direction, turn around 100 meters back. Stop, chest heaving, his lungs bursting.

Manuel picking him up, the same shit, 100 meters in one direction, 100 meters back bouncing on Manuel's shoulders like a sack of potatoes. He had stopped thinking of himself as Kevin, he was just a he, and then he was no longer a he, he became just a fucking number. Exactly what the army wanted you to be, just a fucking number. Property of the government and so much so that, if you got blisters resulting in light duty you got charged for abusing state property!

'I'm going to take that bitch whistle and push it up that fukken corporal's arse. Not pointed point up, not lying edgeways, but lying flat so it tears his arse open like a fukken tin of sardines,' swore Manuel with hatred in his eyes.

He used his hand to illustrate the whistle position, finger up, edge of hand up then back of hand up. This drew a smattering of laughter from the exhausted men as they gulped down water during a water break. And then the sonofabitch whistle blew and they started to shit off again.

They staggered up to the top the road where a lance corporal was waiting for them. As they reached him he stuck his right arm out indicating the direction they should take. They ran down a slight slope and there waiting for them was a sergeant, a swarthy thin-lipped individual. He had no expression on his face other than a hint of contempt. They had been subjected to a "chasey" for an hour before they arrived at sergeant Thin-Lips. So they were exhausted, covered in sweat stains and dust. The thin-lipped sergeant shouted a halt, bringing the exhausted, running men to a standstill.

'Cunt-faces, this is your fucking fiancé, each of you wet farts is going to choose a wife for yourselves now. Isn't that a decent thing for the army to do, to "fink" of you in such a considerate manner don't you fucking fink?' he screamed in a snarl.

Kevin was amazed that such a loud sound could escape through those bitter, little fucking lips, squeezed together in a dead straight line. The fact that he said "fink" instead of think was not lost on Kevin.

He felt a spiteful sense of triumph; another dumb Dutchman, he thought; not that he thought of his Afrikaans mates as dumb Dutchmen, only the men with rank and Afrikaners who gave him a hard time were dumb Dutchmen as far as he was concerned.

Fink, think….for fucksakes!

Thin-Lips pointed to a heap of kerb stones, lying haphazardly in an untidy jumble.

'What you see here is a gigantic fuckup, a total cluster-fuck. These are previous wives, dumped here by men who are a disgusting bunch of fucking whoremongers who cannot be faithful to their dear wives,' he snarled.

'Now pack this pile neatly in rows and do it gently or I will kick your arse so hard you'll taste your own shit for a fucking week, do you fucking understand me you useless fucks!'

'Yes, Sergeant!' they shouted back.

'I can't fucking hear you; what did I fucking say?'

'That you will kick our arses so hard we will taste or own shit, Sergeant!' they screamed back.

So they packed the kerbstones into three neat rows, with a metre gap between each row as instructed. Kevin vaguely noted that they had numbers painted on them. When they had finished packing them Thin-Lips inspected the stones.

He walked up and down the rows, inspecting them as if they were soldiers on parade. Then he turned on them, his eyes slitted, and a thin triumphant look on his face. 'I see a monumental fucking problem here; do you see it?' he asked.

Before anyone dared respond he continued.

'You half-witted fucks were selected because you passed the physical tests, hey? Also, because you supposedly passed the fucking aptitude test. But it is very obvious that the fucking army psychologists have fucked up badly, allowing you lot into this camp was a great, big fucking mistake!'

'SO WHAT IS THE FUCKING PROBLEM THAT I CAN SEE AND THAT YOU FUCKING MORONS CAN'T SEE?' He screamed the question.

No one dared to venture an answer.

'Well it seems that I'm going to have to tell you,' he said, dropping his voice so that they struggled to hear him.

'Do you see the little numbers painted on each of those stones, well in the army everything has to be in order, and those little "wives-to-be" you see lying there are not in the correct order. So PUT THEM IN THE RIGHT FUCKING ORDER!' he roared.

Once they had put them in numerical order they were ordered to stand in a squad formation, at rigid attention. Sergeant Thin-Lips turned to a lance corporal instructor,

'These fuckers are yours,' he said matter of factly.

The corporal inspected the stones and froze. He turned towards the men saying,

'We have a bloody problem; marble number 23 is missing, you shitheads will have to find it now!'

And so began another 30 minutes of running to the obstacle course, running back, being chased all over the battalion, ostensibly to find the errant marble. Kevin wondered how the hell, he could find a little glass marble while being chased around at the same time?

The men were ordered to stop under the aapkas, the ape box; a mock-up designed to train paratroopers how to exit out of a plane.

The corporal stepped up and said,

'These are referred to as marbles. They are not round which is baffling. They are more or less block-shaped as you can see. For the next week or two, depending on how I feel, your marble will be with you at all times. In the shower, on parade in your bed, do you understand?'

'YES CORPORAL!'

'Your marble weighs 25kg, so this is a very skinny wife and any man is capable of handling a 25kg woman, which means you carry your marble at all times, you never put your marble down on the ground, ever. Your marble is a tense, fucking bitch and wants to go everywhere in a rush, so you always run, you never walk when you are carrying your marble, DO YOU UNDERSTAND?'

'YES CORPORAL!'

'Go pick a marble now'!

So began the love affair with the marble; push-ups with it on your back, lying on your back in the dirt, lifting it up to the whistle, lowering it to the chest with the whistle blast ringing in the ears, lifting it to the whistle, always the bloody whistle, running with the marble, on the shoulders then in front of the chest to the ever-present beat dictated by the bloody whistle.

Chapter Five: **Attrition**

If you should go skating
On the thin ice of modern life
Dragging behind you the silent reproach
Of a million tear-stained eyes
Don't be surprised when a crack in the ice
Appears under your feet.
You slip out of your depth and out of your mind
With your fear flowing out behind you
As you claw the thin ice.

Rodger Waters

Three days later Manuel threw the marble to the ground

They were told to halt and mark time, standing in one place, running on the spot, left right left right, hutt, hutt, hutt, hey!

Kevin looked at Manuel, he was shaking, his brown uniform white with sweat stained salt.

'Pick your marble up you useless fucking sea-kaffir, pick the fucking thing up now,' ordered the instructor.

'You have ten seconds to pick it up, pick it up now you piece of shit!'

Manuel began to sob, his shoulders jerking and his eyes to the ground looking at the marble.

'Come, boet pick it up,' called a voice, then another and Kevin heard himself saying,

'Come brother, come man you can do it!'

'Shut up all of you,' commanded the instructor.

'Pick the fucking thing up Porra or you can fuck off now!'

'Foda-se isso é o suficiente. Merda eu odeio o exército foda-se tudo,' swore Manual, his voice hoarse with exertion as he uttered a string of expletives in Portuguese.

'Speak Afrikaans, you Porra fuck!' yelled the instructor.

'Afrikaans, do you hear me, AFRIKAAAANNNSSSSS!'

Manuel plonked himself down, a puff of dust huffing from under his backside.

'You soft cunt,' swore the instructor as he turned to the squad, the whistle shrieked as he indicated the edge of the parade ground.

That evening when they got back to the bungalow Manuel's kit was gone, his bed stripped. Kevin felt shit, oh so shit. He wanted to cry, fuck this army; fuck this army!

Of the 21 there were 20 left.

'You, Englishman, where is your little friend?' demanded staff Sakkie at roll-call the next morning.

'RTU, staff,' responded Kevin.

'What?'

'Returned to unit, staff.'

'Well go and find yourself a little buddy, now!'

But before Kevin could react the staff took matters into his own hands.

'Ek soek 'n spaarpiel om met die Engelsman to speel, who is a spare cock? This skinny fucking Englishman's Porra buddy has run away so he needs a playmate. Don't be shy, come-come now!'

A hand was raised, and so Kevin met his next buddy, Beyers. Kevin had met him on the train journey to Bloemfontein. The army relied on the buddy, buddy system; two men teams to cover each other, to back each other up, always there in support during training and later in combat. You would learn to trust your buddy with your life. As a result of the pain and danger, the shitting off during training and the experiences shared, the bonds between buddies became literally forged by the furnace of suffering and war.

Manuel would have been a great buddy if hadn't cracked, thought Kevin with real regret.

Beyers was a patriot; enthusiastic to the point of irritation.

He spoke with the thick West Coast accent, the RRR's rolling out from the back of his throat.

'Fuck Englishman, I'm happy as a pig in shit to be here. I've decided that when jump course is over I'm going to volunteer for Pathfinders. I want to become Permanent Force, my brother, going to do my BMil degree, become a fucking general! Who knows, the sky's the limit,' he enthused one day.

Kevin rolled his eyes,

'You're fucking mad, you dumb Dutchman, who the hell wants to become part of all this,' his hand sweeping across in the direction of the battalion as he spoke, 'this…shit, as part of your life, especially forever?' he asked.

'Jeez man, you're fukken mad. I'm out of here as soon as fukken possible!'

Beyers was fit and slightly shorter than Kevin; they made a good pair in the endless grind of training and being fucked around. Beyers was a horny bastard and spent most of his spare moments talking about pussy and his shagging exploits of yore. He was also as funny as hell and his sense of humour was brilliant, his eyes gleaming with mirth from behind his glasses. He had them all in stitches more often than not.

'When we get a weekend pass, I'm going fuck my lungs out. I'm going to pump my girlfriend until her pussy farts,' enthused Beyers to an enthralled audience in the bungalow one night.

'I'm going to fuck her doggie style, I'm going to take her from behind until she squeals like a piggy, *oink, oink, oink*,' he said making pig grunting sounds his eyes gleaming.

One man sneaked up behind Beyers, grabbed him, bent him forward in one surprising movement and pretended that he was doing the dastardly, doggie style with Beyers. The bungalow degenerated into chaos, some men pretending they were shagging their buddies, it was ridiculous.

'Oh by the way,' said Kevin after lights out. 'If any of you get any clever ideas tonight I'm sleeping with my bayonet.'

Spirits were lifted; things weren't going to all that bad after all thought Kevin.

Morning roll-call and breakfast done, staff Sakkie addressed the severely depleted A Coy.

'The Commandant wants to speak to you this morning. So we are going to march you fucking girls down to the Commandant's office, because he feels that you fuckers aren't good enough to grace the hallowed grounds of our parade ground. Every morning, when he looks at you motley chunks of shit, you useless fucking homos, and he sees how shit you are he becomes worried.' He paused, then continued, 'You see men, he is very fucking worried at the rate of R TEE fucking U's pouring out of this gate and he is also very worried that this crop of Parabat wannabees fuckups, are too soft to make the grade.' He continued, looking at them with disdain, 'So he wants to have a little chat with you girls and wants to give you a little pep talk, WHICH AS FAR AS I AM CONCERNED IS A WASTE OF FUCKING TIME!' He finished with a roar.

And so what was left of A Coy was marched down to the Commandant's office, but first they were marched past the aviary housing the battalion emblem, the eagle. The corporal calling out time,

'A left right left right a left right hey, a left right hey, huk, huk, huk, huk, huk, huk, hey... eyyyeeesss rrrright,' as they saluted the eagles,

'eyyyyyeeeesss frrront, huk, huk, huk, hey.

Compaanneeyyy HALT,' and they crashed to a halt.

'Squad will advance riiiggght tuuurn. One two three one,' feet coming down with a crash. And so they stood waiting at rigid attention for the Commandant to appear.

'I wonder what the fuck is going on?' whispered Beyers out of the corner of his mouth, head not moving. It was a big mistake, Sergeant Thin-Lips caught the slight movement and marched to up to Beyers. His nose was almost touching Beyers' nose he screamed at him, the spit flying.

'What the fuck are you talking about troop? Why are you talking while in the ranks, you know that you cannot talk in the fucking ranks while at attention, you fucking stupid fuck!' the spit flying into Beyers' face.

Beyers started to answer when there was a loud crack, as Thin-Lips hit him on the side of the face. Beyers staggered sideways, corrected his balance and stood at attention. Thin-lips turned around and resumed his position.

And so the Commandant addressed them. He expressed concern at the attrition rate; there were too many falling off the programme. He spoke about their morale, explaining that low morale was a killer. On and on he went, trying to build them up and to arrest the flow of candidates leaving the unit.

He didn't swear once, his voice remained at an even tone and Kevin almost believed that he was sincere. He retrospect he probably was sincere. After the address Beyers was strangely silent. He stayed that way for the rest of the day.

Pole PT, two men to a pitch-coated telephone pole while the third man carried the much loved marble.

The whistle, always the fucking whistle!

Poles up, poles down, poles up, poles down always to the whistle; running the Moller's marathon, 10km of it with poles and marbles and the bloody whistle blasting incessantly.

Sit-ups with the pole across the chest, the third man the same, with the marble on his chest. Changing places, Kevin's turn to carry the marble, on and on it went.

Always the whistle, everything was done to a cadence inspired by the mind numbing, hateful fucking whistle.

Five men dropped out, two were from the Kimberly crew, Kevin noted through the salt burn in his eyes.

Of the 20 there were 18 left.

That evening there was no mirth, they were too physically exhausted, too tired to anything other than prepare for morning inspection. Kevin noticed that Beyers was still strangely quiet, sitting on his "trommel", the military chest showing one or two dents from previous abuse.

'What's wrong boet?' asked Kevin, concern in his voice.

'Fuck them all,' was the response. 'Fuck them and fuck that Thin-Lips, I'm going to shoot the fucker, I'm going to kill him. I've decided that the army can go and get fucked, I don't mind swallowing all of their shit, I know there's a reason for it to make you stronger, fitter and so that you can function under fucking stress. But that cunt hit me, he's not allowed to do that, I'm going to lay a charge of assault against the prick!

Watch me, you think you've seen guys skive about to get out of doing stuff, watch me I'm going to become the laziest fucking soldier in this fucking army, they won't know what to do with me!'

He raged on and on until Kevin walked off and left him alone, to vent his fury until he fell asleep. The next morning, Beyers reported for light duty and he stayed light duty for any and every possible reason. He was an intelligent man so he quickly worked out how to buck the system, becoming the biggest skiver or sluiper in the unit. A title he carried with pride until ultimately, he was kicked off the course and issued with a one piece boiler suit and a white steel helmet. The helmet had a bright red cross painted on the front and the back of it, denoting permanent light duty.

Until finally, he was transferred to the vehicle park to act out the rest of his service doing what he had learnt to do best, and that was to do as little as is humanly possible, or in army parlance ... fuck-all.

Of the 18 there were 17 left.

Kevin had lost two buddies and decided that from now on he would just focus on getting through the selection course. No more attachments because every time a buddy fell off the course it just made life tougher. Fuck this shit!

Your new army wife

And so musketry training started; and Kevin had been looking forward to it, rather stupidly he was soon to find out. They were issued with FN rifles, designated R1 rifles by the army. They had wooden butts and not the coveted jump rifle with foldup butt, which was to be issued later before jump course. Staff Sakkie looked at them, an amused glint in his eyes.

'This is an R1 rifle and is your new wife,' he shouted, his moustache bristling.

'Your marble is your other wife but this is your favourite wife. Consider yourself to be like a fokken Zulu. They are lucky buggers, those Zulus, because they can have more than one wife and you are lucky as well because we have allowed you, yes all of you, to have two wives in the battalion. You are spoiled rotten by the South African Defence Force and you should count yourselves to be a bunch of very lucky troops, because you can fuck two women at once!' he roared, his face going red, the veins blue in his neck.

Kevin was shit-scared of the man.

'If I hear any of you useless fuckers calling this thing a gun I will personally push it up your arse, do you fucking understand me?'

'YES, STAFF!' They shouted.

'Now every one of you hold your rifle in your left hand and lift it up, like so,' he yelled, lifting his rifle in his left hand.

'Now place your right hand on your cocks and grip your block and fukken tackle tightly, like so!' he roared, his right fist clasping his groin.

They all obeyed, Kevin held his equipment in his hand and he noted that his cock had disappeared in fear, like a tortoise retracting its head into its shell.

'Now repeat after me. This is my rifle and this is my gun, this is for killing and this is for fun.' He alternated between lifting his rifle up and shaking his groin vigorously in time to the verse.

They repeated the verse,

'This is my rifle and this is my gun this is for killing and this is for fun.'

'I CAN'T FUCKING HEAR YOU, YOU PIECES OF SHIT, SAY IT AGAIN,' he roared.

'THIS IS MY RIFLE AND THIS IS MY GUN,

THIS IS FOR KILLING AND THIS IS FOR FUN!'

'I CANT FUCKING HERE YOU, SAY IT AGAIN!'

And so the next phase of being thoroughly fucked up began. They rolled in the dust with their rifles pressed to their bodies. They were taught to leopard crawl with the rifle across their forearms until their elbows were rubbed raw and bleeding. They had to tie a car tyre to their web belts, with the rifle slung across their shoulders and the marble held in their arms they had to run dragging their tyres behind them. The ever present whistle shrieking, it's demanding cadence dictating their every step. They had to do sit-ups holding the rifle, stand marking time with arms stretched out horizontally and any man lowering his rifle was immediately forced to fall to the ground and start rolling. Four rolls, four push-ups. Ten rolls ten push-ups and so it went on and on for hours.

'One minute, around the packing building,

PAKKERS GEBOU GAAN!' he roared.

And so they ran up the hill, around the parachute packing hanger and back again, over and over again.

Finally the first day of musketry drew to a close,

Of the 17 there were 12 left.

Kevin was fucked and slept that night like a dead man. And so musketry continued; how to strip the rifle and put it back again, clean it until it gleamed, only to roll in the dust until it was covered in sweaty mud. Rifle inspection became the bane of his life and Kevin began to feel the serious need to divorce his new wife!

The shooting range fart

The day had ended, the men had showered and roll call was over. They were lying about on their beds, some reading others playing cards while some were talking shit or "chewing the tobacco", as they would say in a cowboy movie. The lieutenant and the corporal walked into the bungalow.

Aaatennnshion!' yelled the first man at the door and everyone leapt up to stand at rigid attention.

'Stand easy, men,' said the lieutenant quietly. 'I'm here to discuss the requirements for our trip to Hamilton's shooting range[4] tomorrow.'

And so he proceeded to explain what the requirements were for the next day. Kevin stood listening with rapt attention knowing full well, that any omission of the lieutenant's instructions the next day would result in some serious repercussions.

'Tomorrow you must take your rifle, your waterbo…'

and his sentence was interrupted by the sound of a loud fart; a fart which resonated in the barrack room. It was a loud and protracted fart, a fart any man would have been proud of. It was a fart which under normal circumstances would have elicited a series of congratulatory comments from any man within earshot. Instead it filled Kevin with a sense of dread and by the expressions on the faces around him he knew that he was not alone. The corporal looked at the Loot with shock. The Loot ignored him and to everyone's amazement paused only fractionally before continuing.

'You must remember to take two water bottles, all seven magazines your steel helmet…'

The second fart resonated through the room and Kevin heard someone whisper,

'Oh fuck!'

By then the first fart wafted across Kevin's nose and it smelt like rotten eggs with just a hint of rancid onion. His trepidation increased tenfold, the lieutenant had to be smelling this as well, he realised. The Loot didn't miss a beat and finished the briefing, turned and began to walk towards the door. Kevin began to slowly let his breath out in

---

4. Hamilton Shooting Range in Bloemfontein.

a sigh of relief which was caught in mid-exhale as the lieutenant stopped at the door's threshold, turned and addressed the still aghast corporal, as if in an afterthought.

'Oh, I almost forgot,' said the lieutenant. 'Fuck them up corporal, one hour for each fart! Give them a good "chasey".'

Kevin's heart sank, the dreaded "chasey" which by now he knew meant that they were going to be chased around, fucked around to the hated whistle until utterly exhausted.

'Oh no, a fucking "chasey", fuck this,' he groaned.

After the Loot had left, the corporal's face transformed, chameleon-like. The aghast, aggrieved look slid off his face and on slid a look of righteous anger. He roared,

'Which one of you fucking morons has just fucked up my date with my girlfriend tonight?' he asked, his voice finishing with an indignant wheezy sound.

'You fuckers!' He screamed, 'I have been trying to get into her panties for the last four weeks and the very night, the very FUCKING night I have it all set up, guaranteed to have my balls emptied, some stupid fuck FARTS IN FRONT OF THE LIEUTENANT! 'NOT ONLY IN FRONT OF HIM, BUT WHILE HE IS SPEAKING!'

His voice tapered off into a silent wheeze.

'So who the fuck did it!' he demanded!

Silence.

'Tell me who it is and the rest of you girls can go sleepy-bye while I will fuck fart-face up, to such an extent THAT HIS STUPID FUCKING MOTHER WON'T EVEN RECOGNISE HIM!'

Silence.

He cast his eyes about the room. No one made eye contact with him; all stood at rigid attention with eyes fixed onto the opposite wall.

'Right so that's how it's going to be, hey,' he stated matter of factly, with a hint of feigned disappointment in his voice.

'Go fetch your trommels and fall in outside!' he commanded.

They did so and were soon standing outside the barracks, each man's steel military chest placed at his feet.

'Pick up your trommel and hold it above your head,

NOW RUN, PAKKERS GEBOU GAAN,' he roared.

And so it was that Kevin and his mates found themselves running in tracksuits and takkies, around the parachute packer's building and back again to the pissed off corporal; over and over again.

'Go and fetch your fucking beds. Put them on top of each other, two men to each set of bed; now run around the packers building,

GO!''Go and fetch your lockers, put it on your beds, put your trommels on your beds as well, NOW GO!'

And so it carried on and on and on…until one exhausted soldier dropped his bed, the steel leg hit the tarred road and a small spark flashed in the night.

'HAAAAALLLLT!' roared the corporal.

He proceeded to address them in a quiet voice, 'Sparks cause fires gentlemen and fires burn down buildings and seeing that these buildings are government property, I take a very dim view of what I have just seen. I am not happy at your poor attempt at burning down this military base. No, not one bit happy,' he spoke, striding up and down chest out.

The man was having a wonderful time observed Kevin through salt blurred eyes. The corporal continued with relish,

'Now because of this blatant attempt at sabotaging the military might of the South African Defence force, by attempting to burning down One Parachute Battalion, you fuckers give me no choice but to fuck you up for a bit longer. Lovely, lovely, lovely; PACKERS BUILDING, GO!'

Finally it ended with the exhausted men having to repack all equipment and kit in good order. All of the contents had to be repacked with some poor bugger discovering polish on all of his clothes. His polish tin had burst open during the chasey.

Kevin sat on the edge of his bed, legs rubbery.

'Why did one of you attempting to *burning* down this military base,' he chirped, mimicking the corporal's attempt at speaking English.

'Why are you's guys attempting to *burning* down this cunt farm, hey? You's is a bunch of pussies!'

There was a smattering of laughter.

'Salt cock,' responded Lappies, 'at least he's trying to speak English, I don't hear you speaking Afrikaans that much, huh?'

'Oh come on Lappies, why are you defending him, he just spent two and a half hours fucking us up, because one of your fucking mates farted in front of the Loot,' snarled Kevin.

'Yes,' interjected the bloke with polish all over his kit. 'Where is the motherfucker who caused all of this? I'll push this boot polish down his fucking throat!'

'He's your mate,' snarled Kevin, looking squarely at Lappies. 'I understand you guys not dropping him in the shit by reporting him to the corporal, but I suggest you sort him out sooner or later, because he's a fucking idiot!'

In the dead of the night Kevin woke to the sound of yelling and the thudding sounds of bars of soap knotted into socks, being swung with vengeful force against the farter's body. He felt so much better after that and drifted off to sleep.

The accidental shiner

The barrack door burst open and in strode staff Sakkie, a nice little "Sakkie" glint in his eye. The barrack room was ship-shape notwithstanding the fuckup of a chasey the night before and the good staff noticed this in the blink of an eye.

He looked a bit disappointed.

'Shoo-shoo,' he said in a hoarse whisper. There was a stunned silence.

'I said fucking shoo-shoo!'

Now the silence became a confused one. This was most uncharacteristic of the good staff. He would normally rip into the barracks screaming, 'GET OUT, GET OUT!' interspersed with whistle blasts. And then it dawned on Kevin, the man had lost his voice, he had laryngitis.

'Troops, I said fucking shoo-shoo!'

None of them knew what to do. Kevin could see heads moving from side to side as they looked at each other, confused expressions on their faces. Then Sakkie proceeded to remove his web-belt, grasping it in his right hand he stripped it out of his browns in one fluid motion, doubled it up in a second, equally fluid motion and struck the closest man across his back, thwapp! There was an explosion of movement and sound as men began to yell while trying to avoid the rampant, belt swinging staff. Kevin looked around desperately for a way out. He was a born survivor and headed for the row of barrack windows; they were small little slits in the walls and he went through one of them in a series of snaky wiggles, leaving the yells and swishing web belt behind him. He could hear that the smaller and skinnier fellows were following suit, plopping from the windows into the dust like falling lemons from a tree.

They all ran to the front of the barrack room before the staff could get there and were met by the sight of a terrified Lappies exiting the building, last man out and sporting an already nice looking shiner. His eye was starting to close up before their eyes. Lappies was far too big to fit through any of the windows, which left him with only one of three ways out! Around, under or over the swinging staff. He chose the latter and as he shoulder charged and flattened Sakkie, Sakkie delivered a real beaut of a punch which connected Lappies sweetly on the eye. To give Sakkie credit he pulled Lappies out of the squad and sent him to the medics. That night Sakkie walked into the mess and bought Lappies a beer. He apologised and meant it; and Kevin knew then that the staff, while being a hard arsed, full of shit and scary sonofabitch was indeed a good man.

Chapter Six: **Time to find your feet young man**

Hey you out there in the cold, Getting lonely getting old,
Can you feel me?

Hey you standing in the aisles, With itchy feet and fading smiles
Can you feel me?

Hey you don't help them to bury the light,
Don't give in without a fight

Rodger Walters

Kevin makes his first stand

'FAALL IN, FALL IN!' yelled a short stocky corporal amid shrill whistle blasts. The men formed up in a squad and stood at ease.

'Attention; arrange yourselves from tallest to shortest, the marker being to tallest man, NOW!' he screamed.

The men did so with the exception of one man who was convinced that he was taller than Kevin.

'Move to the left dick-head, I'm taller,' said "not so tall" man.

'Bugger off, I'm taller, and who's your bloody dick-head?' snarled Kevin in response, his voice reflecting the panic beginning to set in. He knew that they had better sort themselves out smartly before the nasty, stocky corporal took notice. Too bloody late!

'What the hell is going on there?' screamed stocky corporal.

'I'm sick of you arseholes making a meal out of everything!'

He strode up to Kevin, his eyes level with Kevin's chin, who by now was standing rigidly at attention. Stocky was a B Coy corporal, left hanging about for some reason or other, his mates on the border and him left to fend for himself. So Stocky Corporal Lategan wasn't the happiest soul about.

Without warning he kicked Kevin on the shin, hard, the boot tip connecting painfully. He did it again, three swift kicks followed and Kevin was forced to break ranks.

'Stand still, I said stand still!' he screamed, his face inches from Kevin's nose. A little switch went click in Kevin's head. He raised his arm thirty degrees up hand formed into a fist, palm down, the signal for a man in the ranks asking to be heard.

'Permission to speak Sergeant Major,' called Kevin, his voice slightly quaky.

'Speak', responded Sergeant Major Tillie.

'Permission to address the corporal'

'Granted'!

Kevin continued, the switch now fully thrown, his voice even quakier and loaded with emotion and rage.

'Corporal Lategaan, you have assaulted me and I do not wish to lay a charge against you.

However, I invite you to meet me at 19h00 outside the main gate, in order to settle this, corporal!'

There was a stunned silence.

Stocky Corporal opened his mouth to speak, then clapped it shut like a mousetrap. He glanced towards the Sergeant Major who, with a faint smile had looked away.

Stocky Corporal was on his own. And Kevin knew he had him when he too looked away, breaking eye contact. It was a clear sign, that stocky corporal wasn't happy being stripped of the protection of his rank.

That evening Kevin was on time at the gate, the initial anger had passed, the switch had been thrown the other way to the off position. He waited nervously until a quarter past seven, until he was sure that the short corporal had clearly gone AWOL. He was relieved, the corporal would have been a tough nut to crack and with the switch switched to the off position, he wasn't feeling all that brave anyway.

He went to the mess and drank the regulation two beers. Another beer was placed in front of him. He looked up and asked the man behind the bar who had bought it. He shrugged his shoulders. 'Dunno, someone told me to buy you as many as you want.'

'Who?' asked Kevin.

'He told me not to say,' and turned away to serve another beer to another troop, wanting to dull the senses.

The bus fight

It was late Friday afternoon and they had only been given a pass for the night. The barrack room was a dour place to be in, the guys were not happy.

'No weekend pass! It's a load of shit, fucking stinking shit,' moaned a bloke called Von Rommel. 'This is typical of these bastards. What's the difference between going home for the weekend and staying in this shithole!' he snarled.

'Nothing's happening this weekend, they're just being spiteful cunts,' added Peter, reclining on his bed.

'Let's go and get pissed!' exclaimed Ronnie, bouncing off his bed enthusiastically. Ronnie was a true street fighter and had provincial colours in boxing. Kevin always felt uncomfortable around the man; he always seemed to have a seething anger hidden just below the surface, like a vicious volcano waiting to erupt. Ronnie and Von Rommel were big mates, both fighters; the difference being that Ronnie was quite bright while Von Rommel gave the impression of being a stupid big thug. In fact Kevin was almost convinced that he was a big stupid thug, although time would show that he was brighter than he looked.

'So you guys coming?' asked Ronnie, his tail up.

There were a few unenthusiastic, 'Nopes'.

The rest did their best to remain incognito, trying to stay off Ronnie's radar. They all knew how full of shit Ronnie could become, his aggression level being directly proportionate to his level of inebriation; and the likelihood of those in his company being involved in a fight directly proportionate to both; hence the distinct lack of enthusiasm in the barrack room.

Ronnie looked around a scowl on his face. His eyes settled on Kevin and a bloke called Naatie.

'You two coming?' he demanded more than asked.

Kevin felt his resolve crumbling, Ronnie was an intimidating shit.

'Yeah. you coming?' asked Von Rommel, all henchman-like.

Stupid fucking thug, thought Kevin, not daring to voice his thoughts. And so it was, that a reluctant Naatie and an unhappy Kevin found themselves boarding a city bus, headed towards the night spots and no doubt, a few sin spots in Bloemfontein. The bus stopped about a kilometre on and on climbed a group of "Panzers", men from the school of armour. They walked to the back of the bus. There were five of them and two of them were built like the tanks they manned; big muscular bastards.

As the bus pulled off Kevin heard Ronnie's voice, clear as a bell above the noise of the rattling bus.

'What the fuck are you cunts looking at?' demanded Ronnie.

'Yeah, what the fuck are you looking at?' echoed Von Rommel, the henchman.

Kevin felt his heart sink.

'Aw, shit!' he heard Naatie groan.

Kevin stood up, raising his hands in a pacifying manner and with his voice adopting a conciliatory tone, he pleaded, 'Guys, c'mon, we're going for a few beers, let's not fuck this up, c'mon man.'

One of the big panzers stood up, his mates following suit.

Jutting his chin forward and looking squarely at Ronnie he said, 'I'm looking at you fuck-face!'

'Aw, shit!' he heard Naatie groan again.

Big boy never saw it coming. Ronnie punched him as quickly as a striking black mamba and Kevin saw the man's nose split open, like an overripe tomato. He squealed as Von Rommel punched him hard on the ear. He went down hard and stayed there.

All hell broke loose! Kevin moved backwards, away from the melee, not in the least bit interested in this shit. Looking to his side he saw Naatie doing the same, although unlike Kevin, had a broad grin on his face. Kevin saw one of the panzers get up and move towards him, Kevin turned to face him and looking him in the eye he shook his head slightly. The panzer looked relieved and brushed past him; clearly he wasn't interested in joining the rumble. Kevin was equally relieved. By this time Peter, Ronnie and Von Rommel had got the upper hand and the three of them had one large panzer in the corner of the back seat, kicking and punching the crap out of him. The big muscle bound man had seized up, he was big and unlike the super fit parabats he had punched himself to a standstill. Kevin looked on horrified as he saw the merciless beating continue, by now the man was on the floor jammed between the seats, begging them to stop.

Kevin wanted to step forward and stop it, he couldn't, he was mesmerised by it. He knew that he if he got closer would get caught in the crossfire, very quickly. By now Ronnie, Von Rommel and Peter were all kicking and stomping the man, three against one and he had stopped moving. Kevin felt disgust build up in him and stepping forward he dragged Peter away. Peter spun around and lunged at Kevin, the bloodlust clear in his eyes. He took a swing at Kevin, who managed to block it with his left hand only just in time and instinctively he hit Peter, hard, with the heel of his hand right on his upper lip.

The blow was beautifully timed, hard and precise, it did the job and Peter went down like a sack of shit. Kevin felt the bus the lurch to a halt and looked towards the driver who was already leaving the bus. There was a blue light next to the bus and Kevin realized with a lurch that the driver had driven straight into the police station yard.

'COPS, COPS, COPS!' screamed Kevin. Four policemen were coming up the stairs, one had a revolver drawn.

Kevin simply leapt past the fighting men, gave the emergency window three hard kicks and thankfully it popped out as it was designed to do, landing onto the road in a silver crash.

Kevin hit the ground and began to run, he watched Naatie, then Peter followed by Ronnie and finally Von Rommel all bail past him. He couldn't keep up, he felt as if a little dwarf was sitting on his shoes and stabbing him in the shins. Lategaan, you little shit, thought Kevin, as he realized that the stocky corporal kicking him the way he did, had done more damage than he had realized.

'HALT, I SAID HALT!' Kevin heard a policeman shout.

He looked back and saw the policeman pointing his service revolver straight at him. 'Fuck, I'm busted!' the thought went through his head as he raised his hands above his head. Hours later Kevin found himself in an interrogation cell at the detention barracks.

The room was bare, only a single government issue wooden chair in the middle of the room. The police had loaded him into a van, very civilly, he noticed, and had driven him back to Tempe. He sat on the chair and waited. He heard raised voices, a man shouting at someone in a room down the corridor. The answers were muffled.

'SOLDIER, I want names, do you get it?' screamed the voice

Muffled response.

Kevin heard footsteps and the door burst open to reveal a short podgy staff sergeant, an MP armband on his upper arm.

He looked excited, he was having fun and Kevin realized that it was because he had a few paratroopers at his mercy. The bats were feared and at the same time reviled by many of the other units in Tempe; too many of them going down in a hail of fists.

Another MP walked in and moved behind the seated Kevin. He didn't like the situation at all, the man behind him didn't make a sound, but his presence there made Kevin as uncomfortable as hell. Podgy-boy looked at Kevin, aggression painted on his face in puffed, flushed red.

'So!' Podgy exclaimed, his eyebrows raised in a questioning arc.

Kevin looked back at him, making sure that his face was blank.

'Are you scared of me, soldier?' asked Podgy in Afrikaans, jutting his chin out, his voice even. It was quite obvious that he fancied himself as the perfect interrogator.

Scared of you, don't be fucking ridiculous you fat little fuck, thought Kevin.

Kevin looked back at him, his face remained blank.

'Don't just look at me, trooper,' said Podgy, affecting a menacing voice. Kevin didn't feel menaced at all. Podgy couldn't be intimidating if he tried, mused Kevin.

'Could you speak English please?' asked Kevin.

Podgy paused He opened his mouth as if to say something then clamped it shut.

He paused.

'WHO WAS WIFF YOU ON THE BUS?' he screamed in English laced with a heavy Afrikaans accent, spraying little droplets of spit on Kevin's face.

'You speak to me decently and I'll tell you,' Kevin heard himself say.

Podgy was so engrossed in the little screenplay he had written for himself, that he didn't hear what Kevin had said.

'I FUCKING ASKED YOU, TROOPER, WHO WAS WIFF YOU ON DAT FUCKING BUS?' he screamed, spraying more little droplets of spittle on Kevin's face. Kevin imagined his fist smashing into Podgy's face.

'If you ask me decently, I will answer you,' responded Kevin quietly.

'ARE YOU TRYING TO BE FUCKING CLEVER WIFF ME!' screamed podgy.

'No staff.'

'WHAT?'

'I said I'm not trying to be clever staff.'

'SO, WHO WAS WIFF YOU ON THE FUCKING BUS?'

'If you ask me decently I will answer you,' Kevin repeated quietly.

Podgy looked bemused. He looked at the man standing behind Kevin almost as if he was seeking reassurance.

Kevin braced himself, expecting a blow on the back of his head or something. Then a puzzled expression developed on Podgy's flushed face. Kevin could see the internal struggle taking place in his podgy head, it was in his eyes. Kevin loved eyes, they were the window into a man's head, into his soul sometimes. He imagined the questions flying about in Podgy's fat head. Why was this man not intimidated? I can't talk to him decently, that means I am not a hard-arsed MP interrogator. It doesn't match my little screenplay! My self-esteem is going for a ball of shit!

Kevin was tired.

It was two in the morning and people had been screaming at him forever it seemed; raised voices in the battalion, always screaming; the shrill of the fucking whistle, running with the marble, sit-ups, the whistle, screaming….spit hitting his face. And to add to it all, here is another man saying 'WIFF' who should be saying 'WITH'. The image of the three men beating the poor man on the floor was vivid in Kevin's head. He felt disgusted, embarrassed to be a paratrooper.

'If you ask me decently I will answer you,' Kevin repeated quietly.

'Who was wiff you on the bus?' asked Podgy, his voice quivering with suppressed anger, the shouting gone.

Kevin was tempted to ask Podgy to say please, but realized that, that would be just plain idiotic. The idea popped up in his head but common sense prevailed, quit while you are ahead Kevin! So he simply gave Podgy the names. It was easier than he thought it would be as they rolled off his tongue one after the other. He left Peter's name out, because he knew that he had probably broken Peter's nose and in some strange way, he considered this to be punishment enough.

Strangely he didn't feel guilty, he didn't feel as if he had betrayed fellow parabats; that he had let the battalion down. The image of the three men beating the poor man on the floor vivid in Kevin's head, the guilt just went away then, gone, poof and away!

Podgy was taken aback He didn't expect the answer that easily. He seemed almost disappointed with the turn of events as he wrote the names down.

Podgy's sidekick escorted Kevin outside to a car standing at the gate, Naatie was sitting in the back seat. They were driven back to the battalion in silence.

'So who's the Polly, Polly, the squawking fucking parrot?' Ronnie snarled the question a week later. Peter, Ronnie and Von Rommel had spent the week in detention barracks.

They had been released that afternoon, pending a court marshal and the three of them were clearly on a fact-finding mission. Kevin had just walked into the barracks when they confronted him. Naatie was sitting on his bed minding his own business but Kevin could see that he wasn't at all happy.

The room fell silent. Everyone was waiting to see what Kevin's reaction would be. Kevin felt like shit, he knew his number was up and he knew that if he denied the fact that he had given the MP's their names, he'd be lying to himself. He'd be a fucking coward in his own eyes and that would be a very bad thing! The image of the three of them beating the unconscious man flashed before him and all guilt flew out of the proverbial window. He knew that he was going to get fucked up solidly, but that didn't matter as much, as being accused by the rest of the company of betraying his mates to the MP's. Kevin realized that a few guys would understand but the majority wouldn't, he'd be ostracised by the whole fucking lot of them. But fuck this he wasn't going to lie. Kevin opened his mouth and said,

'I told…'

When suddenly, Peter interjected, his eyes still a greenie-black from Kevin's blow to the nose, and he held Kevin in a stony look.

'Vossie would never blurt on us, never!' he said matter of factly.

Kevin's mouth snapped closed; he couldn't believe what he had just heard.

'Kevin here,' said Peter, turning to the others and jerking his thumb at Kevin, 'would never drop us in the shit!'

'You see my fucking face?' he asked the group touching his nose gingerly, 'Well that was KD here, who gave me a poeshou, a cunt of a punch, to stop us from killing that bloke!'

He paused before continuing, 'If KD hadn't stopped us we'd be in shit up to our fucking foreheads, actually over our fucking foreheads and so he did us a fucking favour; so leave him the fuck alone!'

Peter turned and looked at Kevin, gave a slight nod, walked over to his bed and flopped down onto it.

Ronnie gave Kevin the evil eye and muttered, 'I'll find out if it was you, Polly!' spitting out the word "Polly" as he turned away. Von Rommel kept quiet; he was strangely subdued.

Kevin was so relieved he almost felt light headed, realizing that by not implicating Peter, Peter had cut him a break. The old adage of one hand washing the other applied for sure.

'Lesson taught, me old son,' thought Kevin as he walked towards his spot in the room. If you live by the sword, you'll die by the sword. Stay the fuck away from those blokes from now on, his inner voice chided him.

Kevin makes his second stand

'Aw, grief,' groaned Brian. 'Why do we have to stand guard at another unit's bloody warehouse? This is ridiculous!'

Brian was an intelligent fellow, one of the unit's intellectuals.

Sadly with this intelligence came a superior attitude which reminded Kevin of the English gentry. Stiff upper lip and all that, don't forget to tilt the head back slightly and look down along the bridge of one's nose at the lackey one is addressing.

Brian had the ability to make Kevin feel slightly inferior and as a result, he tended to be a bit nasty to Brian. A bit of the old defence mechanism kicking in, Kevin would come to realize, but not quite yet.

'It's because we are paratroopers and the arseholes stationed there can't look after shit, never mind their stupid warehouse,' responded Kevin.

'Well consider this, Kev-vie,' responded Brian testily, saying Kevvie as if it was two words, 'we are not paratroopers yet, so don't try and pretend to be one if you don't bloody mind.'

Brian had a point, so Kevin shut up. They still had to do evaluation, then selection course and then jump course, it all seemed to be a hundred years away. So Kevin carried on cleaning his rifle.

'You know what guys, it makes no bloody sense,' complained another man, launching into a bitching, moaning diatribe.

'First we have to pass guard inspection, it's a pain in the arse, I mean, why does your rifle have to be spotless, your uniform spick 'n span and your bloody boots shiny? And now I have to bloody-well shave at this time of the afternoon. What a pain in the arse. And all of this shitty, fukken rigmarole so you can stand for two hours on and four hours off, in the freezing cold, trudging about the perimeter of some god-forsaken, shit-hole of a warehouse to stop imaginary terrorists from pinching imaginary shit!

Fucking army shit which as far as I am concerned is as of much worth as a pile of stinking, bubbling horseshit!'

When he had finished his face was bright red. There was a ripple of laughter and Kevin felt a bit better. At least someone was feeling a lot more miserable than he was!

'A left right, left right, a left right, left right, hey, a left right hey, hutt hutt hutt,' the cadence called in English by the corporal; which was as odd as a wart on a dog's arse, thought Kevin, the corporal shouting out commands in English, as they were marched towards the parade ground for guard inspection.

Sergeant Thin Lips was waiting for them and Kevin felt his heart sink. Thin Lips was renowned for finding fault with at least one man, no matter how well turned out he may be. They stood at attention, while Thin Lips inspected them and miraculously he found no fault.

'For inspection, present arms!' snapped Thin Lips.

They each removed the magazine, made the rifle safe and with moving parts in the back position, each soldier placed his thumb into the breach with thumbnail facing forward. This made a pretty effective mirror, reflecting light up the barrel and making it easy for inspection. Thin Lips moved from one man to the other, looking into each barrel, nodding his satisfaction, until he got to Kevin. He grasped the muzzle of the rifle and looked down it. He looked up at Kevin, his lips had reduced themselves to a thin pencil line and got even thinner, until it seemed as if they had snuck into his mouth and hidden away. He looked up at Kevin, malicious intent clear in his eyes.

'It looks like an elephant has had a shit in your rifle barrel, Vos,' he snarled. 'Why didn't you clean your fucking rifle, you lazy bastard?'

'I did sergeant,' responded Kevin.

'No you did not, do you understand me, YOU DID NOT!' and with that he slapped Kevin on the side of his face with a loud crack. It hurt like hell and was so hard that for a second Kevin felt totally disorientated.

Then the little switch in Kevin's head went click. He saw an image in his mind, of Beyers Fourie, the red hand emblazoned on his face that day. It seemed a century ago and the memory of it ensured that the switch was well and truly thrown in his head!

CLICK it went.

He took a step forward with his left foot and as he followed with the right he swung the rifle butt straight at Thin Lips' head. Kevin swung it with precision, exactly as he had been trained to do in bayonet practice.

He prepared himself for the feel of the impact, the crunching sound of hardwood smashing into bone. He had already instinctively mapped out the second movement, right foot forward and the reversal of the strike, rifle up to the left and butt end smashing down onto the head!

But suddenly he was brought up short; it felt as if the rifle had been snagged in a bush, he couldn't get it past the first strike!

He kept trying to free the rifle and watched in fury as Thin Lips retreated out of range.

And through the rage he heard one of his buddies shouting,

'KD, KD, no, don't do it, stop!'

He heard Thin Lips yelling at him, screaming the command,

'Attention troop, stand still, I said attention!'

'I will fucking kill you, you fuck, do you understand me?' screamed Kevin.

He tried to free his rifle, but by now two people had grabbed it and he felt another pair of hands on his shoulders, holding him back; strong hands restraining him.

'If you ever touch me again I will fuck you up, you stupid fuck!' Kevin screamed.

Thin Lips kept screaming back,

'Attention troop, attention!

Kevin could see just a hint of alarm in his eyes, and that only made him more the hell-in, it put more fire in his belly!

As his buddies held him Kevin calmed down… slowly.

Kevin stood there breathing hard, by now they had all fallen back into formation and were standing at attention. Thin Lips asked Kevin,

'So are you going to report this, Private?'

'No, Sergeant.'

'Why not?'

'Because it leaves me with the assurance, Sergeant, that you will know from now on, that if you ever hit me or any one of my buddies in front of me again, then I will drop you in the shit and I will report you to the Commandant, SERGEANT!' responded Kevin, the last word spat out loudly with sarcastic respect.

It didn't happen again.

Kevin never saw Thin Lips hit anyone. Perhaps he did with later intakes as the years went by, but he never struck a member of A Coy, 1975 intake again. Well at least Kevin never saw nor heard of it.

Later in Angola Mally Wolverson would punch Thin Lips down a flight of stairs sending him back to "the states", so justice would be served ultimately!

* * *

Chapter Seven: **Hey Junior!**

Hit me with your best shot
Why don't you hit me with your best shot?
Hit me with your best shot
Fire away.

Pat Benatar

The turning point happened quite suddenly for Kevin, without him even realizing it. He learnt that it wasn't just about *vasbyt*, an Afrikaans word which means, "grit your teeth".

As they all began training in earnest, he learnt that there would be no respite from the physical pain the army wished to dish out. The course was designed to weed out the weak, to select only the men with suitable physical and mental strength. The instructors did everything in their power to crack them. Physically exhausted most of the time, they were subjected to a barrage of little tricks, designed to break the spirit. And, as more men were dropped from the course and Kevin saw the Kimberly crew being steadily depleted, like the rest of them, he became all the more determined to stay.

Of the 12 there were 9 left.

Of the 9 there were 7 left.

Strange, the more you shat off, the more determined you were to stay. Kevin reached a state of bloody mindedness! He learnt to suck it all up, discovering a place he called the "zone" and quickly learnt to seek refuge in the zone. A safe place to be, where the pain, the exertion, the constant screaming and even the hateful whistle, *nothing*, could penetrate the invisible walls of the zone. Just look ahead, just ahead of your feet taking one step at a time.

The burn is your friend, the fire in your muscles as you desperately cling to the marble, palms chafed, arms aching, trying to prevent it from falling on your feet.

In the zone the pain is pushed to the back of the mind. But Kevin realized that this was only the beginning. He was reminded of the road ahead one night when a senior came and sat with them at the mess pub. He wasn't a bad bloke, pretty decent and he reminded them of the Biggy, the big one which lay ahead.

'You think you guys are shitting off now, just wait until you do the PT course! That's going to sort the boys from the men, let me tell you!' he said with relish, taking a gulp of his beer.

'Two weeks, guys,' he continued, holding two fingers in the air.

'Two weeks, eight hours a day of pure fucking, shitting off, AFKAK!' he said in Afrikaans, dragging the KAK out to sound like KAAAK.

'Marble PT, pole PT, buddy PT, tyre PT, rifle PT, you guys just have to zone out man, just go to the right mental place and you will make it, I promised,' he said reassuringly as he nonchalantly accepted a junior's offer of a beer.

Kevin felt apprehensive but at the same time he felt good. He had already found the zone the senior was speaking of. The zone was his place. It was then that it dawned on him, that he would win the maroon beret; he would wear the wings on his chest.

He had what it takes. He just knew it, deep down. Stuff them all, they can't break me! Parachute Battalion was the only unit in the army where there existed a unique relationship between the "oumanne" and "roofies", the "old men" and "scabs".

The old men were referred to as seniors and Kevin and his mates were called juniors. The seniors were jump-qualified, they had passed the selection course while the juniors were younger, of a later intake and still aspiring to become parabats.

Staff Sakkie had made the junior-senior thing clear to them all when they had first arrived, in his indomitable Sakkie manner.

They were standing in a squad, and a corporal was calling out their names checking if they were all still there. Roll call, to make sure no one had gone AWOL, absent without leave.

'Corporal, stop, wait!' commanded Sakkie.

He had spied a soldier jogging past. Everyone ran in the battalion without exception. The only people allowed to walk were the civilians working there during the day and the poor buggers on light duty. The light duty buggers were generally issued with a white plastic helmet, a large red cross painted on it, and spent endless hours brushing the streets in the battalion with tooth brushes; on their knees, brushing tar, day in and day out.

No place for the sick in Parachute Battalion!

'Trooper, come here!' called Sakkie.

The soldier changed course and stopped, military style his right foot crashing to the ground. He stood at attention before Sakkie.

'Stand at ease soldier.'

Kevin was aghast. Sakkie was speaking civilly to a private, a man without rank, almost as if he were an equal!

Sakkie placed his hand on the man's shoulder and gently turned him to face the squad.

'Pay attention you PUSS-FACED FUCKERS!' he roared. 'This is a senior. Note he has no rank but if you blind, little shits, care to look closely, you will notice that on the left side of his chest he's got something that you little homos don't!'

'LOOOKKK!' screamed the staff, pointing to the man's left breast and indicating a indistinct set of black wings, sewed to his uniform.

They all looked.

'What do you fucking see?' asked the staff, his eyes popping out in their sockets, his moustache bristling.

'Fuck!' thought Kevin, 'even his moustache is scary!

It's a pair of wings?' ventured a hapless soul.

'YES, it's a pair of fucking wings, and those wings are hard earned. This man is a qualified paratrooper and by virtue of that fact,

HE IS YOUR FUCKING SENIOR!'

He paused for effect.

'If you run past a senior you stop in your tracks and you brace him, do you understand? You treat him like any other non-commissioned officer in the battalion, he is your superior, he is a parabat and you lot are a bunch of kraal dogs straight from a KAFFIR KRAAL, DO YOU FUCKING UNDERSTAND ME?'

He finished, his voice at the same level as a steam engine blowing off steam, although not quite at the same high pitch; that would be too girlie like for staff Sakkie.

'YES STAFF!' they all yelled.

The senior was dismissed and as he ran off Sakkie had one more thing to say.

'Those fuckers are not allowed into your lines. If any of them come into your bungalows after hours you come and tell me and I will fuck them up,' he finished.

One lesson learnt, Sakkie was a fair man.

The seniors were passing through; the battalion had learnt long ago to keep the seniors away from the juniors. Bravo Company was Alpha Company's senior and they were getting ready to go to the border.

Kevin imagined them to be bigger, stronger than him and his buddies, and most of them were. They were all a year older and they had finished the gruelling training and selection course, they had more muscle packed on them and they had an air of menace.

And so inevitably one day they paid Kevin and his buddies a visit at three in the morning. The barrack room door crashed open and Kevin awoke the voices yelling.

'GET UP JUNIORS, WAKEY FUCKING WAKEY', screamed the voices.

Kevin and the others found themselves standing at attention at the foot of their beds. As Kevin's eyes cleared from the sleepy fog he realized that these were not their instructors, they were seniors, a group of about forty of them squeezing and jostling their way into the room.

The thought crossed his mind, fuck them they have no right to fuck us around, Sakkie told us they can't do this. But he wisely stood still at attention. A senior stood before him, and ugly bastard and he looked as hard as nails.

He asked Kevin a question, soon to become THE question.

'Can you *vasbyt* junior?'

'Yes senior.'

'I can't fucking hear you, junior, CAN YOU *VASBYT*?' he screamed.

And with that, he punched Kevin hard, just below the belly button. Luckily Kevin saw it coming and managed to tense his stomach muscles just before the blow made contact.

It was like punching a rubber mat. The senior moved over to the next man and he was replaced by another senior. This one was just as ugly and the whole process was repeated.

'Can you *vasbyt* junior?'

'YES SENIOR!'

PUNCH IN THE GUTS

Next senior.

'Can you *vasbyt* junior?'

'YES SENIOR!

PUNCH IN THE GUTS

Next senior.

'Can you *vasbyt,* junior?'

'YES SENIOR!'

PUNCH IN THE GUTS

Luckily they had split up to left and right of the room and moved out the other end. Kevin counted twenty punches to the gut as the last man went by. They left with a passing shot.

'If you fuckers say a word about this we'll be back, get it, you fucking wannabees?'

The next day the whole lot of them took strain, stomach muscles bruised and battered as they battled to get through the day. Each sit-up brought a stab of pain in his guts but like the rest of them, Kevin shut up and made it through the day.

Ah, were it not for the zone!

None of them said a word about the senior's visit that day, nor any day after that. Not a word. Other visits followed over the next few weeks, varying in numbers and intensity. From the old punch in the guts routine to being taught by the seniors how to shuffle step as you would while exiting a plane. The difference being that the exit took place from the top of the army chest with a steel helmet, inner removed, placed on the head. The result was that when you landed on the ground the loose steel helmet would follow a fraction of a second later … KLANG, onto the head with painful results.

The seniors lapped it all up. They enjoyed themselves immensely.

As with all "fun times" things were bound to go south, downwards, downhill to nasty time. And inevitably it did go south.

One morning the seniors burst in for the usual rigmarole, but only this time the juniors were exhausted from the previous day. Kevin found himself standing at the foot of his bed as usual, but only this time he was totally "*deur die kak*", (through the shit), or alternatively as half awake and as confused as a ball of shit! Not that that made much sense but he heard the senior yelling at him, screaming and swearing.

'ARE YOU A CONFUSED PIECE OF SHIT, JUNIOR, WAKE THE FUCK UP!'

And before Kevin could focus, the senior punched him, plumb on the nose and knocked him stone cold.

Kevin woke to someone shaking him and mug of cold water being chucked over his head.

'You OK, KD?'

'Feels like it.'

'You sure, that senior knocked you the fuck out man, looks like your nose is broken?'

'Yep I'm sure, I'll be okay,' responded Kevin. His nose felt like it had been smashed, he couldn't breathe as it was clogged up with coagulating blood.

The next morning at roll call, Kevin stuck out like a sore thumb, or rather in this case, a sore nose.

'What the fuck happened to you?' asked Sergeant Thin Lips.

Kevin looked at him, expecting to see some pleasure in his eyes. But nothing. All he saw was a tiny, little, inkling of a fraction of concern, but oddly no malicious satisfaction.

'Who hit you?' he asked again. Strangely he didn't swear this time.

'No one, sarge, I fell in the shower and smashed my nose on the floor,' responded Kevin.

'I'm not your fucking sarge, call me sergeant you fucking moron,' he hissed, loud enough for the rest of the squad to hear.

'I'm asking you again, what happened to your fucking nose?'

'I FELL IN THE SHOWER, SERGEANT!' yelled Kevin in response.

Thin Lips stepped back, with just a hint of respect in his eyes, just a flash of it which came and disappeared before it really made itself clear.

'All of you. Lift your shirts up!' he commanded.

They all did, to reveal different shades of blue, evidence of the seniors' visits; badges of honour.

Thin Lips mouthed the words silently, anger flooding his face.

'Fucking seniors!'

Later that day A Coy watched, rather slyly and without making it obvious, as the B Coy seniors were given a chasey of note.

Hours later they came running up the road from the parade ground towards the packers building, each grasping a hated marble and chanting, 'We will not *vasbyt* the juniors, we will not *vasbyt* the juniors, we will not…'

Thankfully, before any of them built up enough resentment to pay the juniors a visit again, they were shipped off to the border.

It would be last time that any of them would see their seniors again.

Chapter Eight: **The training ground**

There's something happening here
What it is ain't exactly clear
There's a man with a gun over there
Telling me I got to beware

- Buffalo Springfield

'Die doel van vandag se lesing is om julle op te fok!' announced corporal Paale.

Oh jeez, thought Kevin as his brain translated it into the English,

'The aim of today's lesson is to fuck you up!'

Paale was a tall man, he looked all gaunt, it was as if he had been born with too many bony protrusions sticking out all over the place. He was cleanly shaved but had so much chest hair it sprouted out from under his collar and had migrated up to the level of his Adams-apple making him look like a bloody vulture!

Like all Permanent Force instructors, he was older and more mature than the poor souls at his mercy, sitting in a semi-circle at his feet. He loved the position of power he found himself in. There was a fine line between training the men and abusing that power, it was always there, a thin maroon line drawn in the sand. And so the first lecture began and soon someone stupidly, moronically fell asleep.

'Ah, so your little friend isn't interested in a word I'm saying,' said the corporal, his face in a self-satisfied smirk.

'See that tree there?' he asked, pointing at a tree in the distance. 'Well, go run around it and bring a leaf back with you!'

After being chased back because an idiot brought two leaves instead of one and then back again, to give all of the leaves back to the poor tree, they were all pretty alert after that.

'Are you stupid arseholes alert now?' snarled Paale.

'Yes, Corporal,' they all chorused.

And so between being fucked around, doing push-ups for whatever obscure reason, being chased around the tree for whatever contrived excuse, they were indirectly taught the skills of camouflage; how to leopard-crawl in the bush, rifle cradled across your forearms, protecting your second wife from the dirt; how to hide without being seen, how to lay an ambush.

'Right, you bunch of useless excuses of the human race, useless pieces of shit, let's see you practice being like a leopard!' The good corporal announced, his hand moving towards the godforsaken whistle.

'When I blow the whistle you hit the ground instantly, no delay, and no fucking hesitation. I want to see you hit the ground like a bunch of *slap piele*, floppy cocks, I want to HEAR you hit the ground, DO YOU UNDERSTAND ME?' He screamed.

'Shit, here we go,' groaned Kevin as the whistle shrilled.

SCHREEP, shrieked the whistle, followed by the sound of men and equipment hitting the ground. SCHREEP, shrieked the whistle and the men all scrambled up to their feet.

SCHREEP Up!

SCHREEP Down!

SCHREEP Up!

SCHREEP Down!

On and on it went until ultimately, an exhausted man dropped his rifle with a loud clatter.

BLOODY HELL NO!

'You, yes you, come here you useless little fucker!' screamed corporal Paale at the hapless trooper who had dropped his "wife". The corporal sounded demented.

'Mark time, the rest of you, hold your rifles above your heads, the first man who lowers his arms will be the cause of all of you fucking homos, getting a fucking whore of a chasey,

DO YOU UNDERSTAND ME?', he screamed, his voice now going hoarse.

'Yes corporal!' was the collective and equally hoarse response.

'I will rip your head off and shit down your necks, do you get me?'

Kevin felt his tongue, dry, sticking to his palate.

'This little fucker who dropped government property, his fucking wife, is the cause of what you fuck heads are going to experience over the next few hours,' screamed the corporal.

Kevin was so exhausted that he didn't care what Paale had to say. And so began an hour of crawling with the rifle, leopard-crawling, until the elbows and knees were bleeding.

The whistle SCHREEP, roll over to the left three times.

The whistle SCHREEP, roll over to the right three times.

The whistle SCHREEP, leopard-crawl.

The whistle SCHREEP, roll over to the right three times.

And so it went on and on, a never ending cycle of whistle, rolling, whistle, crawling. Field craft, fuck field craft, fuck the army, and fuck that fucking whistle.

FUUUUUCCCKKKK!!!!

The all-knowing genius of a sergeant major.

Sergeant Major Tilly stood before them. As A Coy Sergeant Major he was the boss man, "the main man what counts!"

He was a short-arse, but this was countered by a voice of thunder and a temper to go with it. But in the same breath it could be said that he was a good man and a fair one to boot.

Kevin knew for a fact, that Sergeant Thin Lips had come close to being bust down to corporal after the Beyers slap. And that Tillie had had a very strong hand in motivating it. He was respected by all and held in high esteem by the whole lot of them.

'*Meneere*, gentlemen, tonight we are doing night-time navigation,' he announced, rocking on his heels, his brown pants too long for his short little legs, overhanging his jump boots and almost touching the ground.

'We are going to De Brug and we will be dividing you into little teams of five. Each team will have a leader, a map, a compass, a notebook and a torch and with this in hand, you will be dropped off at a starting point. Your objective is to find five different locations, where you will get your book signed. Thereafter you will navigate to the next point and so on!'

'DO YOU UNDERSTAND ME?' he suddenly roared.

'YES, SERGEANT MAJOR,' they all responded with a shout.

Tillie seemed pleased. 'Nice, very nice,' he said almost as if to himself.

'At 04h00, yes, for those of you who are stupid idiots, that's at Four in the morning!' Your transport back to the battalion leaves at that time,' he paused for effect, rocking on his heels, his boots hidden by his browns. 'Yes, the vehicles will leave promptly and those who are not back or those who have not found all of the check points, WILL HAVE TO WALK HOME!' he finished with a shout.

'DO YOU UNDERSTAND ME?'

'YES, SARMAJOR!' They all responded.

And so it was that they found themselves dumped in De Brug at sunset. One by one the teams were dispatched into the pitch blackness to find the checkpoints.

When it was their turn to leave Tillie beckoned to Kevin.

'Hey troop, come here-ip!' he commanded beckoning to Kevin with a crooked finger. Tillie almost always ended sentences with an 'ip!'

Like, 'Do you understand-ip?'

Or, 'Run around the packers building, now-ip!'

'RUN BEFORE I KICK YOU IN THE ARSE-IP!'

Kevin stood before him, rigidly at attention.

'Here's the book, you're in charge-ip!' said Tillie, thrusting a little hard covered black book at him.

And so it was that Kevin found himself in charge of four other men, stumbling about on the kopjes of the Orange Free State; looking desperately for five checkpoints, each hidden away from sight by the black, black night.

'Typical of these fucking permanent force pigs,' groaned someone. 'They go and choose a night where you can't see your hand in front of your fucking face!'

'Well, what happens if you're really in the bush, stranded and you have to move in a pitch black night; this is what this training is all about,' said a man in response.

'Well, aren't you just the fucking boy scout then,' responded the first bloke in an overly exaggerated sarcastic tone.

'Well, why don't you go and fuck yourself,' was the response in an equally sarcastic tone.

'Fuck you!'

'No, fuck you!'

Then, as if they didn't have enough challenges on their hands, the two antagonists began to shove each other around, which soon degenerated into a full blown scuffle; verging on a brawl actually.

'OH FOR FUCKSAKES GUYS, STOP YOUR FUCKING SHIT!' yelled Kevin.

'Just now one of you arseholes falls onto a fucking rock or something and then we have to carry your stupid arse out of here, jeez guys!' he finished, his tone as exasperated as all hell.

They stopped.

And so it wasn't too long before they got the hang of it; map, distance, compass, stars, cluster of stars, faint silhouette of a kopje; all markers and reference points.

'See those stars, yes there, that cluster of stars, that's northwest and that's our direction,' was one man's contribution.

'Oh you mean that cluster-fuck of stars,' was the response, followed by giggles of mirth.

'Come on guys, let's get serious, or we are stuffed, c'mon I don't want to walk back

40 kliks for fucksakes,' whined Boy Scout.

'Stop complaining,' responded the bloke who had given Boy Scout shit earlier.

'Look guys, I'm walking,' said an irritated Kevin as he began to walk towards the "cluster-fuck" of stars. They all followed. They found four checkpoints all in good time and the little book was dutifully signed by the officer at each point and then they hit a flat spin. They could not, for the life of them, find checkpoint five. They wandered up and down, stumbling, swearing and getting all the more frustrated.

After about an hour of this Kevin had, had enough!

'Fuck this!' he announced. 'We're going to the pickup point!'

Surprisingly there was no protest from any of them. They took a compass bearing on another smaller "cluster-fuck" of stars and headed back. Soon they arrived and found one other group sitting there. The rest were all still out on the Free State *vlaktes*, probably all bitching like a bastard, mused Kevin.

'Okay, KD, what now?' asked Boy Scout. 'We don't have the last bloody signature.'

Boy Scout was starting to get on Kevin's nerves. And then he had it. A little globe switched on in Kevin's head. A bright idea, ping! He remembered. Being an artistic fellow and having an aptitude for forging signatures, he had made a pretty penny at school forging parents' signatures in his classmates' homework books. Being a boarder, or hostel dog as the day scholars called them, Kevin had two things in his sixteen-year-old brain which totally overrode most other thought processes. Food and Pussy, in that order.

So as is the case with most schoolboys of that age, he was permanently hungry and in a perpetual state of horniness so forging signatures became quite a lucrative little business which satisfied the first need. It paid for countless "quarter mutton bunny-chows" from the Dawnside Café in Stanger.

The second had been sadly stymied by the array of acne he had splattered across his face back then. And so like most sixteen-year-old schoolboys Kevin quickly developed a raging affair with Mrs Palm and her five daughters.

So with his bright idea in his head, Kevin sidled up to the leader of the other group, who with his mates was languishing in the dirt.

'Did you guys also battle with the last checkpoint?' fished Kevin.

'Nah it was easy,' responded the other man.

'Well, we struggled,' responded Kevin, 'actually we didn't find it.'

After a pause Kevin ventured, 'I need a favour, boet, I want to borrow your book for a few minutes.'

'Why?'

'I want to forge the last signature.'

'Fuck off, you're joking!' was the incredulous response.

'No,' Kevin responded, his voice even.

'I want to see this,' was the sceptic's response as he handed the book over to Kevin.

And so it was, that with the aid of two torches held steady by willing hands, Kevin produced an excellent forgery of the last signature into his group's book. Satisfied with his handiwork, they lay in the dirt and slept as the other groups dribbled in throughout the rest of the night.

At half past three in the morning the trucks arrived at the pickup point, grinding to a halt in a cloud of dust and exhaust fumes. The headlights blinded them, making them blink like rabbits caught in the hunter's spotlight. Tilly bounced from the lead truck, all energised business.

'Come here-ip, all of you team leaders!' he commanded.

And so, Kevin found himself in a line watching, as Tillie scrutinized each book, his torch moving down the list slowly.

'Shit, he's being thorough!' Kevin heard the man in front of him mutter worriedly. Kevin realized why the man was worried when Tillie, after a cursory glance at the man's book announced, 'you have only four signatures! Corporal take this man and his bunch and make them sit back there, they're walking!'

And then it was Kevin's turn. His heart rate up, he handed his book to Tillie, amazed at how steady his hand remained as he did so. Tillie seemed to take forever and when his torchlight hit the last signature, he paused.

He fucking paused.

And at that moment Kevin's pulse went up by twenty beats per minute. Tillie looked up at Kevin and grinned. It was a wicked grin, which changed amazingly into a mischievous one, as he handed the book back to Kevin.

'Nice work on the last one, Vossie,' he said, winking as he did so. 'I like a man with a bit of initiative. Corporal, they can board,' he commanded as he turned to the next poor soul and his grubby book clasped in his hand.

Kevin was elated as his buddies piled on board, slapping him on the back. A repeated, "Nice one KD" ringing in his ears as they did so.

How the hell did Tillie know, Kevin asked himself?

He would learn as time went by, that sergeant majors always know, somehow they know everything!

Chapter Nine: **No pain, no gain**

'Relax,' said the night man,
We are programmed to receive.
You can checkout any time you like,
but you can never leave!

The Eagles

And so the time had come and the moment of reckoning had arrived.

'Right gentlemen, we have reached the stage in your little lives, where we determine if you lot are made of paratrooper stuff, to see if you can make the grade,' announced Thin Lips.

'Today and tomorrow we do evaluation, and those of you who don't pass the evaluation don't get onto the selection course!'

He paused for effect, his thin lips getting thinner as he prepared himself for the next sentence. Kevin felt utter dislike for him, standing there with his thin fucking lips and shit attitude. Kevin imagined his lips getting thinner and thinner disappearing into his mouth; all the while dragging the rest of his face into it, nose, eyes, forehead the lot until all that was left was a featureless lump on a pair of shoulders! Thin Lips' voice rudely interrupted his romantic train of thought.

'Do you dumb twats understand what this means, first you have to pass the evaluation tests, then you do the PT course and then you have to pass evaluation again, lovely hey?' He finished with relish.

Kevin went through the evaluation tests in his mind, he had passed them all over and over again, but some of the guys had a few psychological hang-ups about the tests. The wall especially seemed to finish a lot of them off.

Thin Lips ran through the evaluation tests with them, his eyes gleaming with enjoyment.

2.4 km in under 11 minutes

3.2 km with full kit in 18 minutes

40 shuttle runs in 90 seconds

200 m fireman's lift with full kit Climb a 6 meter rope

Climb over a 2 meter wall with full kit

50 push-ups without resting

67 sit-ups in 2 minutes

120 squat kicks without resting

And so it began with Kevin progressing well. He almost came short when Thin Lips decided that he wasn't doing the sit-ups properly. Peter sitting on Kevin's feet, grasping his boots at the ankles and Kevin doing the sit-ups. Back must touch the ground, right elbow must touch left knee, back to the ground, up left elbow touches right knee, up down up down.

Thin Lips counting, '48, 49, 50, 50, 50, 50'….

Fuck you, you motherfucker, Kevin under his breath,

'51, 52, 53….67!' You're lucky Vos, you're fucking lucky!' snarled Thin Lips.

Kevin hated doing the 3.2 km with full kit. It was uncomfortable and if the kit wasn't fitted properly just that alone would finish you. But he made it in time and watched the men coming in one by one and in small groups. Typical of the malicious bastards, they made sure that the finish wasn't on a flat stretch; everyone had to run the last bit through the gates and up the steep hill to the packers building. Jan Bloem came into sight and to a man they stood up and began to shout.

'C'mon Jan, c'mon my man you can make it, c'mon!

It was the first time that the army had called men up directly to Parachute Battalion and it had been a total disaster, with most of the recruits falling out very quickly. So they had to go back to basics and send out selection teams to recruit volunteers like Kevin and the Kimberly crew. Jan had been one of the direct call-ups and when he arrived at the battalion he was tall and fat. About 1.9m and over 130kg, no-one expected him to last a week, let alone the course. But he did!

Week in and week out Jan hung on with grim determination; a determination which even earned him the grudging respect of the instructors. Every Thursday afternoon Jan would stand in front of the quartermaster's store and get a smaller set of browns issued to him. So the next cycle of utter dogged stubbornness would begin with the shrinking Jan hanging onto the course with total bloody-mindedness.

And so it was that every man, including the permanent force instructors, began to cheer Jan on. And then an amazing thing happened. Thin Lips broke ranks and began to run the last stretch next to Jan. He was shouting at him, telling him he can make it, encouraging him. Just like the man with the pistol, at the finish line of the comrades marathon; an instructor stood with his back to the struggling Jan, his eyes fixed to his stopwatch. Kevin could see the stress on his face; everyone wanted Jan to make it. Once the man with the stopwatch looked up at Sakkie as if asking him for some signal. Sakkie shook his head, rules were rules and even if he could have helped Jan he wouldn't have.

'JAN, JAN, JAN,' the men began to shout in unison and Kevin couldn't stand it any longer, he screwed his eyes shut.

Then the whistle gave its hated THREEEEEP and Kevin's eyes snapped open to see a fallen Jan, collapsed in a heap.

He was across the line! There was a collective roar, hoots and whistles as the men helped him too his feet.

Kevin looked at Thin Lips. His face was expressionless, unreadable.

'You strange fucker,' mused Kevin.

They were issued their programs after evaluation was done and that night they sat in groups discussing what they saw. Neatly typed out, day after day for two weeks the programme was set before them. The more Kevin read the more he began to shit himself. He heard Peter exclaim,

'Fuck this, guys, I can't do this!'

'Fuck off, of course you can, it's a piece of piss!' snapped Ronnie in reply.

'Yes, a piece of piss,' echoed Von Rommel, the henchman.

Stupid twat, thought Kevin, looking surreptitiously at Von Rommel.

'Listen to this, guys,' said Lappies, tapping the typed sheet.

'Day one, 12 km run with boots and browns, Log PT, Buddy PT. Day fucking two, 21 km run with telephone poles. Shit look, marble PT and bloody rifle PT!' he finished his little diatribe, slapping the sheet hard with the back of hand.

'What the hell is this?' exclaimed Syd. 'Surprise number one, and it's for the whole bloody day!'

'Yes, check here,' said another, 'Week two, surprise number two!'

They went down the list; boxing, soccer, wrestling, rugby with car tyre as a ball. The horrible list went on and on.

Kevin became worried. The self-doubt began to creep into his head. And then he remembered his friend the "zone". A safe place to be, where the pain, the exertion, the constant screaming and even the hateful whistle; nothing, could penetrate the invisible walls of the zone.

He knew then that he would be OK.

The days began to blur, marble PT, the whistles shrieking and the tall, vulture-like corporal Paale, resplendent with his bloody megaphone.

'You stupid wankers want to become Parabats, hey, hey? Well so far none of you useless bastards have a hope in hell of making it! You are fucking useless, the worst fucking crop of recruits I have EVER had the displeasure of training!'

And so it went on and on, the physical pain, the constant whistle, the megaphone and the negative diatribe designed to break you down mentally. Kevin was in the zone; he was comfortably ensconced in it and he knew he was safe. But as always they knew how to get to you, no matter where your mind took you.

Kevin was marking time, left, right, left, right, left, right, clutching the marble to his chest. The thick smock they all had to wear, chafing him but at least it prevented the marble from cutting into the skin of his forearms.

Then Paale walked up to him, the megaphone at his lips, screaming negativity at them all. Suddenly he stopped shouting and stopped before Kevin.

'Come, follow me, Vos,' he said, his voice strangely at normal volume and Kevin wondered if he had switched off the megaphone. He was acting all reasonable like and it made Kevin as worried as hell. His trepidation increasing as he followed Paale, away from the other suffering men.

'There, stop, stand still,' commanded Paale as they reached the canteen. Kevin did as he was told.

'Put the marble down on the floor and stand at ease,' Paale instructed. Once Kevin had done so, he stood at attention, facing the instructor who had by now switched the megaphone off.

Paale spoke to Kevin then, his voice was filled with kindness. Placing his hand on Kevin's shoulder he pointed towards the canteen. Kevin felt the fear creeping into the back of his mind, spreading slowly forward in his head, inexorably taking a firmer hold as Paale skilfully brought him out of the safety of the "zone".

'Look Vos, we all know you want to be a Paratrooper,' he continued. 'But sadly we all agree, the whole lot of us, that you are not Parabat material. You lack the physical attributes, you're too skinny for one thing and you definitely don't have the grit, the balls, and the fucking guts to do this, really!'

He paused, looking at Kevin kindly.

'I tell you what, Vos, you throw in the towel now. We know that it's not that you're giving up, but just acknowledging that you are not up to this. It's no shame to drop off the course we know that you've tried your best.' His hand began to jab in the direction of the canteen.

'You call it a day now and you walk in there. You can have beer, chocolates, cokes, the lot, all on us. The medic will put a drip on you, I can see that you are dehydrated and you will feel on top of the world Vossie.'

'*Vossie, who's your fucking Vossie, you piece of shit,*' the thought rang in his head. Kevin wanted to say it out aloud.

Instead he swallowed hard. His throat was dry as if he had licked the chalk off a schoolroom blackboard.

'And once you're feeling better, you can have a lekker shower and we will send you home on pass for fourteen days. Not just seven days, Vossie, fourteen days!'

'Vossie, who's your fucking Vossie, you piece of shit!' He could feel the zone mounting a counterattack.

He looked into Kevin's eyes before continuing, 'And then we will send you back to your unit to be with your friends, "*Jou matjies*, your little buddies, where you can finish your national service and be done with parachute battalion and all of its shit.'

Kevin remained silent, he stood there swallowing the chalk in his throat.

'What say you, Vossie?'

Kevin swallowed more chalk dust and tried to answer, all that came out was a croak. Paale led him to a water tap and pointed at it. Kevin opened the tap and started to swallow delicious gulps of cold water, until Paale rudely shut it.

Kevin stood up and snapped to attention.

He slipped back into the "zone" just as Paale asked, 'And so Vos?'

'I will stay and complete the course, corporal.'

'You will what?'

'I will stay and complete the course, corporal.'

'I can't fucking HEAR YOU, YOU STUPID FUCKING TROOPER!' he screamed into the now fully functional megaphone.

'GO AND FETCH YOUR MARBLE AND JOIN YOUR LITTLE FRIENDS, MOOOOOVVVVVE!' he screamed, the megaphone inches from Kevin's nose.

Surprise number one, Wednesday morning, found them standing in their smocks at attention in a squad. Kevin felt his muscles aching, the lactic acid build-up making every movement a mission.

'Go back to your little pigsty and change into PT shorts, PT vest and takkies. Also bring your hand towels,' ordered Paale.

They all ran off and a few minutes later they were back in the squad, attired as ordered. 'Get into rank from tallest to shortest, from left to right, three deep, MOOOVE!' He roared.

They all obeyed, shuffling until they were standing from tallest to shortest. Kevin had learnt to get this right sharpish, the kicking corporal Lategaan had made his mark on him in more ways than one.

Paale continued. 'Today we are going to a small farm dam to swim and row canoes. We are going to load you lot into the vehicles there and the instructors are going to tie down the tarpaulins. Any man who opens the tarpaulin is off the course, instantly,

DO YOU FUCKING UNDERSTAND ME?' he roared into the megaphone.

'YES CORPORAL!' they all screamed in reply.

Two hours later the trucks ground to a halt. There was silence.

Then the megaphone squawked, 'FUCK OUT, FUCK OUT AND GET A FUCKING MOVE ON!'

They all leapt from the trucks to be greeted by a horrible sight; two nice heaps lying in the dust; a pile of marbles and a pile of black telephone poles, stinking of creosote; not a patch of water in sight, just the Orange Free State *vlaktes*, stretching, as far as the eye could see. Paale and the rest climbed into the trucks with a parting order.

The megaphone squawked. 'THE POLES AND MARBLES ARE NUMBERED. I HAVE THE LIST WITH ME. SEE YOU FUCKERS BACK AT THE BATALLION FOR SUPPER!'

And with that they left in a cloud of dust and diesel smoke, leaving two instructors to shepherd them back to base. Over 20 km later and at nightfall they staggered into the battalion. Too exhausted to eat, they staggered into the showers, fully clothed and let the hot water bring them back to life. The instructors dragged them out of the barrack room and to the canteen, forcing them to eat.

'You can't finish the course on an empty stomach, you stupid fucks!' was the gem of wisdom left with them as they forced supper down.

Exactly a week later, Wednesday morning, after days of suffering, the morning light found them lined up in a squad. Limping and battered they formed up, waiting for the advent of surprise number two.

'Go get those shitty smocks off those disgusting scrawny bodies and I want you back here in five minutes!' Paale yelled, pausing, casting his eyes across the exhausted men. Somehow he looked taller, more gaunt and more vulture like thought Kevin.

He lifted the megaphone to his lips and yelled, 'AND ONCE THOSE SMOCKS ARE OFF, GET DRESSED IN YOUR STEP-OUTS AND FALL IN HERE ALL SHINY AND BRIGHT, NOW MOOOVVVVE!'

Four to five minutes later they had reformed, in step-out or dress uniforms, green berets on their heads and standing rigidly at attention. They were marched to the canteen and ended up watching World War two para drops, live footage of brave men dropping into Nazi lines. Black and white images of men dropping into the face of the enemy.

Kevin could hear the snoring of men all around him as he drifted off to sleep.

Thursday and Friday was spent doing physical evaluations:

2.4 km in under 11 minutes

3.2 km with full kit in 18 minutes

40 shuttle runs in 90 seconds

200 m fireman's lift with full kit

Climb a 6m rope

Climb over a 2m wall with full kit

50 push-ups without resting

67 sit-ups in 2 minutes

120 squat kicks without resting

The agony of it as they were battered by then, exhausted but those who had not dropped out were by then mentally conditioned to face anything! The only concession granted was that they were allowed to fail one power and one speed test only. Kevin managed to pass them all and this time Thin Lips gave him a clean count on the sit-ups.

That Friday afternoon they were given pass with the parting words,

'Don't get lost at home, lads, jump course starts next week!'

Strangely soft words for the army, thought Kevin. As if they were being given a grudging acknowledgement of having made the grade.

Chapter Ten: **Jumping out of perfectly good aeroplanes**

Don't let yourself go
'Cause everybody cries
And everybody hurts sometimes

R.E.M.

Kitching's World

Kevin remembered seeing pictures of posters placed on walls during the Great War showing the British general Lord Kitchener, finger pointed at the reader and saying,

"Your country needs you!"

He also remembered a parody of the same poster, Kitchener pointing at you and saying, "Be alert, your country needs Lerts"!

'Good grief!' said Kevin out aloud, his voice filled with awe. 'Check that bloke's bloody moustache, reminds me of that Lord Kitchener poster, they used to stick on the walls during the First World War.'

Kevin gazed at the man with awe. He had a moustache the like of which would make the job sported by Lord Kitchener, pale into insignificance.

'Kitchener was a *doos*, a cunt,' responded a bloke called Dreyer, his gaze fixed on the staff sergeant standing before them. Dreyer continued, looking at Kevin almost accusingly as if the damn Boer War was Kevin's fault,

'Kitchener was the fucker who started the concentration camps in the Boer War, he was a *soutie* like you, who murdered women and children in the concentration camps. It was the only way the fokken Engelse could win the war, fuckers!' He spat out the words, 'fokken' and 'fuckers' with equal venom.

Kevin looked at Dreyer, keeping his face expressionless. He didn't wish for a confrontation and in any case his body was still far too sore from the selection course. And in any case Dreyer was almost twice his size. It amazed him, that after almost a century some Afrikaners still harboured so much anger and bitterness about that war.

Dreyer was still staring at Kevin, when he averted his eyes and looked at the Staff

Sergeant. The latter opened his mouth and said, 'Welcome to my world, gentlemen, this is where we will teach you how to jump out of perfectly good aeroplanes.'

'My name is Staff Sergeant Kitching, I am in charge of this course and if you want to become jump-qualified I am the man to help you to get there.'

You have to be kidding me, thought Kevin. He almost laughed out aloud, Kitching versus Kitchener; their fucking names were almost identical. Maybe Kitching subconsciously wanted to emulate Kitchener. Kevin gazed on in awe of it, that massive moustache starting under his nose and sweeping outwards in a wonderfully symmetrical sweep, outwards towards his cheeks. No! Not towards, but right past his cheeks.

Kevin almost turned to Dreyer wanting to say, 'See he's also got an English name and considers himself an Afrikaner, you moron!' But chose not to, there was no point in it.

The "Jump" hangar belonged to Staff Kitching, lock stock and barrel and he made sure that they all understood that clearly. It wasn't just his moustache that was impressive, it was everything about him. He was the epitome of the career soldier, the professional soldier.

And so the jump course began, with endless drills; hanging in harnesses, swinging and being dropped onto mats, learning the paratrooper roll, exiting mock-ups, sliding down slides and rolling when they hit the mats, rolling and rolling and rolling; until it all became muscle memory.

And so the day came when they stood on a small field next to the training hangar and to a man they gazed upwards with trepidation at the *aapkas*. The "ape cage" stood on four legs and stretched above them menacingly. Supposedly set at a psychological height, it had ended many an aspiring paratrooper's journey of obtaining his wings. And so Kevin soon found himself exiting the front door, dropping into space and being arrested with a jerk by the cable attached to his back, sliding along a cable and ending the trip with a para roll in the dirt.

Chin on chest and shoulders round Feet together, watch the ground.

Fitting the parachute, standing in a row as the instructors came down inspecting the harness position and fixings; over and over again until it became second thought. Or so Kevin thought. He found himself standing in full gear, the parachute harness digging uncomfortably into his groin, waiting for Corporal Paale (he of the megaphone kingdom) to inspect him.

Paale stood before him, his gaze following the path of Kevin's harness.

'Englishman, why did you put the FUCKING safety pin into the release clip, WHEN YOU KNOW FULL BLOODY WELL THAT IT MUST STAY OUT UNTIL I CHECK IT AND I PUT IT INTO POSITION!' He yelled.

Kevin flinched as Paale yanked the pin out, rotated the safety clip and smacked it with the heel of his hand. The blow sent Kevin back a pace as the whole parachute slid off him and onto the ground. Paale stepped up to Kevin, and jutted his head forward until his nose was millimetres away from Kevin's nose, yelled.

'If you fuck up your harness, and you exit a plane, you will hit the ground so hard that *jou trill soos 'n huisorrel sal brill!* Your schlong will SOUND LIKE A FUKKEN DINNER GONG!'

Kevin wanted to laugh, he fought it back as hard as he could and Paale could see the internal struggle in his eyes. Paale grinned and stepped back.

'Turn around, you stupid fuck, I'll help you put your chute back on.'

And so at long last one afternoon, Kitching announced, 'Tomorrow, gentlemen, you do a flight experience. This is your last chance to pull out without being placed on orders. If after the flight experience you say you will not jump then your will go RTU, returned to unit. Any man who says he will jump and then does not will be charged, sent to detention barracks and then sent back like a fucking kraal dog to his unit of origin. Do you understand me?'

'YES, STAFF,' they all chorused.

The old Dakota was cruising at jump height, its engines roaring as it headed towards the drop zone. One of the old war horses from World War Two, it still remained in extensive use as a cargo plane and as a mode of transport for paratroopers.

The all sat in their seats and Kevin felt like a trussed chicken, sitting tight up between his buddies. It was cool yet he was sweating and his mouth was dry with nervous tension. They all sat and most had their eyes fixed onto the jump lights, red and green mounted above the exit door. The despatcher stood at the door and screamed out the order, the words which would from that day on and for the rest of his life, always make Kevin's hair stand on end.

'STAND UP, HOOK UP!' screamed the despatcher, his voice could not be heard above the roar of the plane's engines all they could see was his mouth moving. Kevin stood up and hooked his parachute's static line to the cable running along the planes roof. He checked the man in front of him, making sure that the static line was not snared and that the rubber bands securing the static line were good and cleanly positioned at the back of his chute. Kevin could feel the man behind him doing the same for him. Buddy, buddy, your life in your buddy's hands, his life in yours; ultimate trust!

'STAND IN THE DOOR!' The red light had come on, switched on by the pilot as he neared the DZ.

One two, one two, one two, one two, one two; they called it out aloud as they shuffle-stepped, the front foot sliding on the floor, back foot up and down, front foot shuffle, back foot step forward, slam down, one two, one two!

The first man - number one - stood at the door, his left hand braced against the edge of the door. The green light came on and Kevin watched, between shuffling forward, how each man was given his flight experience. Soon it was his turn and he arrived at the door. The despatcher screamed at him over the roar of the plane,

'DO YOU WANT TO JUMP?'

'YES SERGEANT!'

'STAND IN THE DOOR!'

One two; and Kevin stood in the door, the toe of his left boot hanging over the edge, left palm against the outside of the doorframe. He felt the despatcher grab the harness of his chute with his left hand, the right hand gripping the jump helmet firmly.

The hand turned his head to the left, to the right, down then up, each movement accompanied by the dispatcher screaming in his ear, 'LOOK LEFT, LOOK RIGHT, LOOK DOWN, LOOK UP!'

He was roughly jerked back into the plane and the dispatcher, still with his hand gripping Kevin's helmet, twisted his head to face him and screamed the question

'DO YOU WANT TO JUMP?'

'YES SERGEANT!'

And by so doing Kevin had unwittingly committed himself.

This agreement or rather this affirmation would change his life forever.

Unbeknownst to him, it would set him up for eleven straight years of call ups, of operations across the border and of reaction force or fire-force; chasing and killing insurgents in Angola and South West Africa.

It would set him up for the biggest engagement of South African troops in a CIA backed operation, since the end of the Second World War. It would ultimately set him up for a series of events would change his life forever. It would allow him to become a member of one of the greatest fighting units in the world.

Parabat!

Half way through the jump course Kevin phoned his cousin in Johannesburg. His parents did not have a phone so he dialled the number waiting for it to ring. After a few rings he heard her pick it up,

'Hi, Kay speaking.'

'Kay, its Kevin, how are you doing?'

'I'm fine, Kev, how are you managing the army?'

And so, after the usual chit chat Kevin asked her to invite his folks to his Wings Parade.

'It's a big thing Kay, I'm getting my wings, family are invited to attend the ceremony!'

'Okay, I'll tell them, bye.'

The Highveld winters in Bloemfontein, away from the smog of Johannesburg were blessed with some lovely weather. It was eleven in the morning and it was a glorious day. They stood, in dress uniforms or step-outs, gleaming and polished. Their green berets dumped, they had earned the right to wear the maroon beret on their heads. Selection and jump course over, he had made the grade.

He had done it; he had earned the right to be called a Parabat!

His eyes moved across the spectators watching, searching. Parents and family, brothers and sisters, had travelled to there from throughout the country, some had even flown in from overseas.

There was no sign of his parents, no one had come. Kevin felt crestfallen; they had not come. He watched out of the corner of his eye as the Commandant pinned the bronze wings to each man's chest, moving slowly up the line from man to man.

One man had the honour of having his grandfather, a paratrooper and veteran of the para drop over Arnhem, pin his wings to his chest. It was a stirring moment, the total respect shown by the instructors and officers towards this old veteran adding to the occasion.

When it came to Kevin's turn he stood proudly as the Commandant pinned the wings to his chest and said,

'Well done soldier, welcome to Parachute Battalion.'

His parents were not there. He was so proud but so sad, they had not come. But it was all right. He was OK, he had made the grade.

Cowboys don't cry, Kevin, especially not in front of their horses!

Later, while standing there amongst the beaming faces and men leaving with families to go on a seven day pass he realized something. It reinforced what they had achieved and made him proud of being part of all of this.

Of the Kimberly volunteers there were two men left.

Of the 21 there were now 2.

Kevin and a short bloke called Andrew.

Chapter Eleven: **The Okapi knife**

Pistol shots ring out in the barroom night
Enter Patty Valentine from the upper hall
She sees a bartender in a pool of blood
Cries out my God, they killed them all...

Bob Dylan

They were camped at the border crossing between South West Africa and Angola, near the town of Santa Clara[5]. A massive water tower, with a spotter's tent pitched on the top of it looming over them like something out of a science fiction movie. There were only 19 of them; one stick of infantry, two mortarists, signaller, and medic the corporal and Loot.

They had been sent there two days ago as intelligence reports had indicated that there had been some terrorist activity in the area, mines planted and the usual shit. The People's Liberation Army of Namibia (PLAN), the armed wing of the South West African Peoples Organisation (SWAPO) had been flexing its muscles, big-time. Time to teach those fuckers a lesson they had been told during a briefing session a few days ago.

'Shit place to be sitting up there all exposed like that,' said someone looking up at the tower.

'Yep, imagine spending your national service up there, in the sun, with nothing to do but stare at the bush,' agreed Kevin.

'He probably sits up there day in and day out, pulling his wire until his dick falls off,' added a bloke called Manie.

There was a ripple of laughter.

'Hours, days, weeks, months sitting up there, I'd go off my fucking head. It's blokes like that who really lose it. Then they go home and they score lank points because they went mad on the border, all *bombefok*. Mommies hero was a fucking glorified gate guard!'

'Like the medics,' added another, 'those poor buggers working with blokes blown up and putting the pieces into body bags, working in the mortuary and shit like that.

---

5. Santa Clara is the capital city of the Cuban province of Villa Clara.

He paused and then went on. 'My cousin was a medic and he was never the same again. I'd much rather be a bat, see action, get fucking shot at and get to shoot people.'

By now he was on a roll, his face going red as he worked himself up. 'Fuck the rest of the army, I'm really over the moon at our situation, really just love the fukken thought of it!' he finished his diatribe, his voice laced with sarcasm.

'Yep, I really would rather be a bat than sit up there like a rock rabbit on a rock!' agreed Kevin. The day was hot and they spent it under a clump of massive trees a clear indication of water, obviously the reason for the massive water tower Kevin observed.

Kevin had an old Okapi penknife, it was a cheap and nasty old thing but he always kept it with him. Old, reliable and razor sharp he'd found it lying in the dirt months ago and it had often came in pretty handy.

He wasn't a knife carrier, but the Afrikaans boys were big penknife carriers and the old Okapi penknife came under fire regularly.

'Jeez Englishman, that is the shittiest knife I have ever seen,' chided Dreyer.

'You salty cocks have no fukken idea about knives, fukken *rooinekke*!'

Kevin felt the irritation rise in him.

'You know Dreyer, you and all the Dutchmen like you are racist arseholes, always referring to the bloody Boer War,' retorted Kevin.

He continued, 'The English were called *Rooinekke* or red necks because the sun burnt the shit out of them when they first came to Africa. But you fuckers were called *Vaalpense*, grey bellies because you lot were so busy slithering around like snakes on your fucking bellies, the sun never got to it'

'Fuck you, Vos!'

'Fuck you, Dreyer!'

'In any case,' continued Kevin. 'My surname is Vos and that's German/Dutch so stop calling me a bloody Englishman, now fukkoff!'

'Ja you see, your fucking forefathers were *draadsitters*, always sitting on the fence, speaking English with an Afrikaans surname, fucking traitors,' snarled Dreyer in response.

'Your grandfather probably fought on the side of the English!'

'Fuck you, Dreyer!'

'Fuck you too, Vos!'

Kevin gave Dreyer a murderous look and turned away, ignoring Dreyer's parting shot, 'fukken fence sitter, *draadsitter*!'

Kevin didn't turn back; he simply shut up and carried on cleaning the old Okapi.

After all, Dreyer was almost twice his size and he had a very strong sense of self-preservation. Caution before valour always, was his motto.

The next morning they were called together by an excited looking Lieutenant.

'Men, we are going to possible see a bit of action today. A patrol of the horse commandoes were ambushed last night about 60 clicks from here,' he said pointing in a north- westerly direction.

'Three of them were killed and our job is to hunt those communists down and kill them. Check your water, check your ammo and get rats for two days sorted, we leave in 15 minutes,' he finished with a flourish.

It was refreshing, thought Kevin, the army never used the race card:

'We fight communists not blacks.'

Only thing was that, every single one of PLAN's fighters was as black as the ace of spades. A lot of the guys called them Kaffirs, a derogatory, racist name meaning unbeliever, a name which the black South Africans hated. Kevin tried his best not to use the word. Growing up in Zululand he'd learnt to respect and love the Zulu culture and as a boy had read extensively about Chaka Zulu, the Black Napoleon as historians would come to call him. He built up a military machine which, even after his death, had given the Boers and the British Empire a bloody nose before the Zulu *impis* were ultimately defeated.

The battle of Isandhlwana was a decisive victory for the Zulus and caused the defeat of the first British invasion of Zululand. The British Army had suffered its worst defeat against a technologically inferior indigenous force. Kevin's knowledge and respect for the Zulus had not gone unnoticed by some of the more right wing blokes like Dreyer, and once when they had got slightly inebriated at the battalion canteen Dreyer had called Kevin a *Kaffirboetie*. Which effectively meant that he was a Kaffir's brother and therefore by default, a Kaffir.

Kevin had also then decided that caution be placed before valour and had not retaliated. Dreyer and a few mates had as a result developed the opinion that Kevin was a *banggat*, a scared arse, which meant that Kevin, while not quite being a coward was really nothing but a chicken-shit.

The two Unimogs pulled out 20 minutes later, the front Mog filled with the infantry and the Loot, the second one with three mortarists, the signaller the section leader and the medic. They had packed sandbags on the floor of the second one as a base for the 60mm mortar with baseplate. The small compact Unimogs were almost indestructible but had the horrible tendency to rock 'n roll from side to side like a drunken sailor at the slightest bump in its path, it felt as if they were going to roll over at any second.

They "rock 'n rolled" for about an hour along the border fence, known as the cut-line, before they ploughed over the fence and into Angola and that's when Kevin first felt a tinge of uneasiness. They were heading directly towards the spot where the poor hapless soldiers had been shot dead the night before.

'This is going to be wild goose chase,' shouted Kevin over the sound of the diesel engines and saplings being smashed over. 'The chances of SWAPO being around are bugger-all, they're halfway back to Luanda by now!'

'You're right,' yelled back a bloke called Jan. 'this is just a sightseeing trip in the bush nothing else, well ride all day and end up wasting our bloody time!'

Kevin had only hooked up with Jan two weeks ago having joined the group late, he had been kept back in the battalion for a court martial after the fight on the municipal bus. Jan was a decent sort who had undergone mortar training with Kevin and they got on well.

'There should be armour plating on the side of these fucking things, there's no fucking protection,' shouted Kevin, very aware that they were sitting ducks on the top of the Mogs.

'Fuck that, and then we'd really *bliksem* over,' yelled Jan in reply, his eyes wide in alarm.

Catch fucking 22 thought Kevin, the irony of it not escaping him, get shot or get rolled on by a couple of tons of steel, lovely set of options for fucksakes!

The vehicles slowed down as they entered a large *shona*, a manmade clearing in the bush about 4km in diameter. As they entered they split up, the front Mog heading slightly right towards a cluster of huts at the edge of the clearing, while the second one headed straight across to recce the opposite side.

The guys were relaxed, after all the ambush had happened a long time ago, nothing was going to happen. The SWAPO terrs had been legging it for all that time so there was no ways they'd be near! With that comforting bit of logic happily ensconced in his mind, Kevin settled down comfortably on the sandbags, gazing idly at the other Mog as it neared the cluster of huts.

And then all hell broke loose.

The sound of the R1 rifles firing, their deeper boom heard clearly over the PUK, PUK, PUK sound of AK47's. A full blown firefight had erupted out and Kevin could see the guys jumping and falling off the front Mog in their desperation to find cover.

It was a well laid ambush. SWAPO weren't too bad as combatants and they generally put up a good fight. They had placed the main ambush amongst the huts with a machinegun to the side, catching the guys in a potentially murderous crossfire. Kevin noticed that the tracer colours were different and then he knew with a surge of adrenaline that this was the real deal. He could see a stream of tracers pouring towards the Mog and the surrounding bush; it looked like someone was spraying the area with a hosepipe, spewing out bright dots of green light. This was the real deal, a fully-fledged firefight and not just some trigger happy bats pouring ammo at bugger-all.

Kevin's gut gave a twist; it felt like a rock python had come to life in his bowels. The corporal was screaming over the radio as Kevin felt the Mog slewing sharply to the right, it felt as if it was going to roll over for a second.

'Fuck, fuck, fuck,' yelled Kevin in alarm, the adrenalin coursing through him as they headed straight towards the tracer stream. The Mog nosedived to a halt, as if it was about to root in the dirt like a warthog. They moved fast. Kevin went onto his knees and grabbed the mortar pipe, a second before Jan got hold of it; always a competition to be the number one on the pipe these young men trained to wage war. The number one on the pipe was the man who aimed while the number two slid the 60mm mortar bombs down the pipe. The number three was in the safest spot, lying on his side, taking the bombs out of the ammo cases, twisting the head to trigger and handing them to the number two who dropped them down the pipe on Kevin's cue.

Kevin screamed, 'GO, GO, GO!' as he clutched the pipe guessing the trajectory and direction to the SWAPO gunner.

Kevin felt the shock of the first bomb leaving the pipe and the baseplate slamming itself into the sandbags. The sound was deafening and his ears began to ring, a high pitched zing which deadened the sounds of the raging firefight. Everyone on the Mog was watching Kevin as he watched the tracer stream, the hidden gunner still hosing down the bush and the other Mog.

'FUUUUCCCKKK!' shouted Kevin in frustration as the bomb went off in the bush, way behind the terrs holding the lighted hose; still spraying deadly lights at the men pinned down near the other Mog.

'FUCK, FUCK, FUCK!'

Muscle memory, the result of countless hours of training took over. He pulled the pipe back a fraction and screamed, 'Go, Go, Go!' feeling the shock and sound as the second bomb left the pipe. This one was close but still beyond the machine gun position.

The lights stopped briefly and then they started up again, this time the stream was wayward as if manned by a child wielding a toy gun.

This is your rifle, this is gun, this is for killing and this is for fun!, rang illogically in his head!

The third bomb went off almost on the lights and they were cut off, as if someone had shut off a tap, stopping the flow of lights instantly. The fourth bomb smashed into the trees above causing a fluke airburst and the lights were doused once and for all. Freed of the lights at last the guys who were pinned down began to return fire towards the huts, moving in a disciplined skirmish line, and firing at will. Moving in the classic buddy, buddy system your buddy firing while you run, you go down, you fire at the enemy while your buddy runs forward, he goes down you stand up you run.

Your life in his hands; his life in your hands.

Kevin always thought that calling it buddy, buddy somehow minimised it, cheapened it all. They should have called it brother, brother that would have made more sense giving the relationship the gravity it deserved.

The mortar Mog had caught up with the skirmish line and the corporal told Kevin to give Jan a gap at the pipe, they swopped and Kevin took over the number three position, twisting the bombs to trigger and handing them over. Lying down on his side was safer so he was slightly less pissed off at not having control of the pipe.

They caught up with the skirmish line and began to put bombs down ahead of them, trying to discourage and hopefully kill any Terrs trying to escape, placing a curtain of steel ahead of the advancing line.

The running men had slowed down, while being super fit this was after all their first contact and first blood, the adrenaline coursed through them at the possibility of killing or being killed. Kevin could see that they were exhausted and they had the look of war on their faces, fear overcome by valour running into the face of death.

FUCK, FUCK, FUCK! The lights were back.

Kevin watched frozen and watched and watched for what seemed like an age, an eternity of only seconds yet, it felt like forever… as he watched the lights coming towards him through the trees.

In a slow arc, up and up slowly the stream of green seemed to be in slow motion.

He wanted to shout; after all they were in slow motion he had plenty of time to shout. But it was an illusion. He couldn't say a thing in time to warn anyone.

As they came closer they accelerated into a blur of green, he could hear the stream of lights passing them only a meter away, and he imagined a crackling sound combined with the sound of a hissing mamba. He heard the corporal screaming orders as the Mog lurched to the left, it hit a small tree and stopped for a moment.

If you stop too long here we're going to all die, move you fucker, move! Screamed in Kevin's head.

It made a grating sound before lurched forward, smashing the tree over with a cracking sound. The skirmish line swung left and Kevin could hear their return fire, a roar in his ears, the sound of their LMG gunner pouring burst of automatic fire into the bush ahead. The firing stopped the Loot screaming, 'Cease fire, cease fire!' his voice hoarse.

They stopped when they reached a second kraal of huts and carefully and systematically went through each dwelling, until they were sure that there was no one there.

The place was deserted, there were chickens and goats about and the large woven baskets of African corn were full, they had had a good crop; deserted for now by the terrified inhabitants who had fled before the approaching sound of war. The enemy had bomb-shelled on the other side of the kraal, the spoor effectively cold and dead and so they retraced their steps to the start of the contact.

While passing through the kraal, the Loot gave the order and they set the baskets alight, shooting the livestock while the corn burnt and popped in the background. Scorched earth, if you harbour the enemy you pay for it!

They swept the area and found four insurgents dead; miraculously not one of the bats had been hit.

 The side of the lead Mog looked like a Swiss cheese, the SWAPO gunner had concentrated his fire at the Mog, his rounds staying high and not going low; missing the men who had been pinned down.

Were they just lucky…or perhaps God did take sides?

They moved the bodies together at the edge of the clearing, and placed them in front of a small church the people had built. It was small and ramshackle but was clearly a church and Kevin found it poignant, weirdly so, that the guys had placed the dead before a church, a subconscious thing perhaps?

'Hey Kev, check this,' beckoned Jan.

Jan put the toe of his boot against a dead man's skull and prodded it gently, the whole skull moved like jelly trapped in a bowl of cracked glass. Kevin could hear a faint crackling sound, the shattered bone fragments grinding against each other.

The man's eyes were open; they were fixed on Kevin; and it seemed as if he was asking *why are you letting him do this to me, am I not dead?*

Kevin turned away and climbed back onto the Mog and sat with his back to the dead men. He could feel a headache creeping up on him like an old lizard inching itself across a sun-baked rock. He was just 18 years old and he felt old; oh so fucking old.

'*Engelsman, hey, Englishman, hey!* Are you fucking deaf, can I borrow your knife?'

It was Dreyer, holding out his hand with an uncharacteristically friendly look on his face. Without thinking Kevin pulled the old Okapi out of his pocket and placed it in Dreyer's hand who walked off without thanks.

Jan climbed up and plonked himself down on the sandbags next to Kevin.

'You okay, boet'? He asked slight concern in his voice. Not wanting to show any weakness Kevin nodded, giving Jan a thumbs-up. The lizard had moved onto the top of the sun-baked rock. His head felt like it was about to explode.

He heard a voice through the headache.

'*Engelsman*, here's your knife, *dankie*,' said Dreyer, thanking Kevin as he handed it over.

The blade was open, it had blood on it. Kevin looked at the blade; there was blood on it, blood, real blood. He touched it with the tip of his finger, it was sticky. Kevin looked down at Dreyer who was still standing there, looking up at him with a strange expectant look on his face.

'What's this Dreyer, is it blood?'

'*Ja*, check this,' he produced an ear, holding it between thumb and forefinger and waving it at Kevin. Kevin felt the rage and disgust well up in him and he hurled the knife hard at Dreyer. The handle hit Dreyer on the chest hard and it bounced off into the sand.

'What the fuck did you do that for, *jou fokken rooinek*?' screamed Dreyer,' his face going red with mounting anger. 'You could have fukken pegged me!'

'FUCK YOU, YOU FUKKEN CUNT!' screamed Kevin, leaping down to the ground. He started to move towards Dreyer when he felt a hand on his shoulder, roughly pulling him backwards. Kevin spun around in a slight crouch expecting the sucker punch from one of Dreyer's mates. It was the Lieutenant.

'What the hell is going on here?' he asked angrily.

'This piece of shit used my knife to cut off a Terr's ear!'

'He did what?' The Loot sounded incredulous turning towards Dreyer. He looked at Dreyer and held his hand out, not saying a word. Dreyer, with a slightly worried look showed him the ear. The lieutenant's face hardened and took on a look of disgust.

'Dig a deep hole and bury it, NOW!'

Nothing was said about the ear incident when they got back to Ondangwa[6]. The word was out that HQ was extremely pleased with the kills, after all that's why they sent the bats in the first place, they expected the kills. Kevin always the cynic saw it for what it was, a whole lot of smoke being blown up their collective arses. The men were in high spirits and were issued a couple of cases of beer to celebrate. It wasn't ice cold, but someone had tried their best to make it as cold as possible. Kevin drank four beers, they made him drunk and he slept like a dead man.

---

6. Due to its strategic airport, Ondangwa became an important staging area for the South African Defence Force during its campaigns in neighbouring Angola. Local road and rail links were also improved by authorities to facilitate the rapid movement of military vehicles.

Chapter Twelve: **Mercenaries**

Now Ziggy really sang, screwed up eyes and screwed down hairdo
Like some cat from Japan, he could lick 'em by smiling
He could leave 'em to hang
'Came on so loaded man, well hung and snow white tan

- David Bowie

'Gentlemen, we're going into Angola,' announced a high-ranking officer from the Armour Corps. He had a nice round paunch and had a general look about him which reminded Kevin of Obelix, of the Asterix and Obelix comics; except that he wasn't wearing blue stripes like Obelix, he was wearing a brown uniform.

Kevin felt a slight sense of nostalgia, thinking of lying on his bed at home, pissing himself at the antics of the Gaul's and the Romans. He felt a bit disappointed that he didn't have an Obelix comic with him. The Obelix lookalike had an air of supressed excitement about him, his eyes almost dancing with excitement. It reminded Kevin of the real Obelix eying a nice, fat wild-boar turning on the spit. The good officer looked as if he had done a few of those porkers justice in the last while, mused Kevin.

The officer Obelix paused, waiting for a response. It was quick to come.

'Ahem, brigadier, we were in Angola a few days ago when we gave SWAPO a bloody nose,' piped up Lappies.

And you should know Lappies, thought Kevin. You and your mate Pieter had to bury the four dead terrs the next day. Breaking an arm set in rigor mortise, to get it to stay under the shallow layer of earth. *Shards of glassy bone grated in Kevin's head.*

Obelix ignored the fact that Lappies had summarily p romoted him, possibly because he fancied the idea of being called brigadier. Obelix continued:

'The government has authorised a push into Angola. Already the Portuguese inhabitants are fleeing, there are thousands of refugees flooding southwards, and some are trapped. There will be a para drop to rescue them but not you, you are going to push northwards by motorised column…'. And so the briefing dragged on.

John Marais takes up the story from this point:

After solid and strenuous training we arrived in Rundu via train towards the latter part of August '75 to relieve Platoon 1 of A coy. I remember clearly that Northern Transvaal was playing Free State in the Currie Cup final - Pierre Spies scored the winning try in the final minute! It was rather relaxed and the Platoon 1 guys, who we were to replace, informed us that not much was happening – "for about 150 km across the border you will be lucky if you encounter any Swapo". We did the normal stuff: PT on the runway to get acclimatized, the odd patrol close by around Rundu - basic and boring stuff like this. However, we went on a trip in Southern Angola via Unimogs as SWAPO were apparently spotted. What stands out about this op is that we never had any contact and that we were extremely hungry and THIRSTY. I can recall that Portuguese soldiers were with us (I think) and I suppose the rookie border element also played its role. We started drinking the drips during the evening and then Des MacGeer shot a magnificent Sable (Swartwitpens) – we all agreed that it was ok as we were starving - we had a feast that evening!

Ewald Jansen van Rensburg, in his own words:

Operation Savannah had been going on for over just over a month. The Reconnaissance Commando or Recces had a severe shortage of adequately trained manpower to support them. It was like manna from heaven, when some of us bumped into a Recce at Grootfontein soon after our return from the "states". We had originally signed on for two years and they allowed us to go back to arrange for studies next year and some had even gone for job interviews.

But back to Grootfontein; arrangements were made quickly, documentation completed and a few of us (C comp. 1 Parachute Bn) were set for an experience we would never forget. Soon we were on a plane en route to our destination, a town called Cela.

From the men's stories, I had a strong suspicion that they were involved in something big or important, but the question was what? Now we understand why it is not documented anywhere. Many books have been written about the border war but the writers' sources were largely other books with little archival material support. Dates are often faulty; heroic incidents where medals were awarded were often focused on an individual's actions and did not take into account other soldiers' involvement; often an officer making the recommendation would be conscious of his chances of being awarded the medal. So a lot of the facts around these actions are ignored and lost in history.

John Marais described the situation thus:

We realized that something was brewing. We saw SM Tillie Smit, SM FC van Zyl (what a gentlemen) and other "famous" senior recces and parabats around – very much off the radar, but there with a purpose. And so it happened that we were called together and Major Coen Upton addressed us. He was a real showman and informed us that we have to sign documents denying that we were South Africans. We were issued with unmarked (green) uniforms and low-cut "tekkies/vellies" as well as unmarked rifles and ammo. All our stuff had to be locked in our lockers and we were to get that upon our return. We left by Flossie[7] and arrived in Sa da Bandeira early September '75. We were informed that the forces were on the way via road and we had the following duties:

** Ensure that Sa da Bandeira remains under our control – by means of vehicle patrols through and around the town.*

** Ensure that the airport remained safe and under our control.*

** Train FNLA and Unita recruits.*

We offloaded rifles and ammo from aircraft and it really looked like someone (CIA?) donated all their old and redundant shit to them. These guys were completely raw with absolutely no training at that stage. Our first encounter with them was at a homemade shooting range in a far corner of the runway. It was absolute chaos: some of them held the rifles above their heads whilst firing, full automatic and no tap-tap – really chaotic and dangerous by the way!

Some of us also went to Mocamedez whilst escorting high ranking officials – Jonas Savimbi and other prominent black leaders were around as well as lots of senior white officials from South Africa. We had to play body guards to them and at one stage we sat in a huge lounge of a Hotel and Savimbi flamboyantly said the bar was open and it was on the house. Now, brandy and rum as we know it was not to be found - the closest to it was cognac and we thought it to be a good second best. However, they did not appreciate us downing the cognac with coke! They also booked us into our own private hotel rooms with hot showers, shampoo and soap! They obviously concluded their outstanding matters as we were on our way back to Sa da Bandeira the soon thereafter.

Upon our arrival we carried on with the above duties and obviously very bored. Next the Gunners, Pantsers, Infantry and other units started coming through Sa da Bandeira and that is when it really started.

---

7. A C130 Cargo plane.

And that was the first time they heard about operation Savannah. They had to hand in all SADF equipment, even their dog-tags were handed in. They were issued with green uniforms, shoes and rifles without serial numbers. A horrible bloody thing called a G3 rifle with the same calibre as the FN or R1 rifle but it rattled like a bastard. Kevin grew to hate the bloody thing and it wasn't long before he found some electrical tape and bandaged its wounds to stop the rattles.

They were told that they were going into Angola as mercenaries; the rest of the world was not to know that they were South African soldiers.

'Under no circumstances will any of you talk Afrikaans; English only. Do you understand?' barked Obelix in Afrikaans.

That cracked Kevin up and he burst out laughing; soon most of the guys saw the humour in it all and started to laugh their heads off. Obelix had no idea what the joke was about and in any case the briefing was over. So he walked off in a huff! Each of them were given a document to sign, a "contract", employing them effectively as mercenaries and stating clearly that they had signed voluntarily…yeah right!

Kevin signed knowing full well that he had relinquished his rights to the Geneva Convention.

'Sign gentlemen, you are going to earn a bucket-load of money as a mercenary, yes, sign here and there, and there……' Two of them refused to sign.

They were called useless chunks of shit, traitors and cowards before they were shipped off. They were not seen again.

Pereira d'Eça[8] was a wreck; it had been shot to hell. Jan Breytenbach and his Fletchers, a rag tag battle group which was the beginning of Zulu force and in essence the fledgling 32 Battalion, had been and gone. They arrived after the main fight and Kevin felt an odd sense of relief combined with strong disappointment. His first taste of war had left him with a newfound confidence; after all they were veterans now! Then again he wasn't too keen to walk into another shit storm that easily.

A Coy had been split up into little groups scattered all over throughout the campaign and some of his mates would disappear out of his life forever. He knew that the only other surviving member of the Kimberly crew, Andy, was in Angola somewhere; where he had no idea. The little colonial town was pockmarked with bullet holes and the scars of the fight were everywhere.

The stink was everywhere as well, the sickly sweet smell of the rotting dead.

They had already been buried, but still there was an oily smell which hung in the air like an invisible smog.

---

8. Pereira d' Eça is a town and commune in the municipality of Cuanhama, province of Cunene.

'We need to find that bloody stink. I can't handle this anymore, groaned Kevin one morning, after they had been there for three days.

Jan nodded in agreement,

'It's fucking horrible and why the fuck are we hanging about here in any case; this is a waste of time for fucksakes!'

Kevin had steered clear of the bus fight boys since they had all come up to the border; he had learnt his lesson well. Then one morning, Ronnie stood up and announced that they were going find out where the stink was coming from, looking pointedly at Kevin as if daring him to say anything to the contrary. Ronnie walked off and came back later picked up his rifle and asked:

'So whose coming with me? The Loot says we can go look for the stink, there are some UNITA kaffirs bivvied out past the old petrol station. He says we must collect some of them. They know where the stink is coming from.'

And so it was that Kevin and Jan found themselves walking in support, carrying the mortar pipe and walking at the tail end of the impromptu mini patrol. Five Paras and two motley UNITA soldiers walked into the remnants of the carnage of battle.

There were craters left from exploding mortar bombs and they were forced to give an unexploded bomb a wide berth. With its fins sticking out of the soft sand, it had a frightening, menacing air about it. Although the battle had been over for a few weeks, Kevin still felt uneasy.

'This is crap, Jan,' he muttered under his breath, I don't like this one bit.' Jan agreed, just nodding, then raising his eyebrow and with a slight shake of his head simply said, 'FUCK!'

Then Kevin understood why Jan had said, 'FUCK'.

Then Kevin also said 'FUCK!'

The UNITA soldiers had moved the lid of and underground water cistern and the smell poured out and hit them like a wet, oily slap. The stench was cloying, it seemed to get into Kevin's nose, ears eyes, every bloody where. The smell felt almost as if it would slide into his guts and sit there like a wet stinking worm.

Kevin saw the front three and the UNITA men reeling back and watched, as Ronnie vomited a yellow stream of partly digested rat pack, with amazing velocity. And then dumbstruck, he saw one of the UNITA soldiers chuck a grenade into the cistern and the thing exploded as if a thousand pound bomb had hit it.

The gas erupted in a huge ball of flame and the concrete lid spiralled upwards and disintegrated. Luckily the force of the blast went upwards and the concrete slab covering the cistern remained intact.

Directed by the cistern walls and the hole the blast didn't kill them but nontheless it was impressive. Kevin didn't hang around, he simply ran like hell, his lanky legs taking him away from the carnage.

He could hear plopping sounds behind him and didn't dare look back; and as he ran he did a "Ronnie", puking a projectile of vomit ahead of him like a yellow flame thrower.

That night Kevin dreamt of flying pieces of flesh and saw the dead SWAPO man staring at him. He woke up sweating, *the shards of glass grinding in his head.*

Rumour had it that the UNITA commander had ordered the grenade-chucker shot while his men cleaned up and buried the mess. Probably a bullshit story, but either way the stink was gone and the place became quite liveable.

Remarkably it hadn't rained for two days and the Angolan sand had quickly sucked up the rain. It was hot and they lay about in any bit of shade they could find.

Kevin lay idly on his side, drawing patterns in the sand, curls, lines geometrical stuff. 'Hey you know what Kev, I'm *lekker* horny and I need a solid pomp,' said Jan out of the blue.

'Thanks for sharing that with me, Jan, I really needed to hear that seeing that the nearest bit of fanny is about seven thousand kilometres away,' responded Kevin with a touch of friendly sarcasm in his voice.

'There's this girl I knew at boarding school,' continued Jan. 'She was the headmaster's daughter and we used to sneak up and spy on her through her bedroom window. That chick was hot and nobody could get near her. She was the snobbiest, horniest bitch I knew. Once me and my buddy were spying on her and she started to rub her pussy, then pulled her panties down, spread her legs and rubbed and fingered herself until she came.'

There was a sudden spark of interest in Kevin and a rustle of movement, as a few of the others lying in the shade turned towards Jan.

Suddenly everyone was interested in the conversation.

'Just check, you *okes*,' chuckled Kevin. 'All of us lying here half dead with boredom and at the first mention of fanny, you blokes are up and about like a bunch of fukken mongooses.'

'It's mongeese, the plural for mongoose is mongeese,' interjected Peter.

'No its mongi,' corrected another.

'What's a fukken mongee, you mean mongaai.'

'I've come to the conclusion that we are all fucked in the head,' interrupted Kevin.

'Here we are listening to Jan talking about pussy and you lot start talking shit about fukken mongooses; since when is a mongoose more important than pussy, for fucksakes?'

There was a roar of laughter 'Okay Jan, tell us more…'

'That's it,' responded Jan.

'What do you mean, that's it. You watched her jack off and then you tell us that's it?'

'Well I don't believe in sex before marriage, it's wrong and that's it,' responded Jan.

'So it's okay to spy on people, no hang on, to be a Peeping Tom then, is okay is it?' asked a critical Peter.

'Hey Jan, did you jack off while you were watching her?' chirped Lappies.

'Nah, his buddy jacked him off while they were watching.'

'Piss off all of you I'm not a bloody homo pervert,' snarled Jan,

'I might be a wanker but I'm not a pervert!'

'Tell me, who of you have never wanked,' asked Kevin.

'Let him who has never wanked cast the first stroke.'

There was a ripple of laughter and they all fell silent.

They followed the shade as it moved with the sun. Kevin thought of vagina, for the rest of the morning his brain was full of vagina. He thought of a book he had read called the *World according to Garp*, where vagina was described as beaver. The book categorised it into different kinds of beaver; plain beaver, then split beaver and finally split wet beaver.

'Hey Jan, you're a bloody arsehole,' snarled Kevin. 'Now my brain is filled with pussy!'

A Coy 1 Parachute Battalion – Operation Savannah, Zulu force.

Chapter Thirteen: The Okapi avenged

Ira furor brevis est: Anger is a brief madness

Inevitably the Okapi incident came to a head. Being paratroopers they were relocated to the northern side of the town, to hold the local airfield. It was a large airfield as the town had been the administrative capital of the province while under Portuguese rule and was large enough for big plane to land. It was reasonably organised as far as battle areas were concerned. Even a temporary field toilet had been set out; a row of "go-carts" placed on a ditch, not fully completed but useable.

It was as if someone had had the bright idea of installing a communal shitter and then, after getting cold feet about the whole thing, simply moved off before it was complete. The "go-carts" were fibre glass toilet seats moulded onto a base, set on poles and sandbags and mounted over a long trench. No privacy, just sitting in a row chatting to your buddies while taking a shit. It was at times like these that Kevin mentally thanked the sappers who always came, did their "shit" and moved on. Toilet construction being one of the more appreciated things they did.

'I need to take a dump,' said Kevin getting up from the dirt and picking up his rifle.

It was late afternoon and the heat and humidity hung over the airfield making it pretty uncomfortable.

'Thanks for sharing mate; enjoy the go-cart and let's hope the flies aren't too bad,' responded Jan.

The standard joke was that toilet paper, or white gold as it was referred to, was not needed after taking a shit in Angola.

When finished just lift your arse, tolerate the buzzing sensations around your backside and in two seconds flat the flies could clean your arse shinier and cleaner than "white gold" ever could.

Sitting on a go-cart was Dreyer, quietly staring into the distance and contemplating life. One of buddies sitting next to him, also gazing into the distance.

Kevin sat down two go-carts away, ignoring them.

'How's it going Englishman?' asked Dreyer, his voice friendly.

Kevin fell into the trap nicely answering, 'I'm OK thanks.'
There was a brief silence.

'I'm constipated,' said Dreyer, 'and when my crap is this hard that shit knife of yours comes in handy.'

He paused. 'Really *lekker* to cut stuck turds away from my arse.'

Kevin ignored him.

'What's wrong Englishman, don't you want your knife back there's only a bit of shit and Kaffir blood on it, it shouldn't be too much of a problem cleaning it up, huh?'

That word again, it cut into Kevin, kaffir, he hated it and he felt just an edge developing in his mind. Ignoring Dreyer, Kevin finished, stood up, pulled his pants up, picked up his rifle and started walking away. Dreyer too had finished and quickly caught up to him.

'Here, take your fucking knife,' said Dreyer, at the same time placing his hand on Kevin's shoulder and jerking him around.

Kevin allowed himself to be swung about, but purley out of reflex and self-preservation, he dropped into a slight crouch.

'Oh, so the Englishman wants to get clever,' hissed Dreyer as he took a swing at Kevin, catching him on the top of his head with his right fist. Kevin went down, his head spinning and Dreyer was onto him in a flash, fists coming down in a blur. He was big and he used his weight in an attempt to crush the breath out of Kevin. Kevin could feel the power in him as he used his bodyweight to pin him down, his forearm across Kevin's chin, trying to get it into the throat.

Kevin managed to ward off the blows and tucked his chin in, knowing that if Dreyer's forearm got to his throat he was done for. He knew that he had to dislodge Dreyer, so he jack-knifed his hips up and rolled at the same time, managing to dislodge Dreyer who hit the ground in a thump of dust.

Kevin was onto him and began to use his elbows against the head, eyebrows, cheeks, eyes. He used them like clubs smashing and grinding them into Dreyer's face.

Dreyer rolled and the two of them were thrashing in the dust each trying to find the advantage. Dreyer was stronger, but Kevin was quicker and so, as Dreyer managed to twist around one more time, Kevin got lucky and managed to get his right arm around Dreyer's throat. Bringing his left arm over the back of Dreyer's head Kevin locked his right hand on his left bicep and managed to wedge his forearm into Dreyer's throat.

The pressure on Dreyer's throat was relentless and he fought for breath, the air in his throat sounding like a death rattle. He thrashed in the sand under Kevin like stranded fish, his nails clawing into Kevin's forearm in desperation. Kevin heard yelling behind him but his rage was all consuming.

The glass bones ground and grated in his head, the shards hurting his brain; the dead man asking, 'why did you let them do this to me? His Okapi, blade red with the man's blood!

He felt rough hands one pair, two, three it felt like a hundred people were pulling him off Dreyer. They dragged him off and he sat up in the dirt heaving for breath, tasting the dust chalk dry in his throat, watching as they revived Dreyer, pouring water on him, slapping his face. Dreyer moved and rolled onto his side facing Kevin, his chest heaving, his face covered in bloody red mud. Kevin felt bad and strangely he felt sorry for Dreyer. *the grinding shards had stopped grating in his head.*

'Vos, come with me, you look like shit and you're in the shit,' said the corporal beckoning Kevin with a crooked finger.

The fight had ended about twenty minutes ago and Kevin was amazed that retribution was going to be this quick. He got up, his legs feeling a bit shaky as the fight had taken it out of him; the shakiness probably more as a result of the adrenalin than exhaustion, he realized. He followed the corporal who walked a while until he reached an area where the 'rankers' slept. The corporal stood at the corner behind the building and pointed down to an open manhole which led to an underground cistern. Kevin looked for Dreyer, expecting him to be standing there as well, also waiting for justice to be meted out. Oddly he was absent.

'Get your clothes off and get in there,' the corporal instructed.

Kevin was filled with puzzled trepidation but he obeyed and climbed down the rungs into the cistern; he fell the last few metres into the water. It was cold and refreshing, actually it was bloody marvellous. The corporal followed, jumping into the water straight from the manhole with a great splash. Kevin's eyes adjusted to the gloom and he noticed that the lieutenant and a few other rankers were in there as well.

'KD, enjoy the swim,' said the lieutenant. 'You deserve it. We were wondering when you were going to do something about that arsehole. Enjoy the swim, clean up and when we get out of here, this didn't happen. Normally both of you would be on orders for fighting, especially in the operational area, but this stays right here, well done, good man!'

Fuck me, thought a relieved Kevin and he certainly enjoyed the swim!

The Billy the Kid syndrome is a real thing and has been the death of many a poor boy, thought Kevin, as he saw Ronnie walking towards him. Ronnie was a true street fighter and had provincial colours in boxing, as quick as a rattlesnake. Kevin had seen him in action plenty of times; not a man to be trifled with. Then there was the bus incident probably festering in Ronnie's mind. Kevin feared the worst. Like the proverbial train thundering through the proverbial tunnel, the inevitable was coming straight at him!

'So now you scheme you're the fucking main man, huh KD?' smirked Ronnie, eyeing Kevin, squinting, his one eyebrow cocked up in a quizzical fashion.

'No I'm not, Ron,' responded Kevin and in the next moment Kevin found himself on his arse in the dirt. Ronnie had skilfully used his foot and swept him off his feet.

Kevin simply stayed on his backside and waited. He wanted to look unaffected so he lay back and placed his hands behind his head.

'Thanks Ron I needed a lie down I'm tired; that Dutchman is strong.'

A ripple of laughter came from the watching men. Ronnie grinned, turned and walked away.

From that day on nobody gave Kevin any attitude, not in any shape or form. The skinny *soutie* had gained a reputation. He'd handled Ronnie as he should have and even Ronnie showed a little more respect.

In the hierarchy of young men, Kevin had moved up a bit in the pecking order and he found the dynamics of it all to be quite amusing.

A few days later they were called together.

'Vos, you and you lot, too, are being shipped back to Ondangwa,' announced the corporal, selecting a group of them. He continued: 'the rest of you lot are destined for other things, but you guys have been trained in support weaponry and are being moved; they need you somewhere else.

There are too many support guys here with us, so that's it,' he finished and simply walked away.

And so it was that Kevin bade his buddy Jan farewell and found himself in a Flossie, a C130 cargo plane, flying over the depths of Angola. An amazing plane it could fly at great heights, carry massive cargoes and had a fantastic range.

And most importantly as a paratrooper he loved it; it was great jumping out of the thing!

John Marais again:

We were then informed that we are heading towards Cela via a Dakota and that we would be briefed there. I recall some well-known brass flying with us - Cmdt Olckers, the OC of 1 Para Bn, Major Joe Verster, Lt Blaauw and more. The Dak was completely overloaded and we were told by the pilots to take the bare minimum – the reality of it struck us as the Dak tried to get up at least two or three times with no success. After off-loading stuff (I cannot recall what it was) it eventually took off. This was definitely the worst flight of my entire life. We flew through a massive storm and at times we went through mountains at 60 m (radar elimination) and the old Dak also fell from time to time. Everybody on board were shitting themselves – it was one of those situations where you don't act and try to be brave anymore – we all showed real fear. A couple of hours later we were jolling around as if nothing happened.

When we arrived at Cela, we moved into a farm house from where we would operate. I was a section leader who operated under the command of Lt Johan Blaauw and some of the guys are Des MacGeer, Mike Erasmus, Jacques Puren, Pote de Villiers, Natie Potgieter, Keith Cross, Jimmy Pitts, Herman van Staden, Alwyn Whitfield, Harold (from Virginia) and some other guys whose names I cannot remember.

We sometimes operated as one large group under Lt Blaauw but we also created smaller sections of five tosix Bats especially when we did Ops. The other Bats worked under Lt Mark Coetzee and Peter Koller, Ferdie Jordaan, Ferdie Vermeulen, Sid Terblanche, Tim Cleary comes to mind. Brian Rogers, another section leader, initially worked with Lt Coetzee but came across to Lt Blaauw.

Most of the time we were busy with reconnaissance work under Lt Blaauw. We did numerous patrols to gather info to be used by the gunners. This was not fun at all as we operated behind enemy lines the whole time. We walked during the night and were under cover during the day when the terrain didn't provide cover. It is very difficult to explain the powerless feeling during these reconnaissance ventures: We could see and hear them, but could not attack as we were operating behind their lines and therefore were always outnumbered – difficult to explain but trust me, it is a test on its own. Many stories can be told about these ventures and two stand out:

We were lying low one day whilst right in the middle of enemy activity. We could spot their choppers flying overhead and hear their artillery nearby. At that stage we were undetected on a kopje and at about ten that evening Lt Blaauw gave orders to move on. Des MacGeer, Mike Erasmus and I were walking recce in front. It was very dark and soon we spotted light and realized that we were on the outskirts of a local settlement. There was a lot of activity as we could hear loud voices, laughter and shouting (party time for them). We stopped, took cover and I went back to Lt Blaauw and asked whether he wanted to turn back. Rightly, he said that we should move quietly forward and pass the kraal without being noticed. As we were about 12 bats it would have created more chaos turning around in the dark – imagine walking into your own men without being able to see in front of you! Also, when I say we were next to the kraal, I mean we could touch the huts. So we advanced and as the four of us who walked recce were next to the last hut, a fucking Cuban or MPLA soldier just about walked right into Lt Blaauw and two other troops. He tried to engage with the one guy and needless to say, he was captured and it was necessary to silence him.[9]

John Marais again:

The other incident occurred the following day when we were walking in quite dense bush. The enemy knew we were around after the previous evenings' run in with the MPLA/Cuban soldier as they would have found him by then. Lt Blaauw asked me and five guys to cross a small savannah, two at a time. There was no other way to reach our destination and we would recce the territory on the other side once we were all there. We crossed two at a time; the first two guys went unnoticed and we could not spot anything from where we watched closely – I especially watched a granite boulder at the edge of the open space. Mike Erasmus and I went next and as we were half way across, I saw movement on the boulder. In fact I saw enemy jumping off the boulder away from us. Mike and I ran for cover and into the bush we were heading towards. We reached our buddies and hit the dirt as we could actually hear mortars being discharged. These guys that we saw obviously notified their mortars and they were giving it to us big time. Once again, the powerless feeling as you could only try and get better cover. As soon as the first attack on us stopped, we got up and ran for about one hundred meters, took cover again as more mortars were going off. But eventually we realized we were getting away as it exploded further away this time. But they were obviously chasing us. I recall a chopper landing close-by but from here onwards I am completely blurred – I don't recall how we got back to the main group.

It might even have been our own chopper evacuating us, but I am not sure at all. What I can remember is that I was really shit scared when the mortars approached us (the whistle sound or whatever you call it) and then it explodes really close-by and you wonder how it missed you – then you wait for the next batch and all you can do is find better protection, and none to be found. Eish man!

---

9. Brian "Waldo" Wallace recalled being out on patrol trying to locate the firing position of the dreaded Red Eye 122 missile launchers and one of the enemy having his throat cut because we could not take a captive or fire a shot which would compromise the mission.

They flew what seemed for ages, sleeping as all soldiers do until the loadmaster came out woke them and told them to strap in.

'We're going to do an evasive landing, gents,' the loadmaster shouted over the roar of the plane. 'That means when we reach the landing strip this plane will cut engines and drop like a stone, so don't shit in your pants.'

He grinned before continuing: 'As we land the cargo door will open, the plane will turn around and stop. You guys will then exit and make a defensive half-moon around the plane until we take off, got it?'

They all gave him the thumbs up.

Kevin wasn't quite prepared for it when it came. The engines suddenly fell silent and the massive plane began to spiral down to earth, dropping in altitude at an amazingly swift rate.

Suddenly it levelled out and hit the dirt runway, its engines roaring as the pilot reversed the props to brake the plane; at the same time, the cargo door opened. The aircraft came to a halt and turned as if on a dime and immediately they all ran out, each alternate man running to left and right to complete the half-moon formation.

Kevin was still running into position when the plane took off, its door closing while it did so, climbing almost horizontally up into the morning sky until all they could see was a dot in the sky.

They moved away from the runway and lay in the scrub until they saw, trundling along a dirt road towards them, an armoured car followed by a farmer's truck, a stick of men bouncing about like rag dolls in the back. The truck ground to a halt and Kevin recognised the men, all bats from the battalion whom he hadn't seen in over a month.

Lieutenant Mark stood up beckoned to them: 'Are you lot going to sit and rot in the bush or are you coming with me?'

They scrambled onto the back and headed toward a town called Cela. The town would be burnt into their memories forever; they just didn't know it yet.

Chapter Fourteen: **The little battle group**

This ain't no party, this ain't no disco,
This ain't no fooling around
No time for dancing, or lovey dovey,
I ain't got time for that now

Talking Heads

It rained every bloody day and Kevin had had a gut full. There was mud everywhere and everything was soaked. But the rains brought its gift to the land, it was a lush and beautiful place; the mountains, rivers, valleys and plains of central Angola were like an Eden. The land was fertile, a farmers' paradise, but a paradise beset by war, death, rape, murder and suffering. They had spent weeks patrolling in the countryside, through forests, bush and farmland; walking, laying ambushes and trying to make contact with the Cubans. However the Cubans had become thoroughly gun-shy.

The campaign had ground to a halt; the combination of American politics and Soviet arms and support, had resulted in a stalemate. The South Africans were backed by the US Government in a clandestine war manipulated and slush-funded by the CIA. Gerald Ford was about to begin his re-election campaign and the risks were too great if the CIA's little adventure in Southern Africa was to leak out.

So the result of this was the current pain in the arse situation which was starting to really piss everyone off; nothing worse than being stuffed about for no apparent reason.

The last of them had been picked up and brought in from the bush and as luck would have it, Kevin was in the final group. Still stinking, they had been summoned to a briefing, most of the others smelt all nice and clean. He was puzzled, you never smelt all pretty and sweet in the bush. The enemy could smell you a mile off considering the fact that they too were all dirty and stinking.

'Gents, we're going to start a new phase in the war. We are going to do something which I hope is going to crack this stalemate and hopefully the boredom of this stupid situation', announced Lieutenant Mark.

Kevin was a tall, skinny fella but Mark was just that little bonier. Kevin had immense respect for the Loot as he cared for his men and while he could be full of shit, he had demonstrated excellent leadership so far.

'Now we need some self-control from you lot. The war which we bats have waged back there with the armoured lads stops! No more of the fighting and shit we had back at the battalion, understand?'

He paused before continuing, 'Because gents, we are going to have to work closely with our brothers from the armoured corps from now on', he paused again, casting his eyes over the men. 'We are going to alternate between vehicle patrols and doing observation posts behind the Cuban lines. The frequency and duration will change as circumstances dictate between each modus operandi, get it?'

There was a rumble of agreement from the seated men, and all Kevin wanted was for the briefing to end, he could smell his own sour arse, fuck, he stank. The aroma wafting from his loins was positively nauseating.

As if reading his mind Loot paused, his nose wrinkling in distaste.

'Briefing is postponed; see you in an hour. Go and find some water and clean your bloody arses, you stink to high heaven. See you lot here later I can't stand the stink of you filthy buggers.'

Amid the ripple of laughter, one man responded, 'If you weren't so tall you'd be able to smell your own arse, lieutenant!'

'Go fuck yourself', responded Mark with a grin as he watched the men file out.

'Oh and by the way, you can use soap; nothing clandestine is going to happen in the next while', he added.

Ah, that explained the rosy posy smelly bit, thought Kevin.

Kevin bathed in a ditch and like the rest of them, he avoided any still bodies of water, manmade or otherwise, like the plague. Experience had shown that more often than not, they held too many fucking secrets, or at the very least the odd nasty surprise.

The water in the ditch was clean and running strongly from all of the rains and he felt a thousand times better when he had finished. He smelt like a daisy, the Lux soap smell wafting off of him like the scent of a thousand lilies in the field.

As he wandered back from his ditch bath, Kevin eyed his buddy Andy Prew. Soon after flying in he had latched onto Andy, the only other mortarist in the group and, as both were of the original Kimberly crew, they quickly became buddies.

'Hey Prew, you smell like a whore,' he chirped.

'Thanks, sexy,' was the retort.

So they were going to do vehicle patrols. Two armoured cars up front, their 90mm guns pointing upwards aggressively like pugnacious bull terriers, a Porra famer's abandoned Mercedes Benz truck in the middle, followed by an armoured car bringing up the rear. Kevin looked at the mini battle group with more than just a little trepidation.

'Look Prew, there isn't even a place to sit on the back of this fucking thing', he commented ruefully as he examined the truck. 'Those boys in the Noddy cars are going to be pretty safe and comfy behind all of that armour, and we're going to be sitting up here like a wart on a fucking dog's arse,' he groaned.

'Well, let's get the best spot before it's too late,' responded Andy, ever the opportunist, as he tossed his kit up front, right behind the cab. 'This is going to be the best spot, my boet, out of the rain, nicely tucked up and all cosy-like behind the cab. What's the bet those fucking farm boy Dutchies are going to want to sit near the back for a better view!'

'Now all need to do is find something to bloody-well sit on,' added Kevin as they jumped down. 'I'm not going to last long sitting on that bloody thing without a decent chair or something to sit on!'

"You're going to need something to protect that skinny arse,' responded Prew as they walked away.

'You're right chubby, with that fat arse you could sit on a bed of bloody nails and feel fuck-all,' retorted Kevin.

But someone had beat them to it.

'Check this out,' shouted a group of pleased-looking men as they staggered past under the considerable weight of a church pew.

'Where the hell did you get that from?' exclaimed Kevin.

'There, from that Porra church, the one with the steeple all shot to hell,' called one of them, pointing to a Roman Catholic Church.

Kevin observed that its steeple had been blown off and it certainly looked like it had indeed been shot to hell; the irony of the hell analogy was not lost on Kevin. So, the seating had been sorted out and in pretty short order. Kevin and Andy gave some of the guys a bit of shit about desecrating a place of worship. Until one of the Afrikaans lads pointed out that, as they were NG Kerk people and therefore Calvinists, they were only doing what their forefathers had failed to do. And that was to fuck up all Catholics as the Catholics deserved every bit of shit they got. The weird bit was that some of them were being serious!

Oh for fucksakes, thought Kevin, amusing as it all was. Andrew just looked at them, turned to Kevin and said, 'Fuck them all, I'm an Anglican,' as he settled his backside onto the now very attractive looking bench.

As it turned out, they had chosen wisely and retained their seats right up in the front of the truck, notwithstanding a concerted effort later by one or two of the lads to move in on their turf.

The little "battle group" had been busy riding about the countryside, looking for shit, just riding around and hoping that some contact with the enemy would come of it. MPLA or Cubans, anything as far as the brass were concerned.

The brass's sentiment was certainly not shared by the members of the little convoy. Kevin felt like a wart on a dogs arse. They were sticking out like a sore thumb and he expressed his views very vociferously one morning.

'Fuck this, this is absolute fucking crap, riding around like this, just waiting to get revved, this is absolute bullshit!' the word bullshit coming out as a wobbly bb..uuu..ll.. shittt as they hit a rough patch on the dirt road, its surface rutted from the rain's runoff.

The Loot turned around and gave Kevin a cold look.

He loved sitting on truck cab's roof on a makeshift padded seat. Unfortunately that meant he was sitting right within earshot of Andy and Kevin, so he had heard very word.

'Stop whining like a little girl, Vos; that's negative shit talk and I don't need demoralising crap from you, do you understand?'

'Sorry lieutenant.'

Kevin looked away and sensed the Loot had done the same. He knew that everyone including the lieutenant felt the same and that these fucking series of jaunts were nothing but risky bullshit.

'Put a member of the brass in this truck with us, Prewsky, and I can promise you this crap would end in the blink of an eye,' he muttered to Andy.

Andy nodded in agreement.

I'd much rather do another OP than this shit,' moaned Andy, this time making sure that Mark wouldn't overhear him. 'At least we can move in secrecy, you know, do the stuff we were trained to do. Not this bullshit sitting on a truck, making a bloody racket and waiting for a bullet!'

Little did either of them realize how fucking terrifyingly, dangerous doing Observation Post (OP) work would become.

Chapter Fifteen: **Pineapple beer, ponchos and a dead cow**

If we can sparkle he may land tonight
Don't tell your poppa or he'll get us locked up in fright,'

David Bowie

Kevin lay there and watched the sun rise. It had rained again for hours in the night, but that was okay as they were bivvied down in a church about ten kilometres north of Cela; a tiny little church serving a little farming collective. Here the houses were almost touching each other and having the strangest design; the interiors had chairs and benches built out of mortar; rock solid furnishings so there was no chance of rearranging the furniture.

The sun drove the night back into the shadows and as the fields were slowly lit up he noticed something. Pineapples, hundreds of them and it looked as if they were ripe. It wasn't long before the boys were munching sweet pineapples, the sweet juice running down their chins and they were delicious. Anything other than rat packs was a treat. When they were finished Kevin looked at the bits of pineapple skin lying all over the place.

'Prew, you know what, we can brew pineapple beer out of these skins,' Kevin remarked.

'Yep, but we need a container to brew it in.'

So the hunt began for a container of some sort.

Later in the day a triumphant man dragged in a milk can, lid intact. The lid was chained to the can and it was a biggie.

'Vossie, here's the perfect job for your beer,' he stated, obviously pleased with himself.

'Okay, first we have to clean this thing up properly, make a fire and boil some water in it, got to sterilize it,' remarked Ferdie the medic.

Lappies the other medic concurred, nodding wisely.

'Guys, we need sugar, lots of it and some yeast,' instructed Kevin, 'see what you lot can find!'

How they found the yeast never ceased to amaze Kevin, yeast of all things.

'Where the hell did you get that?' he asked Lappies when two blocks of yeast were placed in his hand. They were cold as if they had come out of someone's fridge, 'Ask no questions and I'll tell you fokkol lies,' was the mysterious response.

Soon they had the brew going and each day there was a mini ceremony. They called it beer inspection. They would gather about and someone would reverently lift the lid and tilt it towards the light.

'Still bubbling guys, not ready yet!'

The can stayed on the truck, and whenever they bivvied down it was taken to where someone could keep an eye on it. The pineapple beer was looked after like a bar of bloody gold.

Mark arrived with a bottle of whiskey, opened the lid and poured it in.

'Officers are supposed to get a bottle of this crap a week,' he stated pouring the contents into the milk can. 'This is the first one I've accepted. I can't drink this knowing you guys can't have any,' he said as the last bit emptied into the can. Kevin looked at him in amazement.

'Are you serious lieutenant?' he asked.

'Yes,' was the response?

Kevin just looked at him. Mark looked back, quizzically.

'Respect, sir,' Kevin said and Mark looked pleased but also embarrassed.

It was true. By that gesture Mark had earned his respect.

All of the shit they had gone through and the split decisions he needed to cement his leadership in battle; and for some reason all of that didn't make as much of an impact as that small gesture.

A couple of days later he poured another bottle into the can and two more over the following few days. All in all about five bottles of hard-tack made its way into the fiercely bubbling concoction.

A few days before Christmas, on about 22 December 1975, the little battle group found itself negotiating a pitted and washed-away road. It was heavy going, even the Noddy cars taking it easy up front. Even Syd had stopped singing. The group were was tired and morose, sick and tired of riding around exposed, expecting a bullet in the bloody head at any moment. Experience had taught them all that things could get fucking hairy in the blink of an eye.

'PHOOONNNT, TKLANKITY KLANKITY KLANK KLANK!!!

The milk can blew its top with a violent, gassy burp, sending the lid off with force, its launch stopped dead by the chain. It rattled and bounced against the can's side.

Kevin jerked in fright. Syd yelled out with joy,

'ITS FUCKING READY TO DRINK!'

Consensus was quickly reached that they would wait until Christmas day before taking the plunge.

The next morning, the day after the beer had announced its readiness, they gathered in a schoolroom, its desks smashed and lying on splintered heaps. Kevin couldn't help but think of the futility of it all, as he imagined the children sitting there taking lessons, only weeks earlier. Oh the folly of man! Wars, driven by the lust for power and by greed, initiated by the few, the terrible price being paid by the many; all such a waste, a bloody waste. His little philosophical interlude was rudely interrupted.

'Right lads, listen up,' ordered Mark, authority in his voice.

'Oh fuck, here we go again,' muttered someone.

'What's that?' asked Mark. The mutterer shut it.

"Right, gents,' he continued with just a hint of irritation in his voice.

'Intelligence has it that the Cuban's are going to target our gun emplacements.'

He unrolled a map with restrained flourish and placed it on an oak table which had only three legs, the missing leg propped up by another old table sticking out at an angle from the corner. He pointed at the map, indicating an area where the guns were placed just behind a low ridge, hidden from the Cubans.

He continued, his finger moving up and down across the map as he spoke. 'Every day a little spotter plane flies over the site, trying to pinpoint the gun emplacement and so far they haven't found it ... yet; because if they had it would have been rocketed to hell by now. However, they must have an idea where it is otherwise the spotter plane wouldn't be buzzing the area all the time. And we also have it from intelligence reports that Cuban Special Forces are going to attack our guns.'

He glanced up, the irritated look had disappeared and was replaced with an excited glint in his eyes. The listening men perked up; being paratroopers, the prospect of matching themselves against Cuban Special Forces added a bit of spice to their lives.

Except Kevin, who before he could stop himself swore loudly,

'For fucksakes!'

'What did you say Vos?' asked the frowning Loot.

Kevin made a quick recovery, 'For fucksakes, that's going to be brilliant if we get to rev a few of them,' he replied with feigned enthusiasm. Luckily the Loot bought his bullshit and moved on.

'Right get your kit and *pisvelle* together we move out in an hour,' he finished, rolling the map up with a flourish.

Pisvelle, foreskins, sleeping bag, Kevin always smiled at the lovely slang used in the army. Afrikaans, the language was so beautifully descriptive!

As they walked out of the door Andy kicked the supporting leg and brought the oak table crashing down.

He snarled, 'This is another fuck-around, just watch and see, glorified gate guards, that's what we're going to be, trust me,' he muttered as they all filed out.

An hour later, to the minute, they left in their farm truck without the ubiquitous Noddy cars. Kevin felt naked, exposed and vulnerable without them as they hit the road.

'If the shit hits the fan now without those Noddys we're in the crap,' moaned Pete, echoing Kevin's sentiments exactly.

The men were silent, uneasily riding the bump and grind as they headed towards the gun battery.

Syd burst forth with Starman, his voice rising above the grinding of the truck…

'Didn't know what time it was and the lights were low

I leaned back on my radio,

Some cat was layin' down some rock 'n' roll 'lotta soul.'

Then the loud sound did seem to fade

Came back like a slow voice on a wave of phase

That weren't no D.J. that was hazy cosmic jive

There's a Starman waiting in the sky

He'd like to come and meet us

But he thinks he'd blow our minds

There's a Starman waiting in the sky

He's told us not to blow it

Cause he knows it's all worthwhile

He told me:
Let the children lose it
Let the children use it
Let all the children boogie

I had to phone someone so I picked on you
Hey, that's far out so you heard him too!
Switch on the TV
We may pick him up on channel two
Look out your window I can see his light

If we can sparkle he may land tonight
Don't tell your poppa or he'll get us locked up in fright,'

As usual with Syd letting rip, they soon felt a lot better…until it started to rain.

It began to pour down in buckets, the rain teeming down in a deluge as if God wanted to wash all the blood away in that war-torn place.

Andy whipped out his poncho, it was a beaut. He'd stripped it off a dead Cuban a few weeks back and luckily it didn't have any bullet holes in it, so it worked a treat. He pulled it over his shoulders and before he could blink an eye Kevin had commandeered part of it.

'KD, fuck off, this is my poncho!' Andy complained.

'So what, we're buddies, we share, boet,' was Kevin's pleading response.

'My side's sticking out, I'm getting wet,' Andy grumbled some more.

'Don't be a prick, Prew, jeez man, your side is protected by the cab, you can't be getting wet,' begged Kevin, trying his desperate best to reason with Andy. But Andy wasn't having any of it and began to haul the poncho towards himself, protesting as he did so. It degenerated into a school yard squabble until the Loot intervened.

'If you two girls don't stop this shit I'll burn the bloody thing, so make up your bloody minds who's going to use it!' he shouted.

The Loot had yelled, Syd had stopped singing, Andy was being a cunt so Kevin shrugged off the poncho and stood up. Grasping the cab roof he simply stood there as they drove through the rain and feeling his face being stung by little wet needles.

'FUCK ANGOLA, FUCK AFRICA, FUCK THE FUCKING ARMY and FUCK THE FUCKING WORLD!'

Kevin turned and tapped Andy on the shoulder.

'The wheel turns you little, short shit, just remember that!'

Andy just flipped him the bird.

They arrived in a slither of mud, slipping and sliding down the track towards the battery of guns. The rain was coming down in a steady roar and Kevin noticed with spiteful disappointment, that Andy's Soviet-made poncho had managed to stem the tide.

It was late afternoon and after the gunners had helped them camouflage the truck they set up their little bivvies. Andy and Kevin had got it down to a fine art; they always managed to get a shelter up that was normally impervious to the rain; Andy always bragging about his Boy Scout prowess whenever the set about erecting the thing, except this time they were pissed off with each other, and the lack of cooperation resulted in an abortion. The bivvie looked like a two-year-old had put it up. It was a miserable fucking night and Kevin couldn't resist one last chirp.

'Remember you short shit, the fucking wheel turns, hey Prew, the fucking wheel turns,' he muttered with considerable venom.

"Go fuck yourself, KD,' was the equally venomous response.

The next morning revealed a sorry looking lot of troopers, soggy, wet and bedraggled, shivering in the early dawn.

They waited until the grey had gone and the sun was fully risen before they stirred and attempted to find some dry kit. It was a waste of time. Kevin started a little fire going and began to brew some tea. He looked across and his eyes fell on a miserable bedraggled Andy, his big nose silhouetted in the morning sun. He looked fucking miserable. Kevin felt sorry; he felt like a shit after overreacting the day before.

'Prew, you want some tea?'

No answer.

'C'mon boet, here, have some tea,' said Kevin, thrusting the "fire-bucket" of hot tea at Andy.

'Thanks, KD'

'Cool, man.' Squabble over.

Mark called them over a little later for a briefing. The battery commander who was not wearing any rank as was the custom in modern war, was a captain they later heard. He was a short, stocky man who had an air of quiet authority about him. He looked like shit just as they did, scruffy and unwashed and Kevin felt right at home just looking at the man.

'Right gents, thanks for getting here, let's hope that this Cuban raiding party thing is just a load of shit, just a rumour,' began the captain. 'This battery of guns has been here for a couple of weeks and we have managed to plaster two half-hearted Cuban advances. So they are desperate to find us and to put it bluntly, fuck us up,' he finished, his face was lined and he looked tired.

Kevin looked at the guns, little 25 pounders circa Second World War, nicely camouflaged and impossible to see from the air; barrels aimed over the ridge in the direction of Luanda.

The short captain continued, 'Every day they try and find us, this little Cessna-like spotter plane, thingamajig thing, comes over the ridge there,' he said, waving his hand at the rocky ridge covered in thick scrub.

'It gets above us, makes two quick circuits above our heads and then flies off, regular as clockwork! There's a couple of spotters we put out each day and all they do is scan the sky for this irritating little mosquito. So when you hear whistles blow and shouting "*gate toe*" which you all know means get into the trenches, then get into the trench and under cover.'

He paused, his eyes taking them in. 'The gunners have dug trenches and covered them in cammo netting, so either you lot start digging in or you can stay in the bush and hide.' But if they rocket us you're going to be in the shit in the bush, trust me!' He turned and walked off.

'Right gents,' continued Mark. I'm going to set you lot out in a defensive perimeter. 'We're going to be stretched as there's not enough of us to really cover this joint properly.' He paused. 'By the way, if any of you are moronic enough to try and shoot the spotter plane a number of things will happen. Firstly you're going to miss, secondly they'll know where we are and then we are going to most probably die and thirdly, if I survive I will shoot you in the bloody head! Do you lot get it?' he asked.

'Yes, lieutenant,' was the smattered response.

Mark didn't swear nearly as much as his peers, so whenever he was serious without the ubiquitous expletives, it somehow carried a little more weight. The lack of foul language got your attention in a weird sort of way!

And so it was that they spent the next couple of days just chilling, safely hidden in their hides and watching the gunners run to ground like dassies. Twice a day, as regular as clockwork, being driven to the earth by the irritating little spotter plane.

They got bored, oh so bored.

'KD, I've got a plan,' announced Andy, the day before Christmas. His eyes were gleaming with enthusiasm. 'Let's set up a booby trap, Vietnam style. They used to set up mantraps and kill the Yanks. Hell of a thing, had the Yanks all fucked up, psychologically. They were so shit scared that they used to stay in their bases, only the marines, green berets and those kind of guys would go out and fight.'

'Who's "they"?' asked Kevin

'What do you mean whose "they"?' Responded Andy incredulously.

'The fucking Vietcong, that's fucking who! You know what KD, you amaze me.

Sometimes you act like a genius and the next minute you act like a bloody moron!'

'It's called the lighthouse effect,' responded Kevin.

'Huh?' Andy looked at Kevin blankly.

'Like a lighthouse,' continued Kevin, his hands making little circles in the air above his head. 'You know how the lamp shines in a sweeping arc, everything's black, blank, nothing, nada and then suddenly "FWOOH" you're blinded by a flash of brilliance. There was an oke at school with us, we called him Goofy, an absolute genius at maths and science and knew fuck-all about anything else.'

'Well that's like you, KD, just telling me about the lighthouse effect supports what I said a minute ago, you're a fucking lighthouse!' he finished triumphantly.

'Go fuck yourself, Prew!' snarled Kevin realising that he had walked right into that one. There was a short silence. Kevin's curiosity got the better of him.

'So how are we going to build a man-trap then?' he asked.

Andy rolled onto his side facing Kevin, his eyes filled with renewed enthusiasm.

'You dig a hole, about the size of double bed and about six feet deep, the depth of a grave. Then you take a couple of hundred sticks and sharpen both ends and stick them in the bottom of the hole, with the points facing upwards!'

Andy fell silent, his brow creased in thought

'Okay and fukken then?' prompted Kevin impatiently.

'Calm down KD, you're far too impatient.

Don't interrupt a man when he's thinking of a plan,' stalled Andy.

Kevin knew exactly what Andy was trying to do; he was trying to get under his skin.

So pretending to lose interest he stood up, slapping the flakes of mud off the back of his pants as he did so.

'No, no, sit down KD, I've remembered how,' said Andy, his eyes earnest.

'Yeah, got you,' thought Kevin as he sat down.

Andy carried on, making little sketches in the mud.

'You take the sticks and push the one sharp end into the ground so they nicely stuck in the ground, with the other end facing up. Then, you smear shit on all of the sharp points, cover the thing with a web of sticks and leaves and when the Cuban steps on it, BANG, he falls into the hole.'

'Okay and then?' asked Kevin.

'Well, the shit gets into the wounds and he dies of infection a few weeks later. His buddies see this and they pull a Yank on themselves and stay in their camp!' He finished with a flourish, looking at Kevin his one eyebrow arched upwards, as if inviting comment.

'So who's going to dig the hole?' asked Kevin, a carefully manufactured blank expression on his face. Andy looked at Kevin. Andy paused, there was a silence.

'We will, KD.'

'No, you will,' responded Kevin, his heart singing, revelling in their love-hate relationship; like brothers, always getting on each other's nerves but woe betide anyone trying his luck with either of them.

'I've dug enough holes to last me a lifetime!' Kevin continued.

'Are you going to pay some Angolan to dig the hole for us, hey?'

'Fuck off, KD!'

Kevin laughed.

'Who's going to smear the shit on the sticks and whose shit are you going to use?' Kevin continued, now on a roll.

'KD, I said fuck you!'

Kevin wanted to ask Andy who was going to sharpen a few hundred sticks and wisely decided to shut his face. Minutes went by in silence.

'Why don't we do something easy,' suggested Kevin.

'Liked what?' was the snappy reply.

'We take a hand grenade, strap it to a tree, tie some string to the pin and tie the other end to a tree, it'll make a perfect tripwire,' replied Kevin.

Andy's face lit up.

'We'll have to flatten the pin so that it comes out easily,' Andy suggested.

'Yep, and when our special forces Cubans try and get to us …

"BOOM"!' responded Kevin.

Andy was now as happy as pig in shit.

'See, KD, that's exactly what I meant, the lighthouse effect!'

'Fuck you!'

'Fuck you too!'

Twenty minutes later found the pair of them with the Loot. Andy told him of their little plan and surprisingly he agreed with only one condition,

'You two go and tell everyone on this site what your plan is and don't do anything stupid!'

'Like what, lieutenant?' asked Kevin as they were leaving.

'Like putting the bloody thing on the path to the shithouse!' was his sarcastic response. They all laughed. An hour later the man trap was set.

'Can't wait for tonight KD, we're going to blow up some Cubans.

In the early hours of Christmas day, 1975, the man trap went WHOOMPAA.

The explosion tore Kevin out of his sleep and had him scrabbling for his rifle clumsily, his brain befuddled by sleep. They lay in silence listening into the night, they knew better than to move or make a sound which would give their positions away.

Kevin heard Andy whispering, 'KD, that was our fucking booby trap, boet, we got them, we fucking got them!'

Kevin felt the thrill of excitement, he wanted to get up and look but his training kicked in. That would be suicide, a wounded man lying there would put a bullet in his head. And so it was a long night, waiting for the dawn to see who they had killed.

The light came on slowly, the black turning to grey and the trees slowly becoming visible in the growing light. They lay in total silence their eyes willing the light to come and when it was light enough they heard Mark ordering them and two others to sweep the area, while the rest would cover them.

The four of them formed a ragged skirmish line and they slowly inched their way towards the trees. Kevin's heart was thumping, every muscle tensed, expecting the sound of gunfire at an instant.

Kevin heard the man to his left say, 'Oh fuck!'

Andy said, 'Oh shit!'

Kevin said, 'Ag no, man!'

They all saw her lying there, her black eyes were lifeless, her body covered in blood. It looked as if a thousand rounds had hit her and Kevin felt saddened by what he saw.

All of that beef lying there, so badly shot up that not a single gram was edible. Loot Mark didn't say a word, he didn't have to. The two *souties* were the laughing stock of the whole fucking gun emplacement. Even the gunner's short captain, thought it was as funny as hell; and that pissed Kevin off all the more!

Chapter Sixteen: **Christmas Day**

Radar: [takes a drink of Hawkeye's home-made gin, and grimaces]
I thought this stuff was supposed to make you feel better?

B.J.: No. It's supposed to make you feel nothing.

*TV Series - M*A*S*H*

It was Christmas Day and they couldn't wait to crack open the pineapple beer. The Loot stopped them, there was a chaplain going to be there at about lunchtime and he was going to give them a Christmas message.

'There's no way in hell, that you lot are going to be pissed when the minister arrives', was Mark's order to the lot of them.

'No way in hell!' Kevin couldn't help seeing the irony of that sentence. The chaplain arrived at midday; it was a humid sunny day. He spoke of the birth of Jesus and miracle of the Immaculate Conception. He spoke of the miracles Jesus performed during His walk on this earth. He spoke of the crucifixion and the miracle of the resurrection and that by the blood of Christ they were all freed from the shackles of the law and their sin; that if they accepted Jesus as their saviour they would have eternal life.

The word "miracles" stuck in Kevin's head. Miracles.

He began to think of his experiences, the miracles.

The lights were back. Kevin watched frozen and watched and watched what seemed like forever, an eternity of seconds as the lights coming towards him through the trees; in a slow arc, up and up slowly the stream of green seemed to be in slow motion. He wanted to shout, after all they were in slow motion but it was an illusion and he couldn't say a thing in time to warn anyone. As they came closer they accelerated into a blur of green, he could hear the stream of lights passing them only a meter away, a crackling sound combined with the sound of a hissing mamba; the glass bones grinding and grating in his head, the shards hurting his brain. The dead man asking, why did you let them do this to me?

All of this and they were still alive, alive … alive. The word "alive" was a soft whisper in Kevin's head … *alive* … being alive is a miracle, a series of miracles had happened, he knew it. He felt the hairs standing up on his body. He felt so alive, so beautifully and fully alive, his heart felt light; there was a lightness within him. Just being alive, it was a miracle!

Was it God's granted miracle that they were still alive?

Then Mark's voice brought him down to earth with a bump!

'Chaplain, would you like some pineapple beer?' Kevin heard Mark ask. The chaplain answered, 'Why, that would be very nice, thank you.'

Kevin looked at Andy for a reaction. There was nothing. The Afrikaans boys, all Calvinists to a man, seemed quite comfortable with the idea of a minister of religion drinking alcohol. Kevin had been brought up in the Assemblies of God Church, a charismatic bunch. So being of happy-clappy stock, he considered it an abomination that a minister of religion would drink alcohol. He almost said it out aloud, catching himself just before he shot his mouth off. So they all took their steel mugs, or fire buckets in army parlance, and dipped them into the milk can.

Five hundred millilitres of pineapple beer at a time, a fire-bucket full and it tasted brilliant!

'Jeez, this shit is awesome,' commented Andy, taking a deep swig.

'This "stuff" Andy, not this "shit" for fucksakes, there's a man of the cloth right next to us ... bloody hell!' corrected an affronted Lappies.

Good grief thought Kevin, and said out aloud,

'What a bunch of bloody idiots, are you shitheads listening to yourselves?'

Andy and Lappies looked at each other. Syd looked at Lappies and then Andy looked at Kevin. They all started to piss themselves, began laughing their heads off at the whole ridiculousness of it all.

The pineapple beer had crept up on them as quickly as a little, nasty *tokkelos* would and they were soon under his African witchdoctor's spell. The chaplain was sitting there smiling, talking to the Loot and the captain; as Kevin quietly fell asleep under a tree.

Later he heard that the chaplain too had "fallen asleep."

Chapter Seventeen: **Tolkien's rock**

Didn't know what time it was and the lights were low

I leaned back on my radio

Some cat was layin' down some rock 'n' roll 'lotta soul, he said

Then the loud sound did seem to fade

Came back like a slow voice on a wave of phase

That weren't no DJ, that was hazy cosmic jive

There's a Starman waiting in the sky

He'd like to come and meet us

But he thinks he'd blow our minds

There's a Starman waiting in the sky

He's told us not to blow it

Cause he knows it's all worthwhile

He told me:

Let the children lose it

Let the children use it

Let all the children boogie

I had to phone someone so I picked on you

Hey, that's far out so you heard him too!

Switch on the TV

we may pick him up on channel two

Look out your window I can see his light

If we can sparkle he may land tonight

Don't tell your poppa or he'll get us locked up in fright…

Burst out Sydney in song, giving *Starman* full voice.

As the weeks went by all of them began to see Syd's singing as a form of release. It gave them all a sense of hope, a link to home and civilization.

He gave the song justice and David Bowie would probably have approved, mused Kevin.

Bean's words:

Sydney, yes good ol Syd, the man with the voice that pulled me, pulled us through the hardships and fun ships of Border duty. Most days his singing talents kept our minds focused on the job and away from what combat lays ahead. Him tuning out a Rolling Stones or David Bowie number, me on the air drum at his side is what most remember.

It was four days after Christmas, on 29 December 1975.

The pineapple beer, the passed-out chaplain and the horrible hangovers - all forgotten, as they drove down a hill on a treacherous dirt road. The two pugnacious Noddy cars in front looking as if they were busting for a fight!

Syd, singing his rendition of David Bowie with gusto, to the amusement and upliftment of all on board as the little battle group ground its way down the road. As is it is with most young men they were resilient and good old Syd's singing gave them just that bit of something extra, helping them all by keeping the spirits up.

Thankfully, it had stopped raining for a miraculous three days and as a result the earth and their collective spirits seemed to be all the better for it.

One of the things his mother had taught Kevin as a boy was to appreciate natural beauty and the countryside; so he took in the beauty of the plains, flanked by mountains between Cela and Quibala[10].

Unbeknownst to Kevin, this terrain was to become etched in his mind with brutal clarity for the rest of his life. It would become burnt and seared indelibly into his mind and many, many years later he would remember it, as if it were only yesterday.

The road sloped down the hill, curving gently to the right, its surface treacherous with the grooves worn by the weeks of rain. On the left there was a steep embankment, crowned by the edge of a forest of trees ending in a deep ditch at the base of the slope. Ahead was a river and the bridge crossing it was unusable, it had been blown up by the retreating Cubans.

To the right was a shallow ditch flanked by a magnificent black rock, the size of a four storey building and rising out of the earth like a lichen covered monster; as if straight out of one of Tolkien's tales. It looked fantastical and Kevin imagined that at any moment, it would lift itself out of the earth amid an avalanche of stone and earth and flatten them…

---

10. Quibala (also written Kibala) is a municipality in Cuanza Sul.

'I'm an alligator, I'm a mama-papa coming for you,'

Sang Syd, his voice interrupting Kevin's daydream

I'm the space invader, I'll be a rock 'n' rollin' bitch for you

Keep your mouth shut, you're squawking like a pink monkey bird

And I'm busting up my brains for the words

Keep your 'lectric eye on me babe …

SCHWAAP…WHOOOMPH … the first RPG rocket glanced off the turret of the leading Noddy car and shattered itself up against the embankment. The second incoming found Kevin half out of the truck and the explosion finding him in the ditch. It was that quick!

He couldn't breathe and he could hear the treble of small arms fire combined with the bass-drum-sounds of the Noddy cars firing their 90mm guns at the unseen enemy. Kevin could hear Andy screaming, 'KD, KD, are you okay, fuck me, KD, have you been hit?'

Kevin lay in the ditch and he couldn't breathe; he was terrified that he had indeed been hit as he lay writhing in the ditch like a gasping fish out of water. And then he felt his breath coming back; he had fallen on his rifle and knocked his wind out. Rolling over he gave Andy the thumbs up.

He felt sick and he was as scared as hell.

'You shithead, you bloody shithead!' screamed Andy in relief.

The firefight had developed into a roar of gunfire and Kevin realized that this was no simple thing, not just a skirmish. It was too heavy and he realized that they had run into something big. He heard Mark screaming something, he couldn't make it out, he only hear the sound of his voice.

The following description of the incident was written later by Mark:

> *The first car came round a hillock and as we came into the flat open terrain leading up to the bridge, the radio message comes through; 'It's blown up.' This seemed to be the signal for the enemy to open up on us, as the 90s (armoured car with 90mm cannon) had to stop for the river. The explosion of the first RPG7 having missed the 90 threw rocks and metal all over the dance floor, commonly known as 'kak en vlamme'.*
>
> *Get off the truck and get cover!' I was screaming at the guys.*
>
> *'They're on the river line.'*
>
> *Ferdie was hit badly in the stomach in the first 10 sec and with troops on both sides of the road.*
>
> *Where the fuck were they?*

Out with the binos, get troops to return some fire, get the radio closer.

'Cleary, get your arse here! Ask the 90s if they can see something.'

'No, but looks like from the edge of the river.'

'Klap hulle!' I scream back into the radio.

'Vermuelen and Swart say Ferdie is in a bad way,' Wright shouts, and says they are behind us.

'Bullshit, that is the crack and thump any rifle makes when you are being shot at,' I decide. I don't have time to explain to Wright so tell him to blow two magazines in that direction and if no response to hold his fire.

'Hold your fire, and ask if anyone can see them?'

'Nothing, Loot,' comes back to me. By now I am looking through the binos and at any moment expecting it to smash and wondering for a millionth of a second whether I would remember anything because I'll be dead. I see some smoke from under a tree.

'Follow my tracer,' I shout. 'Half a mag each.'

I fire a tracer. I get Vermeulen, who was a medic and good with the RPG7, and tell him to fire a round where my tracer hits as I had seen smoke. And so I put a tracer into the branches about two metres above the ground, give the order to give covering fire and watch Vermeulen stand up, aim and fire as calmly as if he was on the range.

True to form the RPG hits the trees and we had ourselves some airburst onto the mothers. Cleary is nearby with the radio. I get the troop commander of the 90s and tell him I got one badly hurt troop and I want one of his cars to come load him up and get him out of the contact zone. He must call for a casevac now on the external radio. The rattle and roar of the 90s and of our own rifles is deafening.

I explain to the two medics the scene to take place and to the two section leaders, Pete and Brian. I see the 90 start turning around and coming our way. It stops opposite the medic and I contact the 90 to say I want covering fire. It all runs smoothly and now I get back to the situation of getting us out of here. I discuss the scene with the 90 commander and we both agree it is a bit pointless to do anything now but to get out of the kill zone. We agreed we would crawl in the ditch on this side for 200m and then get onto the truck.

Fuck, the ditch was teeming with goddam ants. I took my chances with the bullets rather than lie down and crawl through that mess. I noticed Sid, Tim and Tony doing the same. I kept thinking that I must be crazy to take a chance like that but the fear of knowing what I would go through if I did get full of ants made me take my chances.

I was behind Cleary, the radio operator, and he just lay down in front of me.

'Move!' I shouted, but he lay there panting, unable to move.

'I can't carry the radio any more, I'm buggered.'

Shit, that left me only as I was last in the line. I had to keep this platoon alive and if it meant lugging a radio so be it. We were still attracting fire and not getting too much back to them as I was two 90s out of the picture (casevac). The bullets were still kicking up those pyramids of ground that the movies are so good at filming.

I got the troops onto the truck and in the process of getting up I banged my knee cap one helluva shot. Shit, it was sore. But I threw the radio up and hung on as the truck pulled away. I got on eventually and immediately got the guys to start grabbing ammo, as well as giving them some target indications to fire at the treeline on the river edge. It occurred to me that you have to aim bloody straight if you are going to get any one cause the amount of copper-jacketed lead that went in our direction in the last 25 mins and none hitting us was amazing. But then again it only has a diameter of 7,62mm which is pretty small. I remember Deon looking back at me and grinning his head off, why I don't really know; maybe it was because we were getting out or that he had survived his first major ambush fire fight and come out OK in all aspects.

He always was one of bravado and cultured his mean-looking appearance.

I grinned back with understanding and warmth.

'You're OK, pal.'

Back to Kevin:

Kevin lay frozen in the ditch, he was paralyzed with terror. He heard Mark screaming something again, this time his voice had a different note to it, almost panicky and Kevin was galvanized into action. He heaved himself up, out of the ditch and onto the road edge, only to get a face full of sand. The dirt stinging into his eyes as a round clipped the embankment next to him. He slid back down into the ditch trying to clear his eyes and looking up seeing the backs of the others firing across the road. Heaving himself up again, he could hear Mark calling for covering fire, his voice a combination of fear and authority and then he understood why. Half the guys were trapped on the other side of the road in the shallow ditch, pinned down by the enemy fire; it was only a question of time before they would all die right there where they lay. Suddenly a calmness came down upon him; he didn't know where it came from. It simply settled upon him like a light, grey shawl would float down onto an old woman's back.

He started to do his share, putting down double taps into any conceivable hiding place, shrubs, bushes, clumps of rock…

There was confusion and unlike the movies nothing was clear. Dust and movement, adrenalin the raging sounds, all was confusion yet at the same time not. The firefight was raging and he couldn't see who was trying to kill them.

He thought he saw movement and put four rounds through the cloud of dust and imagined he saw something going down; one kill … perhaps?

The guys came out of the opposite ditch and started scrambling across the road and amid the dust, the sound of fire and the roar of the 90mil guns.

He saw one man twist and go down, hard; his buddy turning scrabbling for traction in the dirt and pulling him into the ditch.

The fire intensified, he could hear the rounds smacking the armoured cars, which were now sitting ducks. One well-placed RPG rocket and all of the guys in there would be roasted, turned to burnt and blackened pork.

He had seen them roasted like that, twisted and black and stinking. The thought of it and the fear under fire dried his mouth up, as if something had snatched away the grey shawl and rammed a fistful of blotting paper into it. He could taste the bile in his mouth and he knew once again the true taste of fear. Fear was not cowardice he had learnt, it was intelligence and only stupid people knew no fear. Overcoming that fear in the face of great danger was courage and to act in a controlled manner in the face of it was heroic.

And to a man they had courage, every last one of them!

The Noddy cars couldn't escape as the abandoned truck was blocking the road behind them and it was only a matter of time before they were going to get revved by a rocket. The road was too narrow and the combination of the embankment and ditch on the left, the shallow ditch on the right against Tolkien's rock and the smashed bridge ahead; all this had cut off any hope of escape or taking the fight straight at the enemy. The enemy were now gaining the upper hand were by now pouring concentrated fire at them from across the river. It was a perfect ambush, a potential death-trap and the kill zone had only two flaws in it.

They had failed to cover the deep ditch due to the curve in the road and Tolkien's rock partly obscured their fire. And it was only this which had saved them. And then Kevin saw an amazing sight. Their truck driver, Chris, leapt up, jumped into the cab and reversed it out of the line of fire, putting Tolkien's rock between him and certain death. How and why he managed to do that without being killed was a defining moment for Kevin.

It convinced him then, there in the cauldron of war that God does exist; an irony that in "hell" you realize that God exists?

He would acknowledge this as divine intervention for the rest of his life!

Jan Bloem:

What I also remember of the ambush was when we were in the ditch under fire, it was identified by Mark that their RPG was fired from the house you refer to.

Mark called on Vein (nickname) Vermeulen who was armed with a RPG, to launch a rocket to the house. Vein, under all this gun fire, stood up straight and took his shot and hit the house through the window. A bull's eye, as this rocket must have exploded inside the house where these fuckers were launching their RPG rockets.

I personally think this bravery of Vein, to stand up and take aim with the RPG, and Chris turning the vehicle, saved lives on that day, including Mark's instruction to fire a RPG rocket to the house. On the follow-up operation going back to the ambush site, we went to the house and could actually see that Vein's bull's eye caused massive destruction inside the house, as well as wounding or killing a few. There was a lot of blood all over. (Maybe you can just check with Mark as Vein was right next to him, and I might not remember all the facts correctly.)

The fire began to be more accurate and intensified and it was then that Kevin realized that they were outgunned, they had lost the firefight. Amid the crescendo of sound Mark was screaming something, indicating with his hand that they must move. Kevin could see the combat medic treating a man lying in the ditch, blood on them both, busy putting up a drip. He had wrapped the man's torso in plastic, and they began to drag him along the ditch, his face ashen his eyes closed. Kevin recognised him; it was Ferdie and he feared that he was dead.

And to add to their woes, out poured the ants, thousands of them in a river of enraged red, large red bastards with a sting in the tail. Kevin watched in horror as they poured out and began to exact justice for their home being trampled upon, biting and stinging with their tail and instantly it felt as if his skin was on fire. It was a choice they had to make, get stung and bitten to hell or get shot to hell, ants or bullets.

Andrew Prew remembers:

When I was in grade 10, I read the book A Bridge Too Far; *that same year in the post I received my army number, (which I can still recite to this day), that was it, I knew which unit I was going to belong to.*

After Ferdie was driven out of the contact zone, and airlifted away, I found myself lying in a ditch next to Brian Wallace; I had just let off about a half a magazine on the enemy and wide-eyed told Brian it was his turn to stand up and shoot. This wasn't too pleasant an idea as you could hear the ping and snap of bullets overhead.

Brian true to form said something like, 'No, fine, I'll do it,' and at the same time, with a malicious glint, he tapped me hard a few times with his index finger on my forehead between my eyes and said, 'This is where you are going to be shot when it's your turn.'

We both cried tears, laughing, it seemed so funny at the time.

That joke didn't last long, but I still treasure it.

My dad had enrolled me into university, and two weeks after leaving Angola, and driving down to Rhodes, I was given a slip of paper to fill in to enable me to keep a car at residence. It consisted of three lines:

Name; Car Reg No; Residence. I knew the answers, but had to get a chap sitting next to me to fill it in for me. The words were jumping about, try as I may I could not do it.

During a science prac, somebody dropped a flask onto the cement floor. When I heard the crash I fell off those high chairs flat on my stomach.

Everybody thought it was a marvellous joke. Needless to say I plugged. It was painfully embarrassing to me; I had never failed at anything before. My dad was most upset, which made me feel like a dog, but fortunately my elder brother who had been to the army nurtured me and talked me into going back to varsity.

C'est la vie!

The fight was lost and once behind the cover of Tolkien's rock they beat a hasty retreat. They loaded the almost-dead Ferdie onto the front of a Noddy car and with some men clinging to it they sped off to get the wounded man back towards Cela. Along the way a helicopter arrived and casevaced him to the hospital at Cela. In their minds, they all said goodbye to Ferdie that day. Kevin had seen Ferdie's face, his grey and dying face and he looked at Mark asking, 'Do you think he'll make it, lieutenant?'

'I don't know, Vos, I can't say,' a haggard look on his face as he answered. The truck's tyres were flat, and they rode it on rims until it could go no further, until they were safe. They sat in the bush in silence waiting for a recovery vehicle, silent and depressed; it was the first fight they had lost. Kevin knew they hadn't run away as cowards, they had simply lost the firefight but still they all felt like shit. Paratroopers don't lose a fight, ever, but this time they had. Kevin had a headache, a monster and his head felt as if an ogre had split it head open with a giant cleaver.

And from that day on he hated red ants with an all-consuming passion!

Ferdie Jordaan recounts his own experiences:

'Accept this or your son will die.'

The voice was so vivid that my mother turned to my father to see if he had heard it too, but he was unaware. My father was driving.

They were returning home after visiting their youngest son in 1 Military Hospital in Pretoria. I had been admitted shortly before, having been wounded in Angola. Moments earlier, my mother had asked God why her youngest son had to go through this ordeal – the one of her four sons least capable of dealing with pain.

'Why him, God? she asked. 'Accept this or your son will die.'

The response startled her, but it changed her life.

29 December 1975 started as just another day in Angola – nothing exceptional. It was morning and the sun was hot, as usual. We were on patrol somewhere in the central part of Angola, not far from where the battle of Bridge 14 had taken place.

There were us, a platoon of Parabats on the back of a Bedford and a troop of armoured cars, two of which were heading the patrol. Accompanying us was a Unimog with a bunch of Sappers, with another Eland bringing up the rear.

I was sitting in my usual spot on the canopy frame behind the cab of the Bedford, right behind the driver. I liked the unobstructed view of where we were going, sitting higher and facing forward.

Our coms were not working. The Elands were talking to each other on their radios, but the messages were shouted to us by the commander of the Eland just ahead of us.

The last message I seem to recall was that the leading Eland had encountered a problem: there was a ditch across the road that we could not cross. We had to turn back.

That was when we saw the RPG.

It came out of nowhere across an open field from our right and I saw it miss the Eland ahead of us, exploding somewhere in the bush behind it. Another was aimed at us – another miss!

I left my perch behind the cab in a leap, rifle in hand.

Two of us ended up in a ditch on the right of the Bedford, while everyone else had the sense to duck into the ditch on the left hand side of the road – further away from the enemy. We were scanning the area ahead of us to see if there was anything to shoot at, but I saw nothing.

Ahead of us, somewhat off to the right, were a number of large boulders with trees growing amongst them. Someone was shooting the crap out of this target, but I don't know if it was one of the Elands, or the enemy.

Leaves were flying and bullets were sending fragments of rock and puffs of dust into the air. The steady stream of rounds passing overhead, made a sharp cracking noise. The machine guns on the Elands were firing non-stop and every time the big 90 mm guns went off, we cheered, but I never knew if they even saw a live target or not.

Undoubtedly, our patrol was in serious trouble. If we had sprung the ambush, very few of the enemy would have escaped, but their aim was off. Out in the open on a narrow dirt road, flanked by ditches on either side which made it difficult to turn around and head for safety, we were certainly in a spot of bother.

At least us, the Bats, were behind solid cover in the ditches next to the road, but the Elands were sitting ducks. The Sappers were behind us and probably out of the line of fire, obscured by the boulders and trees I mentioned before.

I remember saying to the other guy, Jorrie, who was from Kenhardt, that we had to move a little to get a better view. I was on my hands and knees, crawling. A loud explosion rocked us. Something struck me in the ribs and I was winded, like a being kicked in the stomach.

I could not breathe. My ears were ringing.

The next thing Ferdi Vermeulen, our medic, was at my side. I was on my back, struggling for air. When I finally managed to take a proper breath, I heard a bubbling sound coming from my ribs.

I knew then that I had been wounded - probably a lung shot.

I knew that sound well. I had seen many a springbuck die from similar shots.

I spat in my hand to see if there was any blood, but saw none.

Ferdi Vermeulen was telling me not to panic, but I was dead calm. I knew what was going on.

Al gaan ek ook deur 'n dal van doodskaduwee, ek sal geen onheil vrees nie; want U is met my.

We scampered to the ditch on the other side of the road, where the cover was better. I was still battling for air and must have said something to that effect. Vermeulen tried mouth to mouth resuscitation, but that hurt, so I pushed him away.

Someone was applying pressure to my ribs, trying to seal off the hole in my chest. Then we were running, bent over to stay behind cover. Lieutenant Coetzee told Chris Mouton to turn the Bedford around. The poor bugger had to do a three-point turn to do so, but due to the ditches beside the narrow road, it took a long time – at least in my book.

I was thinking that I was glad it was not my job to get back in that truck with incessant machine gun fire in our direction. All the while, leaves were still dropping from the trees behind us. The Bedford was providing cover as we ran, but how far, I don't recall. On several occasions Vermeulen would pull me down and work on my wound. Eventually, I was heaved onto the front of an Eland, but had to move aside as I was obstructing the already limited view of the driver.

Vermeulen was by my side, possibly running, possibly also on the Eland.

We made it to the Unimog. I was loaded on the back, lying on my back, looking up at faces I did not know (Bielie Naude, a guy who was in primary school with me, may have been there, but I cannot be sure). The Sappers were staring back at me, probably wondering if I was going to make it.

Vermeulen had finally managed to seal off the wound with an air tight bandage, but was still applying pressure.

The sapper lieutenant was driving like a maniac, trying to get me (and his section) to safety. The back of a Unimog is never a comfortable place to ride. It bumps like crazy. The potholes we went through jolted me into the air and made me cry out.

That caused Vermeulen to swear something fearful at the Sapper lieutenant.

I did not think the Loot could have done much better anyway. There were many large potholes on that piece of road. They were the result of very accurate 5.5 fire that followed the fleeing FAPLA and Cuban forces who were trying to get as much distance between themselves and our gunners at the battle of Bridge 14.

When we finally stopped, it was for me to be transported to a medical facility in an Alouette.

Again I was surrounded by people I did not know.

One, presumably an officer in an unmarked uniform, commented on my new boots. He was probably trying to take my mind off my current situation. When we first went into Angola, we were issued with olive green uniforms and takkies. After a few months in the bush, the takkies were finished.

And they stank! A few days before, I had been issued with a new pair of boots. These were now the subject of the officer's attention.

'You can have them,' I told him, 'I won't be needing them any time soon.'

It was probably an hour since I was wounded, but I was feeling OK.

Maybe Vermeulen had given me some morphine. I had never been inside an Alouette and was looking forward to the trip.

I was operated on at the small village of Cela, where a field hospital had been put together. Someone cut the laces on my new boots to remove them and that is about the last thing I can remember from before the op.

The damage, caused by a piece of RPG shrapnel, turned out to be far more serious than just an injury to my right lung. Afterwards, I recall trying to yank a variety of tubes from my body, but I was weak and a medic pushed me down. Then I was in a Flossie in a bed, on my way back to the "states[11]".

We landed at Swartkop Airforce base at night and I remember lying in the back of an ambulance, being aware of the flashing red lights.

I finally signed my release papers from the army in Bloemfontein on 2 June 1976, but my story does not end here.

What follows is the part that matters.

When we visited my folks on the farm a few years later, my father told my wife-to-be that around the time I was wounded, he was in his bakkie, doing his normal farm chores. He related how he was suddenly overcome by concern about my safety. He stopped the bakkie, got out and onto his knees and there, on the hard Free State soil, prayed to God to keep me safe. He drove home and told my mother that something had happened to me. He then sat down next to the telephone, waiting.

When it finally rang, it was an army officer, informing him that his son had been shot.

Many years later, my mum and I discussed the Angola incident. I commented then that I had not been traumatised by what had happened to me.

I experienced no anger and blamed no-one.

Still, since I had given my life to Christ even before going to the army, I saw no purpose to it. My mother was quiet for a while and then, almost overcome by emotion, said: "Son, you may have been saved, but I was not.

Your being shot, saved me!"

Afterthought - *What happened to me in 1975, was war. To be shot at, was to be expected. That is what we trained for. The sad reality of South Africa today is that thousands suffer fates much, much, worse than mine and in a country where there is supposed to be peace. I dedicate this to them, the ones who suffered and still suffer so unjustly because of crime.*

May God help us all.

(Rifleman Ferdie Jordaan, 1 Parachute Battalion)

---

11. *Slang for home.*

This is what Mark wrote:

Ferdie had his diaphragm ruptured and lost a lot of his internals but survived. I went to see him at the field hospital about four days later, having asked all the guys to write some kind of notes to him that I could read to him. I found Ferdie propped up in bed really buggered-looking and the first thing that went through my head was 'Is he going to make it?' My jaw started to wobble because I was not good at these emotional scenes. I tried desperately not to show how I was feeling and thank god he was in such a poor state that he did not notice.

'Get well,' I urged him and said that he was going to be OK. He kept asking if he would catch the next plane out of here in three days' time. I battled to read the letters because of the tears welling up and the quaver in my voice was very noticeable. Thank god I had insisted on going alone. The letters were touching from a group of men/boys who were of the toughest in the SADF. I suddenly found myself suppressing all those feelings of guilt frustration, helplessness so as not to allow myself to feel that for fear of losing the troop's confidence in me as being weak and thus unable to lead effectively. I realise now that it was probably better to have expressed myself then but that is what we have with hind sight.

General Dippenaar writes to Ferdi:

I might well have said that I cannot remember it but in reality I did not connect your name with the incident because the incident itself is so vivid for me that it could have happened yesterday (or the day before yesterday?)

In any case, I delivered a talk to the South African Military History Society on 9 July 2014 on the medical experiences during Operation Savannah and your incident among others came up. The marginal comment in the official War Diary against the factual description of this event reads:

'This was heroic surgery!' So two days after the operation I loaded your bed and everything on the C130 so that you would be handled as little as possible as I was dead scared you would weer aan die bloei sou gaan. I later heard that you had to undergo a further procedure to drain an abscess that had formed under your diaphragm and remove a bunch of kunsspons that I had plugged in your liver to stop the bleeding.

This was not a case which I didn't know how to handle but it was something that I had never personally come across before (or since). I knew damn well and the laws gave me grey hair if the deed became known!

I think you are in error to attribute the injury to an RPG 7. The piece of cast iron that I took out of you was about 15mm x 7.5mm, and about 3-4 mm thick - an RPG projectile does not create so much shrapnel according to the hollading *principle, en die wand is maar essensieel blik. At the time I was of the opinion that it came from a 76mm tank defence gun (like those used against us at Ebo) and I still think so.*

I have often wondered what became of you, and now I know. You were declared medically unfit not so much because you were so badly injured but rather because you had done your duty. They say that lightning never strikes twice in the same place but must one ever tempt fate? Such was the saying from "Saving Private Ryan".

Ferdie being dragged along the ditch after being shot in the ambush

Pencil drawing by Author

The anesthetist for your operation was Lt Andre Boezaart, a conscripted surgeon, and he deserves the credit for keeping you alive in spite of everything. When the drama was over and I began to close you up I looked up and there he stood at the head of the operating table with a grin on his face like a full moon!

I remember saying to him, 'Shit, Andre, that was George Sava stuff!' (Sava was a writer of popular medical thrillers with a high melodramatic content).

Why do I suddenly think as if a bunch of E Posse came together to form the framework of a short story?

What is the saying?   'Is life worth living?

That depends on the Liver!'

Best wishes, Tony Dippenaar[12]

That night, when they had got back to the outskirts of Cela, they encountered fresh troops

for the first time; young men who had been conscripted in June, from an infantry unit fresh from the *States*. They were fresh faced, wearing clean "greens" and steel helmets.

The steel helmets were ridiculous, thought Kevin, what the hell is the point of a bloody steel helmet in this war?

In comparison Kevin and his fellow bats looked like the veterans they were, dirty, scruffy-looking and wearing castoff cammo gear appropriated during the months of fighting.

Hair long, topped with an assortment of headgear ranging from hats to crumpled caps, unshaven, unkempt; they looked like mercenaries.

They stank like kraal dogs. The interior of the Noddy cars also stank to high heaven and the armoured boys looked just as rough. By contrast the new boys looked clean and raw, perfect cannon fodder imagined Kevin. He noted a mixture of fear and awe in their eyes. Fear at their first brush with war, albeit indirectly, awe at the paratroopers who had just survived an ambush.

Kevin began to strip and clean his rifle.

One of them walked over to him and said, 'Howzit,' offering his hand in friendship. Kevin took his hand and shook it.

'My name's Geoff,' he continued, 'Are you guys mercenaries?

'What just happened - we heard you guys just survived an ambush?'

Kevin didn't answer he kept cleaning his rifle.

Fuck the dogs of war we are better than any fucking mercenary, thought Kevin.

'I hear you guys lost the fight and had to run away?'

---

12. *Col (retired Gen) Tony Dippenaar was a surgeon with the 3 Para Bay and later 3 Mil in 1982 with Medical Command S Transvaal in Johannesburg.*

Kevin continued cleaning his rifle, the words *run away* bouncing around inside his skull like a pinball.

'I hear one of your buddies got shot. I hear he's dead.'

Kevin stopped cleaning his rifle. He looked up at the man standing in front of him.

'Fuck off now before I shoot you in the fucking head, move, fucking now!' he snarled venomously.

He looked back down at his rifle and sensed the other man moving off. He felt a deep sadness in him and began to cry.

He cried from the relief of being alive, he cried for Ferdie; seeing images in his mind of his grey and dying face, in the blood and the ditch amongst the ants, while being dragged through the dirt.

He cried for all of those he had seen dead, the civilians, the Porra refugees who had lost everything, the UNITA, FNLA, MPLA and Cuban soldiers dead and bloated next to the road.

He didn't care who they had fought for, why they had died or who had killed them. He cried for them all.

He felt oh so stupid at this upwelling of emotion. Brought up in a country where the remnants of Victorian English rule and culture still prevailed; a society where men don't cry and men don't hug, where keeping a stiff upper lip is the order of the day.

He felt guilty at all of this, but he couldn't help it, and there was absolutely nothing he could do to stop it.

He cried that night as well.

And if Andy had noticed it, he was civil enough not to say a word about it the next day. That was the thing with Andy, a good natured little shit and quick to rib someone given the slightest chance. But he was a decent man, a good buddy to have your back.

Jan Bloem's words:

> *Thinking back to our training at Tempe, Operation Savannah, the other operations*
> *during camps, the survival of Ferdi and adapting back to civil life,*
> *I can see the hand of our Heavenly Father in this. He looked after us,*
> *kept us safe and provided all we needed.*
> *I thank Him for all that and I know our Saviour is Alive!*

The next morning Kevin wandered over to the driver and shook his hand. His name was Chris Mouton, a Southwester of German stock and one of the bravest men he would ever have the honour of serving with.

An hour later they were called together and Loot Mark made an announcement.

'Gents, we're going back to the ambush site. We need to clear the area and see what's going on over there.' He continued, 'We are taking the newbies with us as backup, just in case those bastards are still hanging around. We don't want a repeat of what went down yesterday.'

The convoy was substantially larger this time as it trundled out of Cela. The two Noddy cars again in the lead, the bat Mercedes truck with the addition of two Unimogs, followed by the last Noddy car.

They stopped about two kilometres from the ambush site, debussed and spread out in a skirmish line, twenty odd bats forming the front line followed by the newbies or *roofies*, the scabs, who were supposed to stay within touch, the distance between them determined by the terrain.

Andy and Kevin were on the left flank of the line and in addition to normal rifle and kit Kevin carried the mortar pipe and Andy the base plate. In addition each of them carried four mortar bombs and each remaining man in the front line carried one. It wasn't long before Kevin got pissed off with the scabs who kept falling behind. Each time the line swung right they had to quicken the pace in order to keep formation, and the scabs kept losing contact.

'Oh, for fucksakes,' snarled Kevin. 'We've lost those arseholes again!'

He gave a low whistle to attract Mark's attention, signalled the problem and they had to wait for them to catch up.

Why bother with the low whistle, thought Kevin. The way these wankers are thumping and crashing through the bush, every Cuban between here and Luanda knows we are coming for fucksakes!

After about the fifth time Kevin lost patience. Turning to a sweating scab who had just caught up, he snarled, 'Keep up or get your arse back to the Noddy cars. You fuckers are useless!'

The newbie just stood there and looked at Kevin. Kevin looked into his eyes and saw only fear and uncertainty. The man was breathing hard and Kevin noticed so too were his buddies. Kevin felt sorry then, he realized that this was possibly the first time that these boys were in a real war situation and they were terrified.

Kevin remembered the first time he had found himself in a similar situation and suddenly felt sorry for them, they were new to this and the last thing the bats needed was for them to panic and end up fucking it all up.

'KD, you need to back off a bit, boet,' said Andy, his one eyebrow cocked up. Kevin had been chastised and to be chastised by Prew was an uncomfortable thing, especially while the one eyebrow was cocked upward. He relented.

'Hey, it's going to be OK, man,' said Kevin, in a slightly kinder tone. The scab looked a bit better after that, but the fear remained in his eyes.

Soon they reached the ambush site, quietly swept the area and went down into defensive positions while Mark and two men went down onto the road, to inspect the kill zone. They carefully checked for anti-personnel mines or booby traps, there was nothing. Kevin could see the drag marks and Ferdie's blood still in the ditch; it had turned black. Kevin felt sick, and he felt as if his guts had twisted into a knot. He indicated the spot to Andy, who simply nodded, shook his head slightly and averted his eyes.

As was expected the Cubans had scarpered, which was standard practice, although one could never be sure, thought Kevin. After all, the SWAPO fighters had waited at the scene of their ambush and had paid a terrible price. It seemed a century ago that Kevin had seen the dead SWAPO man's eyes, staring at him.

It felt so long, long ago - *the glass shards grating in his head.*

Mark climbed back up the slope.

'Vos, Prew, put a few bombs on that house there,' he ordered, indicating a house nestled in a little gorge near the river.

Quickly they assembled the pipe and base plate and as Kevin sat down and grasped the pipe, Andy bumped him out of the way.

'What the fuck are you doing, Prew!' snarled Kevin as he returned the favour, shoving Andy into an untidy sprawl.

'It's my turn to hold the pipe,' growled Andy as he lunged at Kevin. It was ridiculous, the same old story, the two of them vying to be the main cat on the block.

Mark snarled, 'Stop that shit, you pair of morons, and put bombs on that fucking house, NOW!'

Andy by now had the pipe and with venom Kevin snarled, 'Tell me when you are ready, you little prick!'

Andy gave him a self-satisfied, victorious look and said in a sweet voice, 'I'm ready Kev-vie.'

The first bomb, the second, third *and* the fourth missed the house, exploding harmlessly in the rocks in the gorge.

'Cease fire, for fucksakes,' ordered Mark. 'You mortarists were supposed to be the hotshots in the battalion, scoring the highest in the country in evaluation and all that shit; and you can't even hit a barn door with an apple at three paces!'

Andy looked crestfallen. Kevin felt triumphant, saying, 'You fucked that up, hey Prew, ha, ha,' he laughed, 'Totally fucked it up, fucking nice!'

'Go fuck yourself, Vos!' Andy responded with venom.

'Wish I could man, if I could I'd have my cock up my arse every night and wouldn't need your fucking blowjobs anymore,' retorted Kevin.

Andy grinned and gave Kevin a solid punch on the shoulder which slid up and clocked him right on the cheek.

'Ow!' cried Kevin rubbing his face vigorously and that was the end of it.

The newbies were aghast; they had never seen anything like it. Kevin heard one of them say to his buddy, 'These blokes are fucked in the head. Watch out, they're bush crazy, *bosbefok*!' And they were exactly on the mark.

Andy Prew:

Yes, I should have aimed the hand-held mortar tube, positioned between my dirty shaking legs, a little bit more forward and one degree to the right ... that would have pleased my best mate KD, who had dropped the bomb down the tube, greatly, and would have saved me a clip on my ringing ear and a good berating from him for missing, as we had played ching chong cha to see who would hold the tube as he was the better mortarist.

C'est la vie!

Chapter Eighteen: **The rocket man**

"I love the smell of napalm in the morning"

Apocalypse Now

"Bean" remembers this occasion involving Sydney:

I fondly recall was an encounter with a hardened 'Recce' that I had the misfortune of being on the receiving end of. Our HQ in Cela is where this GV gave me the PK of all PK's. Thinking about it today, almost 42 years later I can still feel the sting across my face when my mind wonders to the good old days of 1 Para Battalion. Months, years and decades later, my Bat buddy's still have a laugh at the event in the abandoned Catholic Church that doubled as our makeshift sleeping quarters.

There we were, battle weary and exhausted, lying in the "straight stripe" along the hard concrete church floor, to my left Sydney, to my right Jabus, the Free State champion wrestler, no neck, just shoulders that lead straight to his head.

A few others were along the wall and opposite to us, more okes, all in the same state of weary exhausted slumber in their straight stripe. Preaching from the pulpit was Aubs, (Sgt Aubrey Cronje) and 'The Recce'. Yes, he was one of the meanest, battle hardened mofo's I have had the misfortune of coming across.

Well, had it been preaching, we may have actually fallen to slumber, dreaming of our loved ones back in the "states". Not this night, no this night these two were worshipping a bottle or two, spreading their sermon across for all to hear.

Syd, always the instigator, always with his wooden spoon in the ready, prodding me on to ssssh them; him saying, 'Bean, tell them, shut the fuck up, we want to dos.' Probably more stupid than brave, I took the bait.

'Com'n guys, keep quiet, we need to <u>dos</u>'.

This I blabbered out, no success, another Syd prod,

'Bean, they're not listening to you, me another 'com'n, guys', another prod,

'Bean, they ignoring you,' and yes, more chirping from me.

I don't recall how long the prodding and <u>sssh'ing</u> went on for but across the passage I had another brave Bat joining my chorus.

I also don't remember whether Aubs and 'The Recce's' sermon fuelled by liquored spirits had finished or whether the interruptions from their congregation sparked them on but I knew hier kom groot kak.

Marching at double pace towards us was "priest" Aubs and his Recce altar boy in tow. Jumping out of my sleeping bag, assuming the Mohamed Ali, Rumble in the Jungle poster stance, ready to 'float and sting', brave as only a Bat can be; gaining courage from Jabus who assured me 'Moet nie worry nie, ek sal hom bliksem, ek sal nie sy kak vat nie,' *made me stand even taller than my diminutive 1.65m; peering over my hoisted fists ready to unleash a hail of "bullets" at the enemy approaching my ambush, one behind the other.*

You always hear the war stories and I was still wondering if Recce's really do move faster than the speed of light; ask me they do. I was still waiting for Aubs to get within striking distance when I heard the Recce say 'jou troepe het geen fokken respek' *then I felt it, out of nowhere, a palm across my face proving to me the Milky Way exists, a cluster of stars bouncing off my head, so white and bright, with a black hole leading to undiscovered universes.*

Me, "enjoying" my spacewalk, Syd, the innocent bystander and shit-stirrer extraordinaire, in hysterical laughter, because the Recce bilksemed *me and Jabus taking cover into his sleeping bag, declaring,* 'ek dink dis nou dossing *time, good night boys.'*

Fortunately another of my Bat buddies has a similar campfire story because my Recce 'friend' swiftly crossed the church floor and acquainted him with the same Milky Way I had just visited...

It had been pouring rain all night and they had, had the luxury of sleeping in a church at Cela; except Andy and Kevin who had the dubious honour of sleeping in a bivvie. This was next to an old Vickers water-cooled machine gun, its barrel pointing in the general direction of Quibala and ultimately Luanda. How this old thing, circa World War Two found itself fighting in a civil war in Angola amazed Kevin.

It was early morning and the sun found Andy and Kevin, trudging miserably back towards the old church.

'What a crap bloody night,' groaned Andy, lugging his water- logged sleeping bag over his head and shoulders.

'You look like a fukken dwarf, Prew,' observed Kevin. Looking at Andy, his stocky frame crowned by the sleeping back, brought back childhood memories of Snow White and the Seven Dwarves.

'Fuck off, Vos!'

'OK.'

'Pity we couldn't have shot that thing,' mused Andy.

A couple of bursts would have made last night worth it all.'

'Crap, you were probably having a wet dream, cumming into Snow White all night, being a dwarf and all,' chirped Kevin.

'Good grief, Vos, that's the weakest attempt, the most PATHETIC attempt at a joke I have ever heard coming from anyone, good grief!' snapped Andy in reply.

'You're just grumpy,' replied Kevin and after a pause he conceded, 'You're right, that was fucking corny.' He wanted to call Andy "Grumpy the dwarf" but decided that that would be pushing it.

They walked past the two recces, both looked at the motley pair and grinned, one commented, 'You two look like shit!'

'We feel like shit,' responded the two of them almost in unison.

Soon they had little Esbit stoves[13] going, safe to use in the town but not in the bush, because the small fuel pill stank like hell and anyone downwind could smell it a mile away. 'Time for some condies crystals and tea,' chirped a passing Syd, referring to condensed milk and tea. It brought a smile on Kevin's face. Syd had that ability, to bring a smile to the dial, the Syd and David Bowie combo, morale boosters!

Kevin made a brew of sweet tea, rich with condensed milk and plonked an army dog biscuit into it. The damn thing was so hard that the only way eat it was to soak it in tea or coffee and eat it as a porridge.

Breakfast done they walked into the old church minus its pews, for a briefing. The lieutenant spoke. 'Before I start I don't want to hear about stupid plans, chirps about cannon fodder and shit like that, do you have that?'

Without waiting for a reply he continued.

'Today we are going on a motorised recce, the same formation of the Noddy cars and the truck. We are leaving in thirty minutes and heading off along the main road towards Quibala, the objective of this mission, gents, is to drive until we pick up shit with the enemy, *a kaksoek patrollie!*'

He held his hand up sharply, 'I know, shut up and don't say a word!' And with that he strode out.

'Good god!' exploded Pete, 'Are these fuckers mad in the head? That's asking to die; that's asking to get blown the fuck up; that's asking to get a bullet in the head!'

'Ag, relax old Pete, my friend, all will be fine,' responded Lappies in his thick Afrikaans

---

13. *Military issue - pocket sized cookers for use in the field.*

accent, patting Pete on the shoulder with a large meaty hand, as comforting a gesture as could be expected from a friendly troll, given Lappies' size and disposition, thought Kevin wryly. They made an odd pair, Pete being a short shit, shorter than Andy even; and Lappies a gangly giant of a man.

Kevin didn't say a word and nor did Andy as they glumly made their way towards the truck. Pete had said it all.

They left Cela and headed out towards Quibala. Kevin sat and watched the milestones rolling by slowly as they drove steadily towards the enemy lines which were just before the town of Quibala. Kevin was apprehensive, as a matter of fact he was terrified and said so. 'Prew, I'm shitting myself; got a bad feeling about this jaunt, my boet.'

'Me too, KD, me too,' responded Andy. 'Check, even Mark looks unhappy,' he said nodding his head towards the Loot who was sitting on top of the cab. Kevin looked and he could see Mark had a worried look on his face. He lifted a pair of binoculars and began to scan the road ahead and the bush on either side. Kevin looked forward and behind and noticed that all three armoured car commanders were doing the same.

He felt a knot in his stomach, it went *twist*!

They passed another milestone, snow white, firmly planted in the ground; it read, QB 80.

He felt a knot in his stomach, it went twist!

After a while it became a ritual, almost a pattern. QB 70, stomach went twist! QB 65, stomach went twist!

A strange thought crossed his mind. All the milestones were undamaged; not a mark on them. Perhaps the only safe thing to be in this war is a milestone.

'Prew, if the shit hits the fan I want to turn into a milestone,' said Kevin suddenly.

'What the fuck are you talking about, KD, that's fucking random!' responded Andy, his eyebrow arched up quizzically.

Kevin realized how random that was and decided to shut his face. QB 60, stomach went twist!

Fuck this!

Suddenly Syd let rip with gusto, and ploughed into another Bowie song; this time Pete was playing the drums, his hands beating a tune rhythm on the side of the truck. Lappies started playing an air guitar…

Ziggy played guitar, jamming good with Wierd and Gilly,
And the Spiders from Mars.
He played it left hand, but made it too far,
Became the special man, then we were Ziggy's Band.

Ziggy really sang, screwed up eyes and screwed down hairdo

Like some cat from Japan, he could lick 'em by smiling

He could leave 'em to hang

Here came on so loaded man, well hung and snow white tan.

So where were the spiders while the fly tried to break our balls?

Just the beer light to guide us.

So we bitched about his fans and should we crush his sweet hands?

Ziggy played for time, jiving us that we were Voodoo.

The kids was just crass,

He was the naz

With God given ass

He took it all too far

But boy could he play guitar.

Making love with his ego Ziggy sucked up into his mind

Like a leper messiah

When the kids had killed the man

I had to break up the band

Ziggy played guitar…

Some of the crew joined in, some couldn't hold a tune but it didn't matter and before
long spirits were up. QB 60, Ziggy Stardust, happy times, no twist! QB 55, Ziggy
Stardust, happy times, no twist! QB 50, Ziggy Stardust, no twist! Syd kicked off with:

War made him a soldier

Little Frankie Mear

Peace left him a loser

The little bombardier

Lines of worry appeared with age

Unskilled hands that knew no trade

Spent his time in the picture house

The little bombardier

Frankie drank his money

The little that he made

Told his woes to no man

Friendless, lonely days

Then one day, in the ABC

Four bright eyes gazed longingly

At the ice-cream in the hand of

The little bombardier
Sunshine entered our Frankie's days
Gone his worries, his hopeless maze
His life was fun and his life was full of joy
Two young children had changed his aims
He gave them toffees and played their games
He brought them presents with every coins he made
Then two gentlemen called him
Asked him for his name
Why was he friends with the children
Were they just a game?
Leave them alone or we'll get sore
We've had blokes like you in the station before
The hand of authority said "no more" to
The little bombardier
Packed his bags, his heart in pain
Wiped a tear, caught a train
Not to be seen in the town again.

QB 45, little bombardier, hint of a twist! QB 40, fuck little bombardier, twist! QB 35, stomach went twist!

Fuck this! Mark started yelling, 'STOP, STOP, STOP!' Stomach went TWIST! The convoy ground to a halt and the men debussed rapidly into the scrub on either side of the road. Hugging the ground, they lay gazing intently into the dense green ahead of them.

Kevin heard Mark talking over the radio to the troop commander, who was now head down in the lead Noddy car.

'Flash of light on the hill at ten o'clock, did you get it?'

Kevin heard the hiss of the radio and the squawky response.

'Right,' stated Mark as he made his mind up. 'You, you, you…' He selected eleven men including the LMG gunner 'Let's go. I saw a light flash on the hill.

We're going to clean it up, and I think it's a Cuban OP! The rest of you stay here, if I need backup I'll radio in; the armoured cars will give us cover with the Brownings,' he finished with a flourish.

'Can't we come along and give you mortar support?' asked Kevin.

Andy looked excited. Kevin imagined that if he were a small dog his tail would be wagging.

'No chance,' responded Mark with some disdain. 'You two were bloody dismal the other day, missing that house; it was a piss easy target and you missed it. The last thing I need is for you two to put bombs on our heads, so no, you two stay here!'

Kevin felt like he had been slapped in the face. Andy's imaginary small dog tail stopped wagging. Kevin remembered the show of lights and how his bomb had put them out, yeah right! He wanted to tell Andy that it was his fault missing the house; he should have left it to him and that house would have been buggered, three bombs max!

But that would be picking a fight with his best bud, no point in it.

Mark turned away and signalled that they should move out. The stick of men left at a quick pace, heading towards the hill about one kilometre away, leaving two pissed off mortar men watching them move off.

They settled down to wait out the hill climb. Kevin thought of the battle of Majuba. 'Hoi, Prew, this reminds me of Majuba, when the Boers fucked up Collie and the English,' he remarked. 'Those poor Brits sitting on a hill thinking they were all okay, till the Boers went up the hill and shot the lot of them.'

'Your imagination is running away with you, KD,' remarked Andy.

Suddenly Kevin felt a burning sensation on his leg, then another and again and again; the fucking ants again, thousands of them biting and stinging the crap out of them. Andrew rolled away, slapping and swearing. 'I wish we had some bloody insect spray to squirt on these little fuckers and let them die like the little evil bastards deserve!' he snarled.

'Or *gogga* napalm,' remarked another cursing man, using the Afrikaans slang for insect.

Suddenly Kevin had an epiphany, napalm! He got up and ran towards the truck. 'Where are you going, KD?' called Andy.

Kevin didn't answer as he sat on the truck scrabbling in the mortar bomb cases, until he found them; a whole bunch of spare projectile boosters, or *laadings,* shaped like little horseshoes. When placed around a mortar bomb's tail piece they gave mortar bombs added distance or *vooma* as they called it. He collected them and ran back to the bunch of cursing, slapping men all bedevilled by the battalions of ants.

'Now you little fuckers, let's see how like getting fucked up!' said Kevin with relish, as he lit the first of the little horseshoes.

The horseshoe ignited and began to melt into a stream of molten napalm. It poured down on the ants like a mythical god's wrath, burning all in a flaming stream of fire and brimstone. Kevin killed thousands of them, following their trail until he was killing them as they exited the nest, dying at their doorway by the thousands in crumpled, steaming, blackened heaps. Some of the guys came over to have a look; some shook their heads while others made a few constructive comments.

'Why don't you open the entrance a bit and pour it into the hole,' suggested one.

'KD, I think you've lost your marbles,' offered Andy.

'Well, I don't hear you slapping and squealing any longer, do I?' retorted Kevin.

A little voice in Kevin's head said, 'Stop killing God's little creatures.' But he didn't obey the voice of conscience; he didn't care and when the last little horseshoe was spent he felt better. Oh, so much better.

The firefight broke out a few minutes later and they all flattened themselves against the earth. They could hear small arms fire and the return fire coming from the top of the little hill, like crackers going off in the distance.

Kevin could see the small figures moving up the hill in fire and movement, buddy, buddy; leapfrogging their way up. Then they heard bursts of fire coming from the top of the hill, the fuckers had a machinegun up there, realized Kevin, and the little leap-frogging figures went to ground, they couldn't move.

Kevin jerked in fright as the three 50 calibre Brownings on top of the armoured cars opened up. The top of the hill turned into a storm of churning dust and chips of rock. The little figures started to leap-frog again and went up and over the brow of the hill and the sounds of the fight ended abruptly. The fight was over on the little hill and it would take a while for the hill climbers to get back, so Kevin decided to make a cup of tea.

Andy disappeared to the front armoured car, ever curious, to hear what had transpired. There was a relaxed air about the little battle group, they had made the contact they had all expected and it was a certainty that they would now head back to Cela. It was only about two in the afternoon, so there would be plenty of time to settle down for an afternoon of *ballasbak*; lie in the sun, spread the legs and let the sun bake your balls. Kevin often smiled at how descriptive the Afrikaans language was, especially when it came to swearing. There was something extremely guttural and satisfying when you used foul language in Afrikaans!

THWOOMPH!

A deep explosion shook the ground, a sound unlike Kevin had experienced before. He'd seen and heard many different explosions by then, but this was a new one.

THWOOMPH! THWOOMPH! THWOOMPH! THWOOMPH!

Four more in quick succession and there was pandemonium.

Geysers of earth mixed with the black of high explosives shot upwards in columns, thin and narrow it seemed that they were all tall as skyscrapers.

THWOOMPH! THWOOMPH! THWOOMPH! THWOOMPH!

They kept coming in landing a few hundred metres away.

'It's a Stalin's organ!' shouted someone, 'Fucking Red Eyes!'

Kevin looked to the sky and couldn't see a thing. If you could see the "eye" then they were almost dead on target.

So he lay on his back looking at the sky like a frightened rabbit waiting for an eagle to swoop down and kill it, looking for the Red Eyes. Another four came in.

THWOOMPH! THWOOMPH! THWOOMPH! THWOOMPH!

This time they were slightly further away and Kevin realized that the rocket launchers were firing blind, sending rockets in speculative salvos. Luckily for the little battle group, the Cuban observation post had been taken out already.

'They're blind!' shouted Andy. Stating the bloody obvious thought Kevin.

'Turn around, turn around!' screamed the troop commander and once again poor Chris the driver, had to brave the rockets to get his clumsy truck turned around. Unlike the armoured cars crews who by now had battened their hatches, Chris was sitting in his farm truck cab; exposed with absolutely no protection.

Once he had the truck about faced, he hit the deck next to Kevin, chest heaving.

'*Mooi*, Chris, *mooi*!' exclaimed Kevin, admiration in his voice.

He heard Andy, 'Nice one, Chris!'

Chris didn't respond; he just lay on the ground, his eyes fixed to the sky as they all were. The column had done a quick about turn, facing Cela for a quick getaway, waiting for the hill climbing stick to get there. There was no ways they could the group leave them stranded, the paratroopers' credo, never leave a man behind dead or alive!

The hill climbers arrived,

THWOOMPH! THWOOMPH! THWOOMPH! THWOOMPH!

More Red Eyes came in and this time they were so close that Kevin almost soiled himself as bits of earth and vegetation were falling on and around them. All the force of the explosions kept going upwards in columns of dirt and Kevin was grateful, realizing that the earth was soft from all of the rains and that the rocketeers had probably fucked it up. The delays were all wrong so by the time the rocket detonated, its head was already buried in the earth. At least he thought that anyway, having no idea if the rockets worked in that way.

The column took off and the already exhausted hill climbers were running hard, struggling to keep up.

'Slow down, slow down!' screamed Andy.

The truck slowed down and Kevin could see the two lead Noddy cars pulling away into the distance.

'Fuckers, fuckers, slow down!' he heard someone screaming fruitlessly at the battened down Noddy cars as they disappeared up the road. The truck was crawling along, and thinking that they were all aboard, Mark yelled, 'Go Chris, go!'

In the scramble Kevin was not in his customary seat up front, he found himself at the back of the truck. There was one man running desperately, exhausted it seemed that he wouldn't make it,

THWOOMPH! THWOOMPH! THWOOMPH!...THWOOMPH!

Kevin ducked instinctively and when he looked up he realized that it was Herman. The guys called him "Canned Fruit" a name given to him by a PF corporal in the battalion. Herman wore glasses which made his eyes look larger than normal.

'Hey you, you useless troop, don't look at me like that, like … like a peach looking at me from the inside of a bottle!' the corporal had roared. Bit of a misnomer Kevin had thought at the time, he should have been called "Bottled Fruit.

Canned Fruit looked desperate and his legs were about to go into a bit of a speed wobble; his webbing had come loose and everything was flapping about. His glasses were steamed up from the sweat and exertion and the desperate look on his face made him look fucking comical. Canned Fruit was just in reach.

Swinging out onto the tailgate, Kevin leaned down and managed to grab the desperate man's hand and wrist and only just managed to heave himself and the exhausted Canned Fruit up and into the truck, landing in a jumbled heap of men and kit.

Kevin realized that he was laughing 'What the hell are you laughing at?' shouted Canned Fruit, 'It's not bloody funny!'

Kevin kept laughing, he realized that he was making and arse of himself but the laughing carried on and he couldn't stop it.

He scrambled to the front and plonked himself down next to Andy. He was laughing so hard that the tears were running down his cheeks.

'KD, stop laughing, stop… STOP!' yelled Andy.

Kevin snapped out of it and stopped. He felt like an idiot. Then he heard Mark saying, 'Vos, good job pulling Canned Fruit aboard.' He gave Kevin the thumbs up.

Kevin felt like fucking hero but also a bit stupid; a stupid, relieved fucking hero.

On the way back they saw some mountain goats in the distance. One climbed on a rock and looked at them. Mark called a halt.

'You guys feel like some fresh meat?' he asked.

It was a rhetorical question. 'One of you *klap* that goat, I'm tired of rat packs,' he ordered.

It was a long shot, but one of the guys took the goat out cleanly; "bang", and it came tumbling down off the rocks.

That afternoon they had a braai, goat meat barbequed on hot coals with only salt as seasoning and no spices at all. Kevin ended up with the shoulder, with a nice hunk of meat on it. For some reason he climbed a water tower and sat there alone, enjoying the view and eating his bit of billy-goat. It was as tough as old boot leather and every time he bit and pulled off a chunk of meat it felt as if his teeth were going to come out with it.

It was delicious; it tasted like manna from heaven.

Brian "Waldo" Wallace[14] has his own memories of the dreaded Red Eye:

The autumn air is cold and the pain in my back from the "red eye" shrapnel is intense; pain that serves as a constant reminder, twisting my thoughts back to Angola, flooding my mind with flashes from the war, throwing me from one scene to the other.

Memories of a man with his foot caught under the wheel of a car that was taken out and him being burned alive. One of his comrades was captured and I was told to guard him as he dug a grave for the deceased. The man mistakenly thought he was digging his own grave and was sick with fright. I hated doing that and the confusion of war.

Memories of a farmer in his cassava field, leaning on his hoe and giving us the MPLA, FNLA and UNITA hand signs because he was not sure who we were and just wanted to get back to farming and on with his life.

Memories of the Cuban killed in an ambush, whose AK-47 bayonet I have and wonder what his family went through; if anyone ever knew where he fell.

Memories of having to transport a wounded MPLA soldier in an old Mercedes 220s and I only had my R-1 with me. Knowing it was too cumbersome to wield in the confined space of the car, I stopped and got a rock to protect myself telling him if he moved in the backseat I would crush his skull. The fear in his eyes, I think he thought I was going to do it regardless.

Memories of going in to set up an ambush position and my hay fever being so bad I could not control my sneezing and the fear that I would give away our position and cost one of my fellow Parabats his life.

Memories of being out on patrol trying to locate the firing position of the dreaded Red Eye 122 missile launchers and one of the enemy having their throat cut because we could not take a captive or fire a shot compromising the mission.

Memories of ambushes and firefights; of friends being wounded; shellings and missile attacks; the smell of the bush and the sound of combat.

---

14. Today he is a missionary and he once told me that his wife, remarking on his journey in life expressed it as, from mercenary to missionary.

Memories of being home in 1976 and trying to shoot two of our tractor drivers because I did not like how they were ploughing the fields. My folks realizing things were not well with me and sending me to Europe so I could deal with it all.

Memories though that give me peace of mind and the ones that I choose to recall are of my brothers in arms; young men who demonstrated amazing feats of bravery against an enemy that by far outnumbered us; brothers that stuck together no matter what it took; men who would have my back, men I was willing to die for.

I salute you. "Peace."

A Coy 1 Parachute Battalion, Some of platoon two – Operation Savannah, Foxbat/Zulu

Back row left to right – Jorrie Jordaan, Chris Mouton, Willie Du Plooy, Jan Bloem, Colin Sawyer, Kevin Vos, Izak Visagie
Second back – Andy Prew, Syd Terblanche, John Vokes, Andre Sonnekus, Vlok Oosthuizen,
Third back – Deon Schoeman, Brian Wallace, Mark Coetzee, Peter Koller, Rian Labuschagne
Front row – Tony Wright, Jabus Viljoen, Danie Blom, Swartz

Chapter Nineteen: **Sneaking around on foot**

When I go home people'll ask me, "Hey Hoot, why do you do it man?
What, you some kinda war junkie?"
You know what I'll say? I won't say a goddamn word.
Why? They won't understand.
They won't understand why we do it.
They won't understand that it's about the men next to you,
and that's it. That's all it is.

Black Hawk Down (2001) Norman "Hoot" Hooten (Eric Bana)

Mark stood and faced them, a gaggle of ruffians sitting and squatting in the dirt. His face was serious.

'Gents, I've got bad news, Naatie got shot yesterday but evidently he's going to be okay.' He paused as if waiting for a reaction.

'So what happened, lieutenant?' asked someone.

'I'm not sure of the facts, but I hear they walked into a bunch of Cubans while on their way to set up an OP post. Fight broke out and being only five of them they lost.

Naatie got shot through both arms, but he's going to be okay. So it's all good they managed to escape and evade and get to safety,' he finished.

Kevin felt his guts give a twist. He remembered Naatie and the bus fight. Naatie was a good guy, not a rubbish nutcase like Ronnie and Van Rommel.

Mark looked at them, pausing and they could see that he was feeling uncomfortable. 'There's another thing, Mally went missing after they bomb-shelled, I'll let you know as soon as I hear anything.'

Kevin liked Malcom Wolverson, also a mortarist, he was the fittest man in the unit. If anyone could outrun the enemy it would be Malcolm, thought Kevin.

'Any news of Ferdie, lieutenant?' asked Syd.

'No, nothing yet,' responded Mark. 'He's still in Cela hospital. Dunno what's going to happen and when I do you guys will be the first to know.'

Mark indicated a person standing to his left. 'Right, you all remember Captain L?'

The captain stepped forward and they all recognised him as their company commander who had disappeared from the battalion during training. He was already a recce operator then, but he had left suddenly left one day, not to be seen until today. Kevin remembered him as an aloof, silent character who never seemed to contribute directly, always seeming to skulk in the background. He treated the troopers with disdain.

The captain looked at them, his face expressionless.

'Right, you all remember me and I'm not particularly displeased to have to work with you here,' he began. He was met with a stone cold response. The backhanded compliment not lost to them.

Unfazed he continued. 'You are going to do a joint incursion with recces behind Cuban lines. The objective is to move in a fairly large group for what is essentially a clandestine operation,' he paused for effect, looking around at the motley group sitting on the ground.

The response was even colder. Kevin thought that while he should be respected for being a recce, he still remained a prick.

'The rest of your lot will be joining us here later today. They have already been briefed so we can save time. We move out early tomorrow.'

He paused again. Kevin had the idea that he paused for effect often because he was a self-serving fuck.

He continued, 'The idea is to move behind Cuban lines and to remain undetected. If we see a likely target we will engage but the main objective is to determine enemy movements and to obtain any intelligence which might be useful.' Amazingly there was no "I love myself" pause this time.

'The enemy is pretty heavy on the ground, and as a result of this the small five men teams of bats and recces we have been using to do this are getting hurt. We need the numbers to counter this,' he continued.

You are a fucking genius, thought Kevin.

He hung a map against the trunk of a tree and showed them the route in, the destination being a large mountain; and the route back. The plan was to spend at least four days on the mountain. Kevin realised with trepidation that they would have to walk eighty kilometres in and the same out. They would be a long way behind the known Cuban lines.

Fuck!

That afternoon the rest of the crew arrived. Up until then, being split up into groups, each under an officer and operating out of Cela, they were the only bats who were being utilised as they should be, as fighting paratroopers.

Kevin would later discover that the rest of A Coy had been deployed in stupid roles, even to guarding banks to prevent them from being cleaned out, a fact lamented in a book written by the iconic Colonel Jan Breytenbach which Kevin would read many years later. Rumour had it that some paratroopers did developed sticky fingers and liberated large sums of money, but this would never be proven and those in the know simply kept their mouths shut.

The next morning they boarded a few trucks and escorted by the three Noddy cars, they headed in the direction of Luanda. Soon they took a dirt road which travelled in a westerly direction and were dropped in the middle of nowhere.

'Vos and Prew, you two need to carry this medical bag,' Mark ordered. 'You're not carrying your mortar with you so you can carry this. You're used to carrying extra, so there you go,' he finished, indicating a rucksack-like contraption lying on the road.

'Dickhead,' thought Kevin. The one time they get to walk without the fucking mortar and its fucking bombs, they get saddled with this shit thing!

Andy walked over and picked the bag up and Kevin saw a startled expression bloom on his expressive dial.

'Jeez KD, this damn thing weighs a ton; we're going to have to take turns man,' he groaned.

'That's cool,' responded Kevin.

And so they moved out walking silently, spread out in a skirmish line, varying its shape with the terrain, Kevin could see that the boys knew what they were doing.

'Thank God I'm with this lot,' he thought. 'Staying with 11 Commando would have been as close to being cannon fodder as your arse was to your balls.'

Once a recce walked over to Kevin and told him to walk on harder ground, not realizing it he was leaving obvious tracks in the sand. Kevin nodded and obliged. The recce corrected him civilly and Kevin respected that. Every day is a school day!

An hour later as the patrol went down for a short break, Andy hit the wall.

'Your turn KD, my back is fucked,' he whispered as he slid the rucksack to the ground, collapsing in a heap next to it.

When the signal came to carry on, Kevin heaved the rucksack onto his shoulders and almost shat himself. It was so heavy that he felt his shoulder muscles pull up to his ears.

It was ridiculously heavy, the thing pulling him backwards off balance. Andy was short, stocky and strong. Built like a solid carthorse, his body was designed to carry heavy loads, thought Kevin. And here I am, all skinny and tall like a bloody giraffe, he thought, as he felt the pain in his back and shoulders develop into a steady, hot burn.

And so a private world of pain was shared between Kevin and Andy for the rest of the day. It was like being on selection course all over again.

The biggest problem being that Kevin couldn't go into the zone, where the pain became relegated to a secondary thing; where the one foot in front of the other was the only focus and fuck everything else applied.

This was a war zone and they were heading straight at the enemy so the zone just had to be relegated to the reserve bench. The pain was real.

When the patrol went down for the night both Kevin and Andy were asleep as if they had been shot in the head.

The next morning Kevin felt as if his shoulders were set in iron bars. They were rigid, every fibre saturated with lactic acid. When he moved it felt like a million little hot pokers were being stuck into his muscles. He looked at Andy, whose pained expression told its story. They both looked at the offending rucksack. It lay there, seemingly benign but full of spiteful venom.

Kevin whispered, 'Let's bury the fucking thing, boet.'

Andy grinned and then asked, 'Whose carrying first?'

'You are,' responded Kevin, a little too quickly.

Andy picked up on the "little too quickly" bit and responded accordingly.

'How about a fucking no, KD!'

'Okay, then how about a bit of "ching chong cha then?' was Kevin's snarled whisper.

Kevin looked Andy in the eye, 'Ching, chong, cha; rock, paper, scissors, best out of three,' he whispered. Andy braced himself, and the two of them fists behind the back set about settling it democratically.

Ching, chong, cha, Andy paper Kevin rock, Andy one up. Ching, chong, cha, Kevin paper, Andy scissors... 'Shit Prew, you've won', groaned Kevin as he hoisted the lump of lead onto his back. He looked across and saw the recce grinning at them, highly amused at their antics. Kevin, feeling his back and neck muscles stretching, the lactic acid turning them into fire, smiled a grimace at the recce and said, 'Fuck you very muchly,' just loud enough for him to hear.

The recce's grin widened, he was enjoying himself immensely.

Later in the day they reached rocky terrain, the soil washed away by the water, exposing the rocks. Kevin stepped down, almost lost his footing and felt a muscle in his left shoulder tear. He went down in a heap, groaning loudly.

The patrol stopped and Mark walked over to Kevin.

'What's wrong?'

'I think I tore a muscle, lieutenant.'

Mark signalled the medic who scuttled over.

'Check him over,' was the order as he moved back into his position.

The medic gave Kevin a painkiller and when he tried to lift the godforsaken rucksack again, the pain was just too much.

Kevin signalled thumb down to Andy, 'I can't.'

Without any protest Andy heaved the godforsaken, piece of shit rucksack onto his back and they moved off.

As they walked in the heat of the day Kevin wished Syd could sing, it made him feel better. The song rang in his head it was Syd's voice, Bowie had been relegated to second fiddle…

> *There's a Starman waiting in the sky*
> *He'd like to come and meet us*
> *But he thinks he'd blow our minds*
> *There's a Starman waiting in the sky*
> *He'd like to come and meet us*
> *But he thinks he'd blow our minds*
> *There's a Starman waiting in the sky*
> *He'd like to come and meet us*
> *But he thinks he'd blow our mind*

Over and over the song in his head,

there's a Starman waiting in the sky… there's a Starman waiting in the sky…there's a Starman waiting in the sky…

Once again it was Kevin's turn, and he heaved the godforsaken, piece of shit, whore of a rucksack onto his back and they moved off. The pain was terrible and Kevin lasted for about an hour before he signalled that he couldn't any more. The patrol went to ground and Mark came over again.

'What's up, Vos?' he asked.

'My shoulder, lieutenant, it's done in,' was Kevin's response.

He felt like shit, Parabats don't give up, ever. He felt terrible, he felt as guilty as hell. 'I'm sorry, lieutenant, I really feel shit about this, but this shoulder is really stuffed.'

Mark looked him in the eye and he needn't have. He knew full well that Kevin wasn't a skiver, not a *sluipgat*, one who drags his arse in the sand, a lazy bastard.

The recce took the godforsaken, piece of shit, whore of a rucksack and as he dragged it onto his back his face changed. He looked at Kevin and mouthed the words, 'Fuck me,' a wide-eyed look on his face. The recce carried the godforsaken, piece of shit, whore of a rucksack for an hour before Andy took over. Andy carried the godforsaken, piece of shit, whore, cock-sucking bitch of a rucksack for an hour and fifteen minutes before the recce took over.

Kevin saw the little competition develop between them with some amusement. He knew Andy well; he could see it in his eyes when Andy got into one of his stubborn moods. 'This is going to be fun,' thought Kevin as he watched things evolve.

The recce, trudging through the bush, shoulders stooped, placing one foot in front of another as if his pace was being dictated by a metronome; his face fixed in a resolute look. Andy trudging, his short legs moving like a clockwork toy; his face set in stubborn aspect, grimly determined.

They reached a river later in the day and after making the crossing safe the tail-enders had to cross the water. It wasn't too deep, about chest high and luckily the flow, while brisk wasn't too fast.

Half way across Andy lost his footing and went under and all that could be seen was the godforsaken, piece of shit, whore, cock sucking bitch of a rucksack sticking out of the water with Andy underneath it. It looked as if a large turtle was trying to swim across the river and Kevin thought it was hilarious.

He jumped in and with the help of the recce they dragged the bedraggled Andy out of the water.

Kevin was weak with laughter. However Andy was not in the best frame of mind as he emerged from the river. He was not amused and when he saw Kevin laughing, he lost it. The trials and tribulations of carrying the godforsaken, piece of shit, whore, cock-sucking bitch of a rucksack and Kevin's incapacity to carry the thing had got to him.

'KD, I'm going to shoot you in the fucking head!' he snarled, tilting his rifle barrel towards Kevin.

A clever response started to form in Kevin's mind until he noticed the look in Andy's eyes, he was thoroughly pissed off and Kevin wisely decided that it was best to shut up. So he kept his clever chirp to himself.

'I see you have fuck-all to say, hey KD?' The rifle barrel was pointed steadily at Kevin's legs, as if waiting for the wrong response before it travelled up to his head. Kevin simply turned away; he had never seen Andy that angry before.

And so ultimately Andy won the battle, the recce gave up on the competition, probably because he wasn't being stubborn, just wise and Kevin felt thoroughly belittled and had been put in his place.

That evening when they went down for the night at the foot of the mountain, Andy patted the godforsaken, piece of shit, whore, cock sucking bitch, turtle back rucksack, and whispered to Kevin, 'Hey Kev, I cracked that fukken recce.'

You mad, tough, little fucker, thought Kevin. But he didn't respond, he felt guilty about not doing his share and he was still smarting at Andy's threat to shoot him.

That night it was cold and Andy asked Kevin if he could borrow his sleeping bag inner, as his sleeping bag had got wet in the river.

'Go fuck yourself, Prew. Remember the poncho story, hey, remember you wanted to shoot me in the head today?

Well you can go and get fucked my boy!' was the snarled response, the buddy, buddy system now truly fucked.

The next day the recce said a few words to Mark, who split the turtle back rucksack's contents amongst them all. It had turned out that it was a vehicle medical bag, never meant to be carried over long distances. It weighed a fucking tonne.

The sulks ended two nights later while they were bivvied halfway up the mountain. It was a full moon and thankfully the rain had disappeared, well, at least for the night. Kevin was woken from a deep sleep.

'KD, KD, fukken wake up! C'mon, KD, wake the fuck up man!'

'Whhhaaat?' Kevin stuttered as Andy shook him awake.

'Listen KD, there's something near our bivvie,' Andy whispered. They lay there quietly on their backs, the bivvies nylon roof about a foot above their faces. And then Kevin heard it as well, a shuffling sound but accompanied by other sounds he couldn't recognise. He quietly pulled his rifle up across his chest and slid the safety off, he heard Andy doing the same. The sound came closed until a shadow fell across the shelter on Kevin's side and when it did he heard Andy whisper, 'Shoot it now KD, rev him!'

But Kevin didn't; to pull a shot now would be a bad thing, a very bad thing. They were behind enemy lines and that would open them to a whole world of pain. And in any case there was something strange about the sounds, a man or men would sound different. And then something touched the nylon, and from the inside of the bivvie it looked as if someone had placed their fist against it and was moving it in little circles across the surface. They lay there frozen, in silence, until suddenly the "fist" snorted.

And when it did Kevin punched it as hard as his skinny frame would allow, connecting beautifully! And as he did so the "fist" made a startled moo sound, followed by a series of loud moo's and brush-cracking sounds as it went thundering down the slope.

The next morning they saw the effects of Kevin's punch, the bivvie was covered in cow snot! The two of them began to piss themselves, laughing at the whole hilarity of it; Kevin had punched the snot out of a cow.

The buddy, buddy system now not so fucked anymore.

John Marais:

Back to Cela. Lt Blaauw called me soon afterwards; in fact, we were very pissed off as we needed some rest after the recce trip as explained above. He informed me that he was going to do another recce patrol and that I had to take five guys and man an OP post. I was to report for instructions at HQ. I recall taking Herman van Staden along and when we entered the Ops room, I immediately felt the negative energy. This relates to a story that Brian Rogers posted about an arrogant (Gunner) Major. We worked extremely well with the Panzer and Gunner chaps. Compared to the culture where Bats continuously fought the Panzers in Bloem, it did not happen here – quite the opposite occurred in real life when you are facing the enemy. We did a lot of work with SSB guys from Zeerust (I think) who had been from the July '75 intake and we got on extremely well (as you will see later). I mean, they were real "rowers" due to their late intake and on top of that we were Bats – bullshit! We worked like one team. So, back to the Ops room. There was a lot of brass present. I cannot recall the names, but a high ranking officer was present and he treated Herman and I with respect although we looked like mercenaries (refer to Jacques Puren and Brian Rogers' photographs towards the end of the doc). But the Gunner Major was a real asshole – once again and I will emphasize it, we worked extremely well with all the Gunners except this little fool.

Comment from unknown:

OP Beatle was the name of a hill with a commanding view of the area. Marais and his team were dropped in a little mealie land with Pumas, about 20 km north from where the Gunners were dug in, and then move south into the mountain range and man the OP. That area was completely flat and their view was perfect from an OP point of view (weather depending, clouds etc). They were to stay there for five days and had to provide grid references to HQ of any enemy movement. Still fucked up from the previous recce exercise with Lt Blaauw, who was already gone on his next assignment, we jumped into the Puma with its fantastic support (I think at least another two Pumas and three to four Allouettes) and off we went.

We were dropped in the mealie land, and scattered for cover. Nothing happened, no mortars, what a surprise. At approximately 10h00 we slowly moved up the mountain to our destination (Beatle). It was obvious when we got to the top that this was the ideal OP except for one thing: it stood out as a pimple on a hog's backside. But the view was just amazing: north east and east was as clear as a digital picture, the rest were covered with bush and mountain. We had running water and life was a blast under the circumstances. We laid low and two guys were always awake. We noticed a large camp right east of us, about twenty large tents, some plaaslike bevolking mixing with soldiers (Cubans and MPLA). Keeping in mind that a river runs along the mountain range and the "camp people" were regularly walking to the river to get water, wash clothes etc.

Comment from unknown:

That very first afternoon from about 17h00 hours they saw a lot of activity on their watch front. Red Eyes were firing from all over the flat stretch of land at our guys in a southern direction towards Cela.

Serious shit and I felt responsible. The team and I plotted and gave grid references back to HQ via the B25 radio. It was also evident that these Red Eyes were dug in and they were firing non-stop. We kept on asking for return of fire based on the grids passed on but eventually the fucking Major said no go

Now, my question is the following: why put these okes up there if you don't believe them, Major Asshole? And if the answer is that we were not trained to maintain the Gunners fire, then why not send someone with us. Brian Rogers had the skill, but was with Lt Coetzee at that stage. This happened every day and the Red eyes were spotted on exactly the same grids every day.

Comment from unknown:

Anyway, after five days they left Beatle and were relieved by another six guys who jumped out of the Pumas before they boarded - Jacques Puren, Pote de Villiers, Alwyn Whitfield, Jack Moolman and Natie Potgieter were some of the guys that took over.

We were called in to HQ by the fucking Major. I asked him why he didn't return fire and he absolutely crapped on me: not knowing map grids, who am I to challenge him etc. I was totally stunned as we worked together as a team and we trusted one another. I guarantee you that the most senior Recce officer would have taken me seriously on that info that we supplied and acted upon it. Not fucking Major Gunner! Most important though, I informed him that the mealie land as well as OP Beatle was a major risk. The only piece of flat land in a mountainous area and a pinnacle standing out was not to be occupied again. In short, he informed me that I was arrogant and short of contempt.

The big brass officer escorted me out and told me in so many words that he was on my side and I should just hang in there. I thought he was a gentleman, but fuck dude, who is in charge here?

Comment from unknown:

What the Major decided was that the OP was to be relieved after a shorter period of time and when Jacques Puren and coy moved out, all hell broke loose. The Cubans and MPLA were dug in and waiting for the chopper above the mealie land. As soon as the PUMA landed to pick them up, they were sitting ducks in a major ambush. Keep in mind that the process is that the fresh guys jump out, secure the PUMA and then the tired guys jump in. However, as soon as the new guys jumped out, the massive, overwhelming ambush kicked in as a fire force from the Cubans/MPLA commenced.

Remarkably, only Natie Potgieter and Pote de Villiers were wounded, but our guys were outnumbered by far. What obviously helped was the fire power of the choppers before the troop carrying Puma landed to drop the guys. Our guys were also exhausted, hungry and extremely thirsty. Of course they were not picked up and had to take refuge in the bush.

I cannot recall how many fatalities there were from an Air Force point of view. I do recall that one Puma went into the mountain and I think another was shot down as well. At least one pilot and some of his crew arrived back at our own forces after spending some time in the bush.

Comment from unknown:

When Marais and his team went back to Beatle at a later stage they counted at least 30 trenches and shelters in the mountain range above the mealie land afterwards and captured AK type sniper rifles and more).

During the ambush and their endeavour to seek safety, Malcolm Wolverson got lost and we were all worried about our lad. Thoughts of him being caught went through our minds and we all hoped he would survive – but to be honest, we expected the worst as we were way behind the enemy lines. He took a route across the mountain in a westerly/south westerly direction and got back to our forces about 10 days after the incident – well done Mally, you're a star!

Now, Major Gunner, don't you think you could have prevented this?

Comment from unknown:

On 23 December Lt Blaauw and Cpl/Sgt Aubrey Cronje received instructions to go and rescue our guys via convoy. There was a pont to the west of Beatle (20 to 30 km I guess). They were supported by four Pantser cars, an old lorry and two

Sabres. They crossed the river and on the way encountered a hut which Lt Blaauw ordered to flatten – one klap from a 90 mil and it was levelled! It didn't take long to find our guys and as stated before, wounded, hungry and thirsty. Remember, they had been ambushed the previous morning, without water, being completely outnumbered and still under threat from the enemy. We also saw a dead Cuban at a nearby hut, but did not move into the mountains at that stage. We were there to rescue the guys and get back to higher ground ASAP. We gathered them and started the journey back to the vehicles on high ground (kept 3/4s way up the mountain as we moved forward).

Des McGeer and I walked recce and we were tired and gatvol. We got to an over-hanging rock (actually two massive boulders very close to each other) and it was extremely steep around it. As I approached it, I saw what looked like a footpath in between the two boulders – rather a shoulder width alley. It led down for about two meters and then doglegged 90 degrees to the right for about four meters before you could get through the boulders. Des was right behind me and I had my rifle in my right hand to keep balance. As I turned right a fukken Cuban was sitting three meters from me with his AK in both hands and finger on the trigger, pointing it right at me as he must have heard our approach. He started shouting and opened fire on me. I was completely unbalanced and turned around at the same time and fell as it was very slippery – this fall actually saved my life. He opened once again but all the bullets went over me. I ran back and recall Aubrey Cronje shouting whether we were safe and we went forward again. However, this mother got away and there were no other Cubans in sight. We maneuvered back to the vehicles and reached the pont without any additional contacts. I have often wondered what I could have done differently. Obviously I should have had my rifle in both hands, or walked around the boulders.

Comment from unknown:

Back at camp they rested for a couple of days before being informed that they were to get up OP Beatle again escorted by a NS Lt from the gunners (Lt Prins). This time they were dropped by vehicle at the foot of the mountain range and approached Beatle from the south. Once again, it was a huge climb and halfway up the mountain a thunderstorm hit them. They took shelter and got to Beatle during daylight

I informed Lt Prins exactly where the Red-Eyes were firing from when I reported it the first time. He did his thing on the maps and at 5 o' clock they started giving it to

our guys again at exactly the same grids that I passed on initially. It turned out that the Cubans drove the red-eye vehicles into man made dugouts and fired from there. Once we were up on Beatle, Lt Prins had a wonderful time – he didn't enjoy the walk through the bush in enemy country and everything that goes with it. However, it was impressive to watch him give orders to fire – upon a hit he then redirected the canons and even got the mothers who tried to get away. It was a huge success and we stayed there for the night and were ordered back to camp the following morning. Lt Prins turned out to be a great guy and we worked extremely well together. He received a HC for this action. I remember running into him during April '76 at the Strand in Cape Town and he informed me that he was studying at Maties. I have no issue with him receiving the HC, but Major Gunner could have prevented a lot of shit if he believed me in the first place; the egotistical asshole.

John Marais recounted some of his impressions of their stay at Sa da Bandeira (September '75):

We got permission to go to the movies - Portuguese without subtitles, but we enjoyed the time out. During the break in what looked like a cafeteria, we saw two guys accompanied by the most beautiful blond and the best body in the business! Each guy took a turn undressing her, talked about what they would do to her etc. As she walked out, she stopped at the door, turned around and said: Boer se kind sit darem nou ver van die huis af – very embarrassed. We followed her and asked where she came from, also offered many apologies. She was a tough cookie though, only laughed and it turned out that she was a Dutch journalist who was following the war (at least, the start of the war at that stage).

We had fresh meat (shot a cow) for a braai at Cela; unfortunately it only happened once. We confiscated Cuban cigarettes (plain and 25 in a packet). We continuously smoked the stuff and it was normal tobacco with some green parts as well. Brian Rogers informed me recently that the green tobacco was indeed dagga – on dagga for a long time during the five months!

Pote de Villiers got hold of an artificial leather jacket (snake motive) in Sa da Bandeira. He removed the sleeves and used it throughout Savannah where ever he went. He was a tough guy with strong and well defined biceps and really looked like a Rambo!

In Sa da Bandeira a bank manager asked us for assistance. Peter Koller and I went to his house for a lovely Sunday meal - we also checked out his daughters but the lack of Portuguese did not help. He was concerned that his safe would be burgled and asked us to guard it after hours. Permission was given and we positioned ourselves at the safe. Pote was at the safe's door the whole time whilst the rest of us were taking turns exploring the town. The next morning Pote asked me to call the manager first thing as he had something to show him. To our surprise he showed the manager that he actually managed to open the safe without force and he gave the banker advice on how to secure it even better. The manager thanked us but never asked us to guard it again!

Comment from unknown:

John Marais recounted an incident when he got back home. His father asked him, somehow embarrassed, whether anything had happened on 23 December.

The reason for him asking was that my Mom, a bank manageress, could not get out of bed that morning as she was very ill with a fever. She insisted on going to work, but he got a call from the bank later in the morning asking him to fetch her as she was unable to drive her car. He brought her home and they made an appointment with the doctor for later that afternoon. He informed me that he thought she was going to pass out at any moment – she was really in bad shape. When I told him that I was nearly killed on that date when I walked into the Cuban, he started shaking and said he knew she was somehow in contact with me as by 14h00 her fever broke and she was instantly OK. He took her back to the bank and she completed her day and drove back home all by herself. By the way, we got back to the Pont just after lunch!

Just something to think about...

Alyn Whitfield was also in the action at the Beatle Hill. He remembers that the weather was overcast and it felt as though they were suspended floating on the clouds. They watched from the high vantage point as the people below went about their business. With the arrival of vehicles they called in the 5.5 cannons to take them out but there was no action from the gunners - they were either out of range or for some other reason were not being able to bring fire to bear on the enemy.

Alyn Whitfield recalls:

On the one occasion they did respond, we directed shell fire right into the camp and they scattered like ants. At this stage we called in Airburst which explodes at height sending shrapnel raining down on the enemy. We returned to the farm and another group went to the OP Post. They obviously got wise to the fact that they were being observed and correctly deduced that it must have come from OP Beatle. It must have been at this stage that they laid down an ambush and attacked our guys as they came down to relieve the OP Post.

This is where Natie got shot through both arms. Back at the farm 9 base camp we were notified that our guys were in trouble and me and a group of guys were flown in by Puma helicopter to go and help out. I was first in the door sitting behind the gunner manning the 50 Browning. As the chopper came in to land we came under fire. I believe the gunner was shot in the shoulder and at the same time returned fire and gave the signal for us to get the hell out of the chopper. Fortunately the chopper was facing the action on the starboard side. I was first to hit the ground, stood up to grab the heavy B25 radio. I am told that a RPG rocket passed through between the chopper and the ground. I was completely oblivious to this as the chopper rotors and machine gun fire drowned out any whoosh it might have made. Had this hit the chopper ... With all the guys now out the chopper the first thing I remember was hugging the ground and getting rid of the extra weight of the twin 60 mm Mortar container converted into a water container.

Comment from unknown:

The Puma helicopter took off leaving them right in the thick of the ambush. The chopper was unable to make it back to base and had to make an emergency landing but luckily the crew made it back safely. The Puma was accompanied by an Alouette helicopter (for casevac purposes) but the pilot took a shot in his foot and they had to abort the casevac.

From here the memory is hazy. I think we stuck it out the night and went back up to the base of the ambush the following morning. I counted 19 or 21 ambush positions where the Cuban had lain in ambush. They must have scattered when they came under fire from the Chopper 50 Browning as they left a helluva lot of gear in position. Amongst this gear was the abandoned RPG and rockets. I retrieved a pair of Russian binoculars, aluminium water bottle and dixi with belt and grenade pouch and surprisingly a US Marines knife. I still have these items today.

We had radioed back the previous day a sitrep. Evacuation by helicopter was out of the question. Lt Blaauw and the boys were coming to fetch us by road. Making our way to the rendezvous point, I recall coming across two dead Cubans. Maggots had already filled the eye sockets and mouth gorging themselves.

40 YEARS LATER:

I am a member of my local church, New Life in Christ Fellowship, Daggafontein, Springs where I am part of the worship team as a Drummer. Our Pastor, Johan Haywood, had also been in the military. Of course I had recounted some of my experiences with him, telling him about OP Beatle and what had happened there with one of our guys being wounded through both arms. He said that he knew of a person that had this experience. Later at a men's weekend get together arranged by Johan, Natie Potgieter and I were introduced to each other by Johan. Imagine my expectation and surprise when it turned out to be Natie from OP Beatle. It was an emotional experience. Natie and I recently attended the Parabat reunion at Hartebeespoort Dam on 25 October 2014 where we met up with Sakkie Marais and Johan Marais.

OP Smokey as experienced by Ewald Jansen van Rensburg.
(In a very short ops during Savannah)
Ewald again on an account by Flip Welman:
A few years ago, Flip Welman described an event where a few guys (eight plus) of our company had been involved in. At a reunion Piet du Preez spoke about this in the early hours of the morning, as I made the decision to get behind the true story and asked the questions. Luck was on my side and I could have a conversation with the officer of spec forces (Maj. Frank Bestbier) who was directly involved in looking for volunteers for this "rescue" operation. With this information, we now have a very good picture of what actually happened. However, there is a loose thread and that is, the role that played by a medic in this whole process. Piet du Preez had the impression that the medic also was a member of the bats, but a later intake than us. Everyone at the reunion agreed that the medic should also have earned a medal. *Here's the story.*

BACKGROUND Operation Savannah: The date, the beginning of December 1975 and the place, Cela. It is about 600km north of the southwest border.

Six weeks before the South African Defence Force task forces with names like Zulu and Foxbat's started their campaign against the MPLA's military wing, Fapla and at times against the Cubans who supported Fapla. Although sometimes experiencing up to eight contacts per day the task forces advanced at staggering speed northwards. The rainy season had begun and crossing rivers later in the campaign would only be done via bridges. FAPLA and the Cubans began blowing up bridges and this, combined with the politics of the day, bedevilled the advance towards Luanda.

THE EVENTS: The road north of Cela to Quibala is hilly and Corporal. Andre Jeffries (Diedies) of 1 Reconnaissance Commando received instructions to establish an observation post near the soon to be famous, Bridge 14. Sources differ, some noted that the bridge was 18km and others 25km north of the front line at Cela. Either way, the area was under FAPLA / Cuban control and it was very risky to move in the area. Yet Diedies with a protective element consisting of FNLA forces (some sources say 15 men) and we now know that there was also a medic accompanying them, went to the vicinity of the bridge. On the 2nd of December 1975, Diedies established an observation post on a mountain near the bridge. Some confusion exists whether it was on Top hat or Hippo hill, as both give excellent views of surrounding terrain.

Seven km south of the bridge the road towards Cela passed over a mountain pass and at the foot of the hills turned left in a northerly direction over wooded areas and ploughed fields. Hippo Hill was situated before the bridge on the left and just across the bridge, on the left (west) was Top Hat. Diedies did very well on his OP and his instructions for the artillery resulted in the destruction of several enemy targets which were erased successfully. The enemy soon realized that the accurate fire was as a result of an OP and began to send out patrols to locate Diedies and his crew, even making use of helicopters to do this.

Some sources say all of the 15 FNLA troops deserted or refused to go along with Diedies to establish the OP, but it was more likely that they left, when they saw the helicopters and patrols of FAPLA becoming a real threat, that their food supply was gone and the radio's batteries were flat. Diedies then sent his medic with a message to HQ back at Cela. This medic was not a coward who had fled, as he later offered to act as a guide for the relief effort. From the available data, I think that Diedies was under the impression that he would be relieved and the OP post would be manned. HQ however realised how grave the situation was and decided to send out a rescue patrol, to escort Diedies out of danger, guided by the medic.

By now his radio's battery was dead, and when the rescue patrol came under fire, I think that this gave Diedies the opportunity to vacate his OP unnoticed and run to safety. Andre Jeffries would be rewarded for his heroism with the first of the two honorus crux medals. Apart the medic the rescue patrol all consisted of members of C Coy 1 Parachute Battalion, 1975 intake.

The following account of the events is by Flip Welman who was part of the patrol, with some commentary of another member of the patrol, Piet du Preez:

It is unfortunate that this story was first told after more than thirty years, because there is certainly information which has become blurred or lost over time.

By 12 December 1975 we had completed two years of military service, and were ordered to guard the bridge over the Rio Queve river, just outside Cela. We had just finished our two years' service, but there was no hint of us going home. From time to time we went on protection details with Recces.

On 11 December, we were informed by Major Frank Bestbier that a recce group about 30km north of the front line was trapped and that we were to go and rescue them. He said that once we had completed this mission, we could go home with the first available 'Flossie' (C130). What was so difficult about that decision, quick in and out and home!

Late afternoon we (I remember only a few names) Groover, Piet, Carl, Dick the Medic, Theo and I think Daan Schutte and, oh yes, me and Jan Recce. I remember Jan Recce because he started getting the jitters and shakes every time the Unimog stopped. And also I remember Pokkels, because he is the guy who worked with Groover and had to turn back when Groover suffered food poisoning. We were taken to the frontline in armoured vehicles to wait for dark. There I bumped into Piet Swanepoel, a cousin of mine. He was an armoured car driver, who in tears told me about their terrible experiences and warned me not to go northwards from their position; it was far too dangerous. We were wearing the same shoes and uniform as the Angolan army. We were ordered to move north, and not to walk on the dirt roads, as they were registered by the Russian red eye rocket launchers. If anything moved on these roads they automatically drew fire. (As we passed we could see the craters left by red eye rockets exploding)

Piet Du Preez:

We also packed our kit as light as possible. I had a packet of "doggies" and one other ration. The rest, as far as I know, had water and ammunition, because we assumed that we would be back soon. Just quickly rescue the guys and come back, no long stories! The medic has also carried his medical bag. I just want to take my hat off for that Medic, he had slipped away from the reconnaissance group to come for help, got help and went back with us to show us where his trapped comrades were and then again returned to safety with us. In total he walked at least 120 km in two days and three nights, WITHOUT REST AND FOOD. These are the types of men who fought that war but probably never received a medal or any recognition and believe me, he earned it.

We left when it was dark. We walked on the right side of the road, with difficulty as it was raining hard and had been for a long time. This and the long, wet grass was a problem. So we decided to walk on the road in order to progress quickly to the mountain, where the men were trapped, hoping to arrive there while it was still dark. After all we'd hear shooting, and have enough time to scatter! We had not been walking for long when Groover van Huysteen started to get terrible stomach cramps. Earlier in the day in his wisdom he had decided to cook a tin of bully beef on a red-hot fire, just like that in the tin. He had to turn around right there and be taken back. Pokkels had to accompany him back, and he was sulking, I remember it well.

To measure our progress, we had two scouts walking on either side of the road and they had to pace off 1 000 steps. In this way, we knew that we had walked about a kilometre each time. Sometime during the night it was Carl's and my turn to wear the scout's shoes. The road went over a hill and descended into a valley before us. As we started to move over the hill we heard a bird whistle, a sound easily mimicked by a person. 'Sounds like an ambush!'

We immediately stopped and the men, who had been walking in single file, staying close enough to see each other, were signalled to go down. Right there and then we started writing our last letters home to our mother and father and brother and sister, especially written to our friends' sisters, to put into our breast pockets in case we were shot dead right there. [Last sentence is bullshit, but sounded pretty cool if you want to make a movie out of this].

Carl and I met in the middle of the road trying to decide what we should do. We could not allow the entire section to walk into an ambush. We decided to carefully walk ahead and see what happened.

At every step we took, the birds continued to whistle. By now we were convinced that we had walked through the kill zone without a shot being fired. Slightly sweaty we came together and surmised that the people who had laid the ambush, allowed us to pass through and were waiting for the rest of the guys to walk into the kill zone.

We decided that each of us would cover a side of the road and go back to the section through the field, zigzagging as we did so; hopefully that by doing so, we would uncover the ambushers. It was a difficult part of the walk, every step you take you have to use your rifle barrel to move grass or a bush, anticipation the sound of a shot at any moment. Understand this, very few soldiers would do that, what a privilege to walk with such men. Returning to the others, we decided to shut that that bird up by throwing stones into the trees. Everyone threw what stones we could lay our hands on into the trees, but nothing took flight. After all this racket had ended we realized that there was no ambush at all. The escapade had cost us at least half an hour and we felt stupid. We continued through the night without mishap.

By 4 pm, we reached the place where we thought we should be. We had counted 30 km, and in front of us was a huge mountain, which was as described as us, possibly the mountain where the other men were trapped. We decided to lay low until dawn and then work out our best modus operandi.

We had gone to ground for a couple of minutes, when we heard a short burst or two of rifle fire coming from the mountainside, and then it was quiet. Someone said it was definitely R1 shots. Little did we realise that the trapped men themselves had fired these shots and by so doing had managed to escape the mountain? We did not know this and still thought that we should rescue the !

By daylight we saw that the mountain was indeed the one we had been looking for. Between us and the mountain was a rocky outcrop which was about 10 per cent of the height of the mountain. We decided to go out there and to observe the area and also, establish a spot where we would lie low for the day. We moved in single file to the rocky outcrop and below its outcrops we were well protected. The medic who returned on his own to look for help, a man of steel, slithered up a sloping rock and with his binoculars, began scanning the mountain.

The crack of a sniper bullet passing over his head and smacking against the rock behind him, had him sliding down the rock as quickly as a lizard would, leaving his binoculars lying still there on the rocks. Nonetheless, we had to get onto the mountain, and decided to do so in single file walking as far as possible from each other. Between the rocky outcrop and the mountain - a distance of about 600 meters - was a plant which looked like a potato plant which about half the height of a man. I remember a lot of weeds and grass, too, about halfway a man's height too I would say.

Carl and I were right at the back of the queue. We were just about halfway towards the potato plant, when a single rifle round from the mountain flew between us. Everyone fell flat and started shouting at each other, asking who fired the shot. After a while we all realize that the rifleman was somewhere on the mountain. We decided to get up, walk a few steps and try to see if we could see where the shot came from. We had walked for about five meters, when we heard the treble of automatic rifle fire and hit the deck so hard, that the dust hung in a cloud above us! And we knew then- this was the party to which we had been invited..

We leopard crawled until we lay right in front of the mountain, each shooting 5 shots into the mountain, with eyes wide open to see if we could see anyone. It was then as if someone had opened the taps fully and the roar of rifles could be heard aimed in our direction. That's when "buddy-buddy" back to the outcrop. The amount of bullets that were fired at us was overwhelming. I was running right behind Theo (I think so!) when he disappeared in an instant. I was still trying to figure out if my friend had been shot, when I fell ass-over-head into a hole, and just above me I could see the potato plant through the opening. On the other side of the hole I saw Theo sitting on his arse with his eyes closed. Neither of us was hurt and we were now out of range of the bullets flying about. My only comment to Theo was that we could stay here for the whole day as no one knows about us - we can get away in the dark.

He agreed and as he said it, the bullets started clipping the leaves above our heads with regularity. We realize that the height of the mountain allowed the enemy to see us. Somewhat distressed we realized that we have to get out! In the first 2-second gap between bullets, we flew out of the hole and ran as fast as we could back towards to the rocky outcrop. I remembered that there was a reasonably sized clump of bushes between the potato field and the rocky outcrop. We thought that if we got into the bushes we would be safe!! Crap! You could hear the sound of mortars incoming left and right or right down on you, and right before us they started to drop mortar bombs onto the bush we heading towards.

I and another guy shouted at the same time 'this one's coming straight at us!' as we took cover. I took cover next to a tree about 8 to 10 inches in diameter and the closer the bombs fell the flatter we lay convinced that the next one was meant for us and we prayed! The next bomb exploded so close to us where we lay that masses of soil, leaves and branches rained down onto us. At that moment we loudly cheered and shouted 'that missed' and flew up to run further. It was then with shock, that I noticed that the tree next to me was missing from knee height up! My second observation was the filthy hole that the bomb ripped out of the soft earth, about 6 meters away from me.

And, guess what, my buddy screaming at me 'here comes the next one!' We hit the ground and lay flat and heard the bomb coming in. After the bomb exploded, this time at least a little further on, we flew, 'broke several speed records for 50m and then again collapsed.

And so we were pinned down for hours it seemed, before we reached the outcrop. I knew that they we could no longer be seen because their bombs were being dropped speculatively on the other side of the outcrop.

Everyone is arriving and Daan Schutte's legs give in, he stoops and begins to vomit from the tension. Someone grabs him by the arm and we run the last 30 meters from the shelter of the rocky hill.

Pale and uncertain, we instructed the signaller to radio HQ and to call in a rescue chopper to get us out of there quickly. Now, we were sitting on the outcrop and we decide is at least safe for a while, and we need to radio in to explain our situation.

We then decided that we could not leave the guys stuck on the mountain and had to come up with another plan, to go back, perhaps with via a detour and complete the mission. Corporal Welman, the signal officer on the other end of the radio, had some interesting information to tell us. He tells us that the enemy have an entire company of men on the mountain, with armoured vehicles hidden to the left the mountain in a coffee plantation. We know where the place is and also that behind us, between the rocky hill and forest, a track ran that at any time could allow a vehicle to be rapidly deployed to trap us. He also tells us that the men who were trapped managed to escape at 4 o'clock in the morning by shooting their way out of the trap and running away from the mountain.

They were on their way back, and we should get back to our lines via the shortest route. There is no way that he could send a helicopter, it is too dangerous. When I realized that we had walked all night, very little food, and we have to walk back at speed...

I believe that everyone prayed like me and begged for angels to escort us out. There was no time for talk. Everyone ate what little they could, I shared my dog biscuits with the other guys and we moved one by one out of the potato land and into the forest. Carl and I are the last under the outcrop. When the last man disappears into the forest, it is Carl's turn. While he was on his way, I realize that this is not so comfortable to be alone. I still think of the uncomfortable feeling when the mortars were being dropped.

Suddenly Carl turns and sprints back to me. Before he could get to me a mortar explodes in the place where he was when he turned! We decided as a man, that this single file thing doesn't work and together we ran so hard we could into the forest behind the other guys.

Once there, everyone realized that those Cubans are going to mortar us again so we begin to "dog-leg" all the time. Run, do not stand still. Best way to get out. We started walking southwards in single file and with dogged determination. As the mortars are fired, we begin to understand the pattern of fire and by dog legging we avoid being killed. It was not long, when a man whose turn it was to carry the radio, sits against a tree and begins to cry, refusing to carry the radio. We explain very nicely that he can enjoy his stay in Angola, we are going home and he changes his mind quickly.

I remember that I told Piet at one point that I could carry on walking like that for a week, the wonder of adrenaline! As the day progressed, I became aware of a few things that I initially did not even realize. A mortar had landed close to us and we hit the deck and I realized that when I got up, I have to pick up my rifle. But where did I leave it? When I focus, the reality of what is happening to us is quite shocking. The next time a mortar approached, I watched everyone's actions and saw a shocking sight; men running around in circles throwing down their weapons, lying on their side in the foetal position. A man stood up, picked up his gun and walked on as if nothing had happened. Due to the rain, and the resultant soft soil, a lot of bombs fell near us and penetrated the soil deeply resulting in less shrapnel.

There were times when hot gravel and bits of shrapnel fell onto us. A bomb demolished a tree and another left a big hole in the ground just behind the tree. We had risen and gone ahead, scratching the ground for shrapnel souvenirs, some were too hot to pick up! We ran together for the whole day. The decision was to run until we could no longer see the mountain because logically they would then not be able to see us.

Late afternoon, I guess about 15h00, we were at a place where we could not see the mountain. By the way that they were dropping bombs haphazardly, we knew that they no longer knew where we were.

We decided to lay low until dark, and then get back on the road to move back quickly. As we lay there in silence I slapping a bug on Dick Roux's raincoat. We got such a fright that everyone raised weapons ready for a firefight.

Everyone was angry with Dick, he just smiled.

At one point we heard a helicopter approaching. Initially we were very excited because we were surely going to be picked up and flown out of danger. After a short while we realized with shock that it was approaching us from behind, from the north!

We were lying in the field and in the open, with really no chance against a helicopter. What could we do? Our team got ready to shoot the pilot as he came near. I was lying down and getting to my feet, looked above the grass and waited, I saw the helicopter for a fraction of a second, and then it turned back!! I do not know what would have happened if the pilot had flown towards us for further 5 seconds. The pilot probably did not think we could have progressed so far so quickly.

It was not fully dark when we hit the road back towards our lines. As we started walking again, I realised that I was really tired and very hungry. That night someone had a terrible fright just behind me, I think it was Janna. Our nerves were still pretty shattered and the next second a firefly passing about three meters to left of us decided to switch on his "hazards". The reader needs to really understand, that we were well drilled in "quick kill" we had been trained by firing thousands of rounds with deadly speed and accuracy.

But when that firefly switched on his light we had our weapons trained on him faster than we ever did in any other situation! We realized what it was just in time and Mr. Firefly was not shot! A few of the guys directed a few choice words at him and I will never know if he understood what they were saying.

We had earmarked a row of eucalyptus trees as a spot where we had to stop to set up a radio link. Beyond the trees, was where we had waited the night before and we were afraid that the FNLA forces ahead would shoot us. (In my opinion it was unlikely that they were in the front line, they were cowards. They ran away like crazy every time there was a contact with the enemy).

Once there, we get the message that there is no vehicle to fetch us, we have to wait until the next day. It was there that I learnt what real swearing was all about. It started raining, we were cold, wet, tired and hungry. We found the best possible shelter and ended up spooning each other as we lay in the wet in order to stay warm.

Not a very manly thing to do but we had to somehow stay warm. It was not a great night. (Funny how in moments of anxiety, but also moments of "comfort", you remember these situations. I remember those two hours lying behind the back of big Dick Roux, I cherish that bit of heat under those circumstances to this day)

The next morning we were ready to be picked up, only to be told we have to walk the last kilometre! When we arrived at the armoured cars, we were told to walk to Cela, there were no vehicles to take us there. Once again we swore until the air was blue. We still had about 10 km to walk! While we are standing and arguing and about to start staging a protest along comes an armoured car with a broken barrel and gets permission to go Cela for repairs. We boarded that vehicle and sat on that thing like a bunch of ticks, refusing to walk another step.

Not long after that, we are on a Flossie heading back home....

Today I know our Creator has a purpose for each of us. He protected us in what I think was in almost impossible situations of a whole day under mortar fire, and none of us had a scratch. (I also remember when we were back in Cela for about an hour, we submitted a report of the events to the Maj. Frank Bestbier.

For the rest of the day we made our food and rested. The most striking thing, however, was that the men were deathly silent. Occasionally if you looked at one of your guys' in the eyes, they just shook their heads.

That night there was a little bit of here and there but the guys were subdued and I think it was just to get over the shock. A day or so later, as we stood in a queue for food or rations someone dropped something with a loud bang and the next moment I dived for cover! Seconds or later I realized what I had done and stood up and guess what, the 7 men who were with me at the "party", had also sought cover. We just looked at each other and started laughing, we were no longer 18 and 19 year old boys we were now veterans.

I have to say here, ALL GLORY TO GOD.

That night I heard an atheist say, *"I'm not so convinced now that God does no exist".*

This, my friend, my version.

OP Smoky 2. As experienced by Mark Coetzee:

I got orders to take an OP patrol out into no man's land out into the plains of the frontline north of Cela and east of Ebo with Quibala in the distance. We were being hammered every time our patrols went out so we knew that they had an op and suspected it to be on a mountain code named Smoke Top which if I recall was east of another hill called Top Hat.

We got orders around 12 pm and I briefed the guys that we would go out as one section and I chose Pete's and left the other section at base. They would come and relieve us in five or six days' time, depending in what the situation required and to bring us either rations or radio batteries.

We had a walk of about 20 km to get to Smoky and we had to pass our own forces' artillery which was entrenched about 15km from the front; that was as far as they could reach.

We got a lift out with a ration truck and the dirt road was quite wet and slippery, but we got to them around four, debussed and got the patrol together. I went to see the officer in charge to let him know I would be leaving shortly and that I would be using the road as a navigation tool as it was getting dark. I would stay on the left of the road and keep walking until I got to position or until I had covered enough ground.

We set off and I glanced back at the area and took a couple of trees as land marks and got an idea of the general lay of the land. When we came out again I would then have a fair idea as to where they would be so as to warn them I was coming out and that they must warn the guards. Considering we had not washed in a couple of weeks and all had a motley accumulation of uniforms that we had stolen, taking the camouflage ones that were really good, as well as having long hair and beards, we could have been mistaken for Cubans. One rule was that if we went into no man's land we took our caps off so that we could identify own forces on that basis.

They were still a good couple of kilometres from Smoky so Mark decided to stop for the night and proceed again at first light. Lo and behold, their worst nightmare got them - the rain started coming down and the red ants found them. They had waged war on the ants in every place they had come across them and had seen them 500mm thick on a sheep they had just skinned and walking 100mm wide on a path. They would take cordite sticks which the gunners used to get range in the 5.5 inch cannon and lay them along the ant path, set it alight and incinerate them all.

We had had about two hours sleep and I awoke with the bastard things all over me and when you kill one it sends the pheromone to the rest and they all start biting; you have to strip down completely and kill each one but first you have to move all you kit cause otherwise you just get reinfested; it is a real fuck up and you can't swear and curse the mothers as you in no man's land. Once we were all cleaned of them I decided to carry on the patrol; by now it was getting close to dawn.

They did not have topographical maps as one would in a normal military situation because there weren't any. We had road maps that we had taken from the petrol stations and shops in the towns we had occupied. I had just marked on a map where Smoky was in relation to the road as we had been able to see Smoky for a good long way away.

As we walked on quietly we were sodden from our waist down from the wet grass and low branches and when we got closer to the mountain, we crossed the road to start making our way up the slopes of Smoky. The sun was up and I had Pete in front with another troop then myself when Pete turned round and gave the thumbs down sign indicating enemy.

'Where, Pete?'

As he is slightly up slope from me I notice a movement past him and see an enemy move and have a piss about 100m away. Pete indicates down to the road. I look and sure enough, there is an enemy patrol walking slowly in single file up the road towards our lines. They had not come to our cross-over point yet and I was nervous that they would see the track as it was still muddy.

'How many?' I whisper to Pete.

'Ten-twelve, I think.'

It is quite difficult to see through the trees obscuring the road. I decide to ask the armour to come up and give some speculative fire into the bush because if they get to our cross-over point we're really compromised.

'Zulu 30, this is Zulu 21. Send armour up the road ASAP as I have enemy visual and need to stop them coming round the mountain and surrounding us.'

'Affirmative, have got a patrol on its way towards you. Their call sign is November 20.'

I get the armour car commander on the radio and explain that I want some heavy machine gun fire into the trees and then some 60mm mortars into the plains about 50-100 m either side of the road and I will direct fire as they continue. Now the plan was that I would get the patrol away from our feet then use the armour to lob some mortars on their OP and so we would could get some cover and take in a position of our own.

'Nov 20, this is Zulu 21. Do you copy?'

Silence.

I look at the battery indicator light and it's flat. Fuck the thing must have got water in it. I change batteries and make contact but these batteries fade as well. Change again. I can hear the commander keep asking what is happening and as soon as I transmit it fades. Fuck, what now? I see the Eland 90 and 60's turn around and start heading back to our lines.

'Pete, come over here. Tell all the guys to get cover. I'm gonna see if I can get the artillery onto their OP.'

I change channels and raise the art commander but very faintly. But before I can explain what I want from a ranging shot the radio goes dead. Now what the fuck to do? It's about 10 am and the enemy has been shot at and must have heard the cars leave. So they would be coming out of hiding as well as the OP about 100m away. Every one stays down and I crawl over to Pete and Vermeulen the medic.

'Pass the word no one is to move; camouflage yourselves very well in case these fucks send someone on a recce and stay put, and then come back here so we can work out a plan.'

This all happens and Pete is back.

'Right, only one way and that is you have to leave at last light and go back to fetch spare batteries and get these charged and then come back in five days with the other relief patrol. Who do you want to take?'

I'm left with Du Plooy, Visagie and a medic, Swart, with Vermeulen going back with Pete and then to lead the next patrol back while Pete gets some rest. I point their Op out to Pete and he looks at me and grins.

'Bit close, hey?'

'Ja, if you fart we'll be heard.'

They waited the rest of the day in the blazing sun, keeping as low a profile as possible. Luckily the terrain was longish grass with boulders so cover was not too bad with a big coffee plantation at the base through which the road ran on which they had come. Mark reiterated his orders of being back on day five.

'Good luck,' and they filter off into the dark. Now we can stand up for the first time in the day cause it is pitch black with no moon and I talk to the three other guys. We make a plan about who is gonna be my buddy and I get the Medic as we always work in buddy system. Generally as the LT you get the Platoon Sgt if he's around or the radio operator. The Sgt, du Plooy, was a big solid Afrikaans guy would never bitch about a thing; the radio man, Visagie, was a *dominee*'s son and prone to get a bit excited when things got hairy but also solid dude. My choice was the Medic, Swart, who was short and thickset with a sense of duty around him and one of those non-flappable guys as I'm sure his training at 3 Military Hospital would have made him.

The next day at first light Mark made the decision to stay in position so they would have visual on their Op and note their movements. Funny, when you think you're not under threat you take things for granted. They saw these guys take out their blankets and flap them loudly, thinking no doubt that when the armour left so did the infantry. Mark's men could hear their voices and hear them report on the radios for their sitreps.

It is extremely taxing on not to be able to stand up and move around and if you want to shit you got to do it right there next to your buddy and bury it under a rock close by. No cooking, smoking or talking and by the time night fall came we were exhausted and wanted to stand up and move around a bit. Nothing happened that first day but that evening we heard movement in the road below us and then digging so we assumed that they were laying mines. I made notes on the time and approximate area and length that it took to dig, when at around 11 there was a huge explosion and some screaming as one of them must have fucked up. We slept intermittently that night and at first light took up our positions again of watching. I was trying to work out a plan to see if I could get to their OP and take them out and having to do it quietly but realized that it would compromise our position cause if their HQ got no response from their OP, they would send someone to investigate.

On day three Mark decided to take a recce patrol further up the mountain and at 3-ish with the sun in their eye he and Swart crawled out from their rock and made their way up and away from the enemy but the terrain was too steep and more exposed so they turned around and went back to their hide. Nothing happened that night other than the quietness of a mountain and eating cold cans and really wanting a cup of tea but not risking the possibility of lighting an Ezbit stove as the smell carries a long way. Day four was bright and they were feeling the tension of lying in one place and the grass was starting to get a bit trampled. I was looking through the binos over the plain and in the distance saw some vehicle movement. As they got closer I saw they were four BTM 21 armoured personnel carriers with a machine gun in the turret and eight men in each. When they got to about 2 km away the men debussed and spread out in extended line.

I say to Swart, '*Kyk daar, wat dink jy?*'

He looked and nudged Du Plooy who snatched the binos away and said '*Fok my.*'

Visagie burst out, "*Ek wil sien; ek wil sien,*' and took his turn.

All this time I'm trying desperately to remain calm and think this one through; do we split when they get to the bottom of the mountain and then let the relief patrol walk into them or do we wait till tomorrow morning and then split at first light? Fuck, I start praying now. 'Dear God, help me get through this. Give me the strength and wisdom, please God. Please help here.' My heart is going flat out and

I'm fighting the panic down; a thought goes through my mind, 'I can run and I'll probably get away but will they? Duty calls and I'm responsible here to these men and if we die then so be it.'

I find it very difficult to concentrate and think of a plan; it's like when you get into a fist fight it sort of goes noisy in your ears and you've got to force your mind to start working because mostly one wants to run. I look at the three guys and they ask, '*Wat gaan ons doen, Loot?*'

We wait till night and we'll take it from there.

Well, as the extended line got closer and closer so did the panic and fear, building up to thought of capture and interrogation and what am I doing here now? Should I not have left when the batteries failed? Jesus, Fuck; the fear, the gnawing cold dread of death and knowing here comes a huge amount of shit. But at the same time not showing it to the troops and explaining quietly that we will wait for Pete's patrol and then duck and take them back or assess the situation tonight, but we must be calm. As it got darker so the enemy patrol got closer till they were in the trees below we and we lost sight of them.

'Pack all your stuff and get ready to rock and roll at any time if the shit hits the fan. Drink some water and eat now because I've got no idea what is going to happen.'

At around 8-ish Visagie says he can hear some movement in the bush below us and I send him and Du Plooy to check it out as it might just be Pete's relief patrol.

'*Nee, Loot, dis die veiand! Ons kan hulle nie verstaan nie en hulle maak te veel geraas. Hulle neem stellings in.*'

OK, well that sorts it for me; I'm going at first light as I have to give the relief patrol as much time as possible because if they walk into this then they're fucked. We did not sleep much that night even though we were dog tired and the strain of the fear makes you exhausted, and at 4-ish I said, 'Let's go.'

Mark took the lead, then the medic, then other two. He went as slowly as he could down the slope and into the coffee plantation, walking very slowly and placing each foot with care because at this time of the morning it was very, very still. A rustle up front; I put my hand up and we can only just make each other out. I indicate enemy in front and turn around and go to the left, hear something similar, back track and it's getting lighter by the minute. I start heading back up the steeper part of the plantation and hear some sleeping bag scratch and a rifle belt drag on a rock. I edge forward cause it looks like we are surrounded and this is going to have to break out and shooting when '*Bon kedn ifhjjoaaj!*' a challenge in a foreign language. I look at the sound and see a face looking at me from 10 m away protected by a rock and drop down and say, '*Vyand voor, volg my.*'

I go left towards the rock and I hear scuffling and murmurs and bushes been pushed around but I keep going with Swart behind me and the other two coming. There is loud talking on their side of the rock so I come round with rifle ready; up to the left on higher ground I see two figures turn and raise rifles. Instinct takes over and the rifle comes to bear sight on the one on the right, slightly lower and I pull. He goes down in a flash, like someone has hit him with a hammer. I shift to the next one and pull another shot. He drops but gets up and starts running towards us; he is 25 meters away and he is shouting. I'm shouting to my guys, 'Let's run!' and we start towards him and our paths collide with him tripping and coming past us. He's bleeding but has lost his rifle and is two meters from me and I bring the rifle to bear but don't pull but keep shouting to my guys, 'let's run as they are gonna put mortars on us.' We zig-zag, run as hard, as fast as we can run, and I have to keep slowing down to wait for the guys cause they're not as fast as me.

The mortars start as I thought they would and they are way off target so we catch our breath and keep walking in an easterly direction, back to our lines, stopping every so often to make sure we are not being followed as they will pick up our track soon enough.

We get to the stream and I tell everyone to fill up because we were a bit low on water and gulped it down now.

'*Het jy daai skoot gesien?*' I ask Swart.

He grins and says '*Ja, Loot; mooi geskiet.*'

I still do not know why I asked that question. Was it to get some kind of affirmation that I had just killed a man or what? I was hyped up on the escape but felt that we were not out of the woods yet. Then there was an almighty fire fight and I reckoned they had walked into each other and we laughed. Little did they know that it was actually Pete's patrol that had come back and when they heard the shots going off earlier they had decided that we were in shit and pressed forward only to come into one of our own patrols. They beat a retreat as they were only a ten-man patrol and did not know what they were up against.

We had by now continued walking and kept the road on our right and were in about 30m so we could just see the road and walked for about six hours. At round midday I came onto the road and thought I recognized the area from our drop off point, where the artillery were supposed to be. We crossed the road and started looking around; then we found the tracks and the cigarette butts and cans and realized they had gone. Now what?

We made tea and it was wonderful, sweet hot tea after cold tins for five days was really welcome. Swart says, '*Loot, ek het Vermeulen se sak gedrop want dit was te veel toe ons begin hardloop.*'

'*Wel, daars niks wat ons kan nou maak.*'

'*Maar wat van sy kamera?*

Now we were forbidden to take cameras but he had slipped one in and it is a pity cause there must have been some good shots but worst of all they would show that we were Para's and in the SADF.

Mark had decided there was nothing to do about that. He was more worried that, although our front line had moved back, he and his men could quite possibly walk into an ambush of our own forces.

With no coms with them who knows what lay ahead. I decided to walk on the road as we were far enough from the front. I made sure we had no caps on and spread the guys out on either side of the road. We started off and just kept trudging, wondering where all this was going to end. After probably three hours I saw an Eland 90mm in the distance coming towards us and behind it the rest of the troop of armoured cars. I told the guys to take cover and I stood in the road with my rifle in the air and waited. The armoured car stopped about 200m away and I noticed the turret move to line the machine gun up on me.

'Please see that I'm a South African,' I kept thinking but knowing that unless they hear me they will not know because we looked like Cubans. It was a stalemate for about a minute and I'm hoping that it was because they were on the radio trying to identify who I was. The hatch opens and I shout in Afrikaans, '*Dis Loot Coetzee van Valskerm Battlejon.*'

A head pops out and the car commander shouts back, '*Is jy OK?*'

Relief as I realize I ain't gonna get the wrath of a Browning machine gun. '*Kom uit manne,*' I say to the guys in the grass. We walk slowly to the cars and talk to them. We catch a ride back with them and when I get back to the lines I went off to the OC and reported in and wanted to know about my relief patrol. They went out last night, he informs me. It then dawns on me that it must have been them that got into the firefight. The OC also says that they had to mobilize a whole bunch of my guys to go out to a chopper that had been shot down so had delayed my relief patrol.

* * *

Chapter Twenty: **White vision mind fuck**

"In the daylight we know what's gone is gone.
But at night it's different.

Nothing gets finished, not dying, not mourning;"

Margaret Atwood - Morning in the Burned House

They walked until the sun was low in the east and one of the recces signalled that they should go down. There were only five of them, three paratroopers and two recces and they were about 30km behind Cuban lines. They moved in a clockwise arc and back-tracked parallel to the spoor they had left. They went down silently and Kevin and Andy lay down facing their incoming tracks. If anyone was tracking them they would walk straight into an ambush.

They lay in a ragged row Andy, Kevin and a recce facing the spoor, the other two facing backwards in case someone approached them from behind. They lay silently, listening to the sounds of the African bush. No lions, no hyenas just the sound of the millions of insects in the brush around them. Between the Portuguese settlers and the black populace any vestige of wildlife, wildlife of any substance, had long ceased to exist; butchered like most of Africa's wildlife. The more Kevin thought of it the more pissed off he became so he stopped thinking about it. He had begun to do that more and more, uncomfortable thoughts just pushed to the back of the mind, so that he could stop thinking about them.

They lay and watched the sun set, a red orb flickering through the trees slowly washing into orange.

Red in the night is the shepherd's delight;
Red in the morning is the shepherds warning.

Tendrils of black flowed over everything until it had driven even the slightest hint of grey away. The moon had not risen and the night was soon as black as ink. They had eaten in the late afternoon and Kevin still had the aftertaste of tinned Vienna's in the back of his mouth.

He whispered to Andy, 'I hate Owampo *piele*'.

He heard a faint chuckle; it always amused them to think that tinned Vienna's were nicknamed Owambo cocks, bloody army food!

Kevin crept into his sleeping bag, pulling the groundsheet over his head, his second wife in bed with him. He moved her away slightly as her magazine dug into his ribs and soon fell asleep to the sound of thousands of mosquitos, trying their damndest to get to him.

He'd learnt a long time ago to sleep that way, covered from head to foot, a small hole blocked by a net scarf to keep the little bastards out.

They had been trained to set up temporary bases when patrolling, a string stretched from man to man; standing guard in turns throughout the night. In a real war they had learnt that if you move right and do right you can sleep right.

So no strings, no standing guard and he was relieved to see that the recces did the same.

Fuck, thought Kevin, perhaps he should have joined the recces…but four years in the army, fuck that!

He woke once to the sound of a bird flapping its wings desperately in the trees. The rest of the bush was deadly, cotton-wool silent. Then he fell asleep again almost instantly.

The light was white; it penetrated through the groundsheet, lanced through the netted breathing hole and into his brain. Kevin's eyes were shut and he screwed them tightly closed, but the light was white and intense. Nothing could shield it. Kevin looked and could see the shapes of the others. Strangely the light didn't illuminate them.

They were only black bumps on the ground. Kevin stretched his arm out and shook Andy. He did not respond. He stood up, blinded by the light and his feet tangled in his sleeping bag, he fell over Andy and landed on top of the recce, who didn't stir.

Kevin opened his mouth to scream and it was soundless, the light reached in and sucked the sound out of his lungs.

He was drawn to the light, inexorably like a moth to a lamp, he had no control. It was intense, a searing whiteness and he found himself stumbling through the bush following it. He realized that he was unarmed, he felt naked.

He heard the sound of war, not the roar of the ambush but a smaller war; rifles crackling in the bush. He could hear the screams of women and children. He watched as the bright light cleared, not faded but cleared, allowing him to see as if looking through a tunnel, the edges blurred with swirling tendrils at its edges, tendrils gently swirling as if the light was smoke stirred by a gentle breeze.

He saw a woman on her hand and knees, her free arm clutching an infant to her breast and watched in horror, as a man shot her through the head. He dragged the infant away from her and crushed its skull under his boot. The man was mulatto, he had a massive Afro hairstyle, its bushiness highlighted by the white light.

He appeared to be in command and his features were hawk-like, he exuded evil. The huts were burning and the men moved through them killing everything they saw, men, women, children, the goats, chickens, dogs everything, everything. He saw a small boy running, his legs pumping, red legs reflected in the firelight, clutching a something in his hand. The Afro man shot him in the back and Kevin saw the boy hit the ground and bounce over onto his back like a rag doll.

The mulatto Afro hair continued to walk away, until he and the others with him had disappeared into the light.

It began to rain, pouring down in a steady roar.

He could hear the thunder and smell the ozone as lightning seared the night sky. He could imagine it all but could not see it, only feel, smell and hear. The rain drove him into the earth and he lay there curled up in a ball, his back taking the brunt of the storm, he remained blinded by the light.

He remembered nothing after that, didn't feel the rain stop nor knew when the light had gone.

He woke with a start, and realized that he still lay where the light and the storm had left him. He was almost dry, his body heat had partially dried his clothes but he was cold to the bone, his teeth were chattering with the cold.

He looked up and he could faintly see the shape of the boy on the ground. The sky was just starting to show faint colour when he began to move. He felt compelled to do it, he had no choice. He was as helpless to fight it as much as a moth could defy the pull of a bright light. He crawled to the boy and stood up, heaving the little body onto his shoulder. The world was soaked from the night's rains and it wasn't long before his clothes were once again drenched from brushing up against the vegetation.

He held the small boy over his shoulder, draped like a sack of potatoes. He could smell the smoke from the kraal fire on the boy, the smell of countless African huts. He bore his burden with ease, his thin frame belying the strength he had, his muscles like cords under his dirty jacket. The small boy was a dead weight and. He slipped once on his way down to the river, dropping the boy on to the wet ground, picking him up with effortlessly ease and making his way cautiously down to the river bank. By the time he reached the river's edge the sky was starting to turn grey and he could see the water, grey like the dawn, flowing like treacle, sluggish, as if the river was resisting waking to the new day.

He placed the boy gently on the ground and as he placed the child's lantern on the boy's chest, disjointed random thoughts crossed his mind, images of burial rituals, tombs and artefacts. The lantern was a work of art hand-made out of old Coca Cola cans and clear plastic. Within the frame was contained a small stump of a candle, Long cold, its wick as black as ink.

Like a child launching a toy boat, he pushed the boy gently into the river and as the current took hold, the body rolled over onto his its side, the lantern falling into the river with a soft plop. On an impulse he grabbed the lantern and tried to put it back on the boy's chest, but the child body had already drifted out of his reach.

The boy's eyes stared at him, lifeless, accusingly, and the thin man regretted not having at least remembered to brush them closed when he could. Water poured into the boy's mouth as the river accepted her bounty; the man turned, placing the lantern in the branches of a small tree; for no real reason, he just placed it there.

He stood and watched the dawn, his face taking on a haggard aspect which belied his eighteen years. He thought of the boy's eyes as the river took him; and the man wept. Kevin woke like a man raised from the dead, the air sucking into his lungs with "whoop" sound. He was lying in his sleeping bag, bone dry, the earth wet around them, the white light nightmare vivid in his mind. He looked at the recce to see if he remembered being fallen on in the dead of the night, but he was lying quietly waiting for the light so they could move.

Kevin looked at Andy and whispered. 'Prewsky, did you hear anything last night'?

'Nope, just some bird flapping about'.

'But I shook you, brother, there was this white light.

I fell over you man right onto the recce lying there!'

Andy looked at Kevin, the typical Prew look of amusement when he was about start winding someone up.

'KD, my boy, I think you are starting to lose your bloody marbles,' said Andy a smirk starting to develop. 'You've been lying in the bush for too long, living like a savage, seen too many dead people. I think maybe I should tell those recces that we need to keep an eye on you, you know, make sure you don't snap and plug someone.'

Kevin felt desperate; he imagined that his eyes were still sore from the light. He knew he had seen the light; it had been too real and it couldn't have been a dream, surely, not just a dream. He remembered the Afro man, the horror of his indiscriminate killing, the evil of the man, surely not just a dream.

He decided to leave it at that; it was pointless pursuing anything when his buddy was in this kind of mood and in any case they were being signalled to move out.

They came out of their hide and spread out, moving silently through the wet bush.

Kevin knew that they had to cross a river ahead and once over that they could stop for something to eat.

His guts rumbled like distant thunder.

They entered a clearing and as the trees thinned out they could see what looked like a small village ahead, partly hidden by the long grass. They spread out and walked slowly towards the huts cautiously, carefully looking for signs of life ahead.

The lead recce signalled a halt and went onto his knee to inspect something in the grass. They went down as well, facing outwards scanning the surrounding bush and grass. Kevin felt on edge and turned to look at the recce, who by now had stood up. His face was grim. Kevin could see the distaste on his face.

He gave a low whistle and they rose and continued to walk slowly forward. Kevin reached a position left of where the recce had been kneeling and looked. A dead woman lay in the grass, her head half blown off, the flies already black on her face, like moving black warts. He looked away. *Strangely this time the glass bones did not grind in his head.*

When they reached the huts they could smell the dead. Bodies were scattered in and around the blackened huts, huts which had been mostly destroyed by fire. The carnage was days old, the stink and rain-washed ash testimony of the time which had passed.

They backtracked and moved away from the huts towards the river, their original plan to cross it still intact. There was no point in sifting through the village. It stank and there was the risk of booby traps, just too much risk. Soon they could see the river and hear its burble, flowing slowly, was almost soundless. Kevin began to feel more and more on edge, a sense of foreboding crept up and over the back of his head until it settled on him like a grey cloud.

They reached the river and two of them crossed, leaving Kevin, Andy and one recce behind to cover them; standard practice, once they had crossed and established a position the rest would come across and join them.

By now the sun was higher in the sky and the humidity was already starting to coagulate into a muggy, invisible cloud. They stood up and began to move down to the river's edge treading carefully, not wanting to slip. Kevin lost purchase and slipped, managing to reach out and stop his fall and as he did so, he caught a glint out of the corner of his eye.

He froze and looked to his right... *the glass shards grated in his head. He could feel their grind; he could sense the dead man's eyes as he saw it* ...The lantern was a work of art, hand-made out of old Coca Cola cans and clear plastic, it contained a small stump of a candle, long cold, its wick as black as ink. It had been placed in the branches of a small tree.

There was an iciness in Kevin after that, his mind confounded by what he had experienced and seen. He could not grasp what had happened and there was no way that he could rationalise his way out of it.

He chose not to tell Andy, not to tell anyone of this. They would never understand; they would be convinced that he was going mad. He actually wondered if he was going insane and so he simply buried it in the deepest recesses of his mind. Over the years ahead he would keep pushing it back until it became a small black dot in his memory.

·

Chapter Twenty one: **Tantrums and depression ended**

To hate them and fear them
To run and to hide
And accept it all bravely
With God on my side.

Bob Dylan

It was pouring with rain, the water roaring down from the heavens and converting the world around them into a sea of muddy misery. It rained almost every day and it was a constant battle to keep themselves dry and to stop everything from rusting. It never ended.

It was as if God was trying to wash the Angolan earth of all of the blood and misery soaked into it. Whether on an OP on the side of mountains, when going down for the night or while walking, going down to sleep and while on a patrol; it rained.

Almost spitefully the rain came down in the afternoons giving them little chance to stay dry. Kevin and Andy had perfected the waterproof bivvie, nylon groundsheets woven together and strung low against the earth. With a low earthen wall and ditch dug around it, once they had crept into it and closed the entrance up, they were in there as snug as a pair of bugs. Andy constantly bragged that it was his Boy Scout training that did it. 'If it wasn't for me being a boy scout we'd be as cold and wet as those dumb Dutchmen, KD!'

Two rules applied; no farting and wanking in the bivvie. This rule was cast in stone. Kevin suspected that Andy wanked in the bivvie on the odd occasion, very cleverly because Kevin never managed to catch him doing it. Andy had the same suspicion and one morning, while they were making their early morning brew, Andy popped the question.

'KD, I heard you catching a wank last night,' stated Andy in a matter of fact tone.

Andy was looking for shit, trying to wind him up, he knew it. Kevin ignored him, watching for the water in his steel mug to boil. His mother had taught him that the best tea had to be made with rapidly boiling water. And she was right, generally mothers are always right, like sergeant majors he reflected.

He missed his mom, the old man too, although mostly the old man was full of shit.

He still loved his folks; he missed them today more than other days.

In later years, he would come to understand why he missed them then, as a child would. He was only eighteen years old. He felt like an old man, like a young man with an old soul; a young man who has seen far too much, far too much for a young man of eighteen. Mom's advice about the boiling water applied; he always waited for it to boil.

The fact that they used rat-pack instant, powdered tea was not lost on them, but they always made sure that the water was boiling. Mixed with condensed milk, it made a half-decent brew.

Syd's tea and condese crystals. After drinking half of the tea they would break an army dog biscuit into the tea, turning the rocklike biscuit into a palatable porridge.

'About the wanking last night, actually it was a wet dream,' responded Kevin, emptying the sachet of powdered tea into the mug, flicking the last bit out.

'Jeez, KD, that's disgusting!'

'Why's it disgusting boet, fuck, I can't help it, it just happens?' responded Kevin.

'Fuck, into your pants, jeez that's horrible,' protested Andy.

'Actually, I got my pants off in my sleep,' said Kevin, sipping the sweet tea. It was delicious.

Andy sat looking into the distance.

'Did you feel that prod, prod in your bum last night, well that was my cock, Mr Prew, my cheesy cock!'

Andy shook his head in feigned disgust.

The morning sparring session over Andy looked to the horizon watching the rising sun.

'Check, here comes the rain again,' he said, pointing into the distance. A pissed-off expression had developed on his face.

Kevin looked past the truck and the Noddy cars, and saw the rain coming, columns of it highlighted by the rising sun.

Kevin cracked then, just a little; yes he lost it, just a little.

All of the wet misery and mud, the mouldy fucking smell always hovering around them, always in their fucking nostrils, got to him; just enough to make him crack, yes, just a little.

He found himself climbing onto the back of the truck and he went and stood in his customary place.

He took a sip of his tea and watched the advancing downpour.

'FUCK YOU…FUCK YOU!' Kevin screamed at the elements. He raised his fist at the heavens and carried on screaming at the rain and at the sky heavens; telling the rain to fuck off, loudly and repeatedly.

He felt someone's hand on his shoulder. It was Visagie the son of a NG Kerk minister.

'Stop that, Vossie,' he gently admonished. 'Screaming at the rain is the same as screaming at God, it's pointless,'

He continued gently.

He managed to calm Kevin down, who suddenly realized that the rest were all standing around watching him. The armoured car crews and bats standing together, watching the skinny fool rant at the heavens.

Kevin suddenly felt stupid. He wanted to apologise, but as he got down off the truck they started to wander off back to their bivvies, to try and stay dry until the fucking war forced them into the rain. Strangely nothing was mentioned again about Kevin's rant. They all knew, and so did Kevin, that it was more than just about the rain.

Kevin slipped into a dark black depression. He wanted to crawl into a comfortable hole somewhere and just stay there. Instead of a hole in the ground, he withdrew into a hole in his head. Ignoring Andy and the rest of them, his mind shut down, denying the reality around him

All of the memories came flooding back into his mind like a puddle of black ink.

The white visions, there were so many of them and they drove Kevin deeper into his black hole of despair.

The little boys red legs, pumping as he tried to escape, his lantern clutched in his hand, the raça cruzada murdering him, cutting him down coldly; his Afro hair silhouetted against the light of the burning village.

The SWAPO man's eyes, the grinding sound of his shattered skull, his eyes staring as the boot moved his head like a sick jelly; Dreyer, handing Kevin his Okapi knife, the blade red and sticky; the lieutenant sobbing in the night, after he slit the Cuban's throat from ear to ear.

One mother's son, his innocence lost, another mother's son, his life lost.

The prisoner screaming for mercy, running away and clinging to a truck's prop shaft; the engine started and the truck lurching forward dislodging him.

The Unita Capitão pulling him out from under the truck and cold-bloodedly shooting him in the head with his officer's pistol; the life ended like a switch pulled.

A fuse pulled in an instant!

The trapped mercenaries, eight of them on a Landrover; the one, clearly a young woman disguised as a man; her terror when she thought they were going to kill them all, when Kevin, accidentally moved into the line of fire.

Andy saying, 'Move, KD, we'll kill you if we shoot.'

The woman thinking that Kevin was moving away so that they could kill her;

Kevin watching, as the dark stain spread across her groin and down her legs, like a drop of ink spreading into blotting paper. He wanted to say sorry and to touch her on the shoulder in comfort. Instead, he looked and laughed, pointing at her wet groin in mockery.

The dead Cuban, his body already subsiding into the earth; Kevin leaning down and claiming the Tokarov pistol and hiding it in his webbing; a trophy, a memento but in reality a symbol of one man's growing callousness as the war began to brutalize him, to change him forever.

The refugees, desperately coming back behind them as the war moved northwards, hoping beyond hope that they could reclaim their shattered lives. Murder and murder again, of black man upon black man in an ideologically driven madness.

The dead, stinking and bloated corpses.

Only God knew where and when the black depression would have ended.
Actually God did know and God ended it very quickly in the mud, six days later.

In later life, Kevin would always reflect on one of the greatest misnomers in military jargon, friendly fire. They were all to discover very soon, that there was absolutely nothing friendly about "friendly fire". Friendly fire was as deadly as any and if directed by competent men it was terrifying in its closeness. It was horrifying and generated a frustrating rage that was palpable. It made raging at the rain and the skies an insignificant thing.

They stood and listened to Mark. The rain had stopped in the early hours and the clouds had scuttled off to rain-land where little men in rain suits, working in a rain factory, topped them up for the next cycle of wet misery. The water was dripping from the trees around them, drip, drip, drip.

The water was gurgling in little rivulets past them, heading towards the swollen streams, towards the swollen rivers and ultimately to empty out into the pounding sea.

Kevin thought of the sea, of Blythdale beach, swimming with surfers out backline; floating in the ocean and body-surfing the waves. He had never mastered surfing but he loved the sea. In his child's mind, he could see the Umvoti River, swollen and brown as it emptied itself into the churning sea, turning the water into a muddy brown. Brown foam whipped into the air by the wind.

He heard his father's voice saying, 'When the sea's brown like that boy, stay out of it. That's when the taxman in his grey suit comes looking for his pound of flesh!' The old man always referred to sharks as the taxman, pinching the odd fish off his line as he was about to land it, taxing the fishermen in more ways than one.

 He longed for the sea, near the place where he had grown up.

He longed for home.

He felt a lump in his throat and fought back the tears with effort. He was still depressed. He felt miserable and wanted to get the fuck away from all of this shit.

Andy had been asking him what was wrong, Kevin just responded that he was pissed off, tired of this crap. Andy left him alone and Kevin couldn't blame him, after all depressed people were poor company and all that depressed people did was depress you.

Mark's voice shattered Kevin's depressing thoughts. 'Today we are going out with some sappers to blow up a bridge,' he stated matter of factly. Kevin could see a faint mist coming off the top of Mark's head. He had obviously spent a miserably wet night last night, mused Kevin. The rain sure as hell didn't respect rank.

'We are going in the direction of Quibala, and here,' he said stabbed his finger at a point on a map, we turn off towards the piggery and cheese factory we found a few months ago.'

It was too far for Kevin to see on the map and in his depression, he didn't care if he saw the position on the map or not.

'Some of you will remember the piggery?' he questioned, scowling in disgust. Kevin remembered it well. They were walking and came upon the piggery. Hundreds of pigs locked up in pens, cannibalising each other, dead and dying. High pitched squeals of agony as they ate each other alive. The stench was unbelievable, hanging in the air heavy and oily like the smell of dead men.

Kevin remembered vomiting until he tasted bitter bile.

And so mid-morning found them on the tar road between Cela and Quibala, heading north towards the place of the dead pigs.

Stuck between them and the last Noddy car, travelled an army Land rover, were a crew of four sappers sitting comfortably inside, safely ensconced between the two vehicles. Kevin knew that they felt safe because they looked safe. They gave the impression of, "Look, we're fucking safe here, what with the Bats and all this wheeled armour looking after us."

As they drove along, Kevin had a sense of déjà vu as he watched the milestones drifting past. QB 70, stomach went twist QB 65, stomach went twist!

This time though, his stomach went into a twist and fucking stayed there.

They headed inexorably towards Quibala, towards the place where he had napalmed the thousands of ants, where they had been rocketed by Red Eyes. Before they reached there, the lead Noddy car took a dirt road to the west and headed towards the place of the dead pigs.

The place of the dead pigs; it had a poetically, ominous ring to it mused Kevin. He watched in trepidation as the Noddy cars began to slip and slide on the muddy road ahead of them and soon they too began to slide sideways. Somehow the miracle driver, Chris, managed to keep the old farm truck heading in the right direction.

Syd let out a whoop and a cowboy 'yeeehaaa!' A joy ride in the mud. The sun was up! For now!

And Syd let rip with another Bowie rendition…

> *Something kind of hit me today*
> *I looked at you and wondered if you saw things my way*
> *People will hold us to blame*
> *It hit me today, it hit me today*
> *We're taking it hard all the time*
> *Why don't we pass it by?*
> *Just reply, you've changed your mind*
> *We're fighting with the eyes of the blind*
> *Taking it hard, taking it hard*
> *Yet now*
> *We feel that we are papers, choking on you nightly*
> *They tell me "Son, we want you, be elusive, but don't walk far"*
> *For we're breaking in the new boys, deceive your next of kin*
> *For you're dancing where the dogs decay, defecating ecstasy*

You're just an ally of the leecher

Locator for the virgin King, but I love you in your fuck-me pumps

And your nimble dress that trails

Oh, dress yourself, my urchin one, for I hear them on the rails

Because of all we've seen, because of all we've said

We are the dead

One thing kind of touched me today

I looked at you and counted all the times we had laid

Pressing our love through the night

Knowing it's right, knowing it's right

Now I'm hoping someone will care

Living on the breath of a hope to be shared

Trusting on the sons of our love

That someone will care, someone will care

But now

We're today's scrambled creatures, locked in tomorrow's double feature

Heaven's on the pillow, its silence competes with hell

It's a twenty-four hour service, guaranteed to make you tell

And the streets are full of press men

Bent on getting hung and buried

And the legendary curtains are drawn 'round Baby Bankrupt

Who sucks you while you're sleeping

It's the theatre of financiers

Count them, fifty 'round a table

White and dressed to kill

Oh caress yourself, my juicy

For my hands have all but withered

Oh dress yourself my urchin one, for I hear them on the stairs

Because of all we've seen, because of all we've said

We are the dead

We are the dead

We are the dead.

There was collective roar of laughter as Syd sang the '*we are the dead*', affecting just a hint of the Bowie voice wobble when he sang, '*dea he hed*'. They all sang out loud

We are the dead

We are the dead

We are the dead

We are the dead

We are the dead

We are the dead

It was all so fucking macabre, thought Kevin, singing '*dea he hed,* '*dea he hed, we are the dea he hed.*' *Dea he hed* , he felt more depressed. Kevin looked at Andy.

He wasn't singing. The depression was starting to rub off on poor Andy too, he surmised. Soon they were all silent, the euphoria over, jerking and bouncing on the church pews, slipping and sliding in the mud. A thought came to Kevin, it was a Vietnam War expression,

'*slippin an slidin, duckin and divin in the mud and the blood.*'

An hour later they came slipping down the muddy road and slid to a halt. The wheels looking double their size, caked in clay. It was misty, the sun had lost its fight with the clouds and mist; and had decided to go AWOL and went back to go and skulk somewhere behind the mountains. The river ran quietly under the bridge ahead of them, it was as grey as the mist and flowed like oil.

The bridge was a sturdy affair of concrete and rock and it looked like it wasn't going to go down that easily, thought Kevin. Across the bridge and to the left of them lay a sea of reeds, marshland stretching as far as the eye could see in the mist. A raised road, like a causeway, ran as straight as an arrow towards the piggery and cheese factory, a blurred shape in the mist. A mountain loomed above them to their right, its slope coming down to the river's edge downstream of them.

'Right lads, I need some of you to make a quick recce across the river there,' Mark announced, pointing towards the piggery.

Kevin made sure that he well out of Mark's eyesight when he started casting about for likely candidates, he didn't fancy depositing his meagre breakfast amongst the dead pigs. Mark dispatched a Noddy car to the piggery, covered in men perched precariously on it like a rash of warts on a dog's backside; give it a sweep to make sure there were no nasties skulking there.

In the meantime, the vehicles were turned to face the way they had come and the men settled down to protect the sappers as they went about their business. The sappers started up a petrol-driven Arbor[15] and began to drill holes in the earth where the bridge joined the road.

---

15. Air compressor.

Some of them began to place plastic explosives under and on the bridge, stringing cortex between the deadly little lumps of plastic. Looks like putty, kiddie play dough, mused Kevin.

The drone of the Arbor sounding like a country club lawnmower, excepting there wasn't the accompanying smell of freshly cut grass.

Soon they were bored.

Then they became more bored.

And after a little while longer they were fucking bored!

And then suddenly Andy piped up, 'Loot, can we catch some fish please?'

Kevin noted that Andy had his most charming look painted across his dial. As always, the expressions Andy could adopt were as varied as they were priceless.

Very few people could resist the Prew charm. Mark looked bemused.

'Where in the name of hades will you get fishing gear from, Prew?' he asked.

'Yes where?' added Kevin, slightly less bored now.

Andy set about scrabbling in his webbing.

'Here!' he said triumphantly, holding up a percussion grenade.

Mark looked taken aback.

'Prew, you're mad!' he snapped turning away.

Andy waited a few minutes. Kevin could see the little gears grinding away in his head.

'Go ask him again,' encouraged Kevin, knowing full well, that if anyone could convince Mark to allow them to use percussion grenades to catch fish, Andy could. 'Um, lieutenant,' Andy broached the subject again. And before Mark could respond he continued.

'Just three or four grenades, Loot and you get the pick of the catch, how's that?' Andy finished, his face a comical mix of "You're being convinced and you're not being conned, I promise you."

Kevin added his voice and in a moment the one-man fishing delegation had doubled in convincing firepower; too much for one little lieutenant to handle. 'Just three or four grenades, lieutenant, there's not a soul within a hundred kilometres of us. We'll make it quick, we'll share the fish with all the guys, I promise!'

The Loot looked at them, shook his head in resignation and nodded, jerking his thumb towards the river. The two of them scuttled down to the river bank.

'Right, KD, you stand on those rocks there and I'll chuck the grenades up there. I'll run down to these rocks here and we catch all the fish floating by, got it?' Prew's instructions were clear.

Kevin always felt slightly irritated when Prew started getting all bossy-like. This time he kept his irritation to himself. In any case catching fish was pretty cool and he felt his mood lighten just a little bit.

WHOOMP! WHOOMP! WHOOMP!

Three grenades were thrown into the river in quick succession. The catch was fantastic, the fish bobbing to the surface and floating by slowly. Soon there were about seven of the crew in the water collecting fish.

'Prew, you're a fucking genius,' called someone.

Andy felt on top of the world, his face could be read like a book. As if the words were written across his forehead, 'Look at me, I'm as happy as a pig in shit, look I'm a clever little fuck!'

Mark soon gave a few of the others permission and soon half of them were whooping and lobbing grenades into the river. After all, they were soon to go home, no Cubans or MPLA fuckers within a hundred kilometres, so it became chill time.

 A little bit of R&R in a war zone.

'Okay guys, get clear, take cover, they're going to blow it!' commanded Mark.

They all took cover and Kevin lay low watching the bridge intently. He could see the piggery and cheese factory in the distance, still blurred by the mist. The bridge blew up in a massive explosion, black smoke and chunks of concrete and rock hurled into the air and landing in the river in gigantic splashes.

Poor fucking fish … and that thought was interrupted as he saw the piggery go up in a fountain of mud and chunks of debris, roofing sheets spiralling into the air already twisted to hell.

It was surreal. His mind couldn't fathom the impossible. How in the hell could this explosion trigger that explosion all that distance away. And all at the same time!

'How the fuck did that happen?' he heard someone exclaim.

Kevin turned to Mark who was close by sitting in line of site between the bridge and the partly demolished piggery.

Mark looked just as stunned. Andy sat there, his mouth agape, just like the fish he'd just caught. He opened his mouth to speak when suddenly the piggery and cheese factory erupted in a series of explosions, the earth churning as the explosions ripped the roof and masonry to bits; geysers of shit flying upwards.

There were pigs in there, pigs in the churning dirt, Kevin thought. Then they heard it, the drone of incoming shells, coming from behind them from their own lines!

The first thing that crossed Kevin's mind was that they had been outflanked, that the Cubans had them trapped and they would have to fight their way out of it.

His gut twisted into an agonising knot of fear as he saw the shells starting to explode in the marshland, spouting funnels of mud, reeds and black smoke into the air. Then the explosions began to "walk" towards them, coming down in rows like an advancing line of mud trolls, raging and hurling mud and reeds upwards into the air.

The drone of the shells coming in over them in waves began to intensify. Kevin was frozen, like a rabbit caught in a speeding car's headlights, blinded, mesmerised; he just lay there in the mud, frozen in fear.

The sound of diesel engines quickly dragged his attention away from the incoming headlights. Kevin the rabbit leapt up, slipping in the mud, terrified as he watched the convoy of vehicles beginning to move.

'They're leaving me behind, they've forgotten I'm here.

Fuckers, fuckers, stop, stop!' he heard himself screaming, running in the mud, the mud clinging to his shoes becoming heavier and heavier, the sound of the shells droning in, explosions coming in closer, closer. He reached the truck and was hauled onto it by willing hands.

The truck's engine was howling as it tried to gain purchase in the mud, and Kevin watched as the shells continued to come in. The truck was wagging its arse, fishtailing in the mud.

'WE ARE FUCKED!' screamed Kevin, and then the rear Noddy car rode into the back of the truck and began to push it out of the mud. Suddenly the truck's wheels found purchase and it lunged forward, sending them all sprawling into a heap.

Kevin crawled to his place next to Andy, and he could hear Mark screaming over the radio. He couldn't hear what Mark was saying, but he could see the anxious fear on his face as he did so. Kevin looked up and saw the gate ahead, whitewashed, pristine, and gleaming like a fucking ghost in the mist.

A gate. A big white gate.

Easy to see. A marker.

Kevin suddenly realised what the gate meant. As a trained mortarist he knew that there were always markers on the firing plan; markers, the coordinates of which were known.

'STOP, STOP!' he screamed.

He heard Andy yelling and Mark looked at them briefly. He turned back to the radio and began to scream into it again, bringing the little convoy to a sliding halt.

As he was leaping off the truck Kevin saw the gate disappear in a whirling black explosion. He could see a series of small red balls in the centre of the blasts; not like the movies, where the eruptions were always red and spouting orange flames everywhere.

This was real; it was blackish grey and the explosion released a sound like a banshee as shrapnel ripped over their heads. He found himself in the mud, rolling in the mud, crawling and slithering, away into the trees. He could see the others doing the same, some crawling and others rolling.

And then the sound changed, the explosions took on a different note, they weren't muffled by mud, marsh and dirt; they were louder; the sound echoing against the mountain. Kevin could hear the shrapnel tearing into the trees and the foliage all above and around them. Kevin heard Andy screaming,

'Airburst, airburst they're using airburst, FUCK! FUCK! FUCK!'

He began to dig into the mud with his hands, clawing chunks of it out of the earth; lying on his belly, digging like a turtle wanting to lay its eggs. He felt the displacement in his ears and the shockwaves, shock waves partially dissipated by the trees.

His grandfather once told him of being shelled by the Germans in the Great War and how they blocked their ears and kept their mouths open to prevent their eardrums from bursting.

He opened his mouth to do the same, perhaps to scream too; and the mud flowed into it, stifling his voice in a muddy gurgle!

And then it stopped.

Suddenly.

The silence hung on them like a heavenly mantle.

Deafening, beautiful silence.

He heard someone sobbing near him and he turned his face sideways both to breathe and to see who was crying. The man stopped crying suddenly, as if he had realised others could hear him. Even in the aftermath of terror men are embarrassed.

Blessed silence.

Kevin lay there, using his tongue to clear the mud out of his mouth, shovelling it out with his tongue. It wasn't a bad taste; it tasted like the earth should, like the taste of dirt eaten when he was a kid. He spat and spat again. He could hear others spitting as well; muddy fucking mouths everywhere, he thought. He realized then that he was rambling in his head; words and thoughts bouncing about in his head like a Ping-Pong ball as he spat the mud out of his mouth; his tongue curling about in his mouth, shovelling out the mud. He tasted blood. He might have bitten his tongue.

He spat the pink mud out of his mouth and then began to retch, dry heaving, wanting to vomit but it wouldn't come. Pink fucking mud!

Slippin an slidin
duckin and divin
in the mud and the blood

They gathered in silence next to the little battle group's convoy and Mark took stock of them. He looked pale. He was in control but Kevin could see his eyes were hollow in their sockets.

He looked drawn and he very different from his usual demeanour. Something had certainly changed in Mark. Miraculously there were no serious injuries and Kevin was amazed at this.

As they began to drive off, slipping and sliding along, a thought began to develop, a realization that slowly dawned on Kevin. Like a light dimmer-switch slowly being turned up, the light growing brighter and brighter until it was fully bright.

He turned to Andrew. Andrew didn't look too bright at all. He had a dark look about him and was gazing into the middle distance. His eyes were a bit like Mark's were a few minutes ago, thought Kevin.

'Prew, there has to be a God,' Kevin blurted out.

There was no response from Andy, he just kept staring. Kevin cast his eyes about and noticed that the rest had the same look in their eyes. Even the ever jovial Syd sat there staring into the middle distance. They looked shell-shocked, the lot of them, stunned, beaten into submission. They looked horrible!

The thoughts began to run in his head, he began to take stock. Two ambushes, both were potential killers; rocketed by the dreaded Red Eyes, now shelled by artillery.

'Oh, for fucksakes!' snarled Syd suddenly. 'Lieutenant, we have to turn around, we left the bloody fish by the river!' he yelled out. There was a ripple of laughter and then the ripple turned into a wave of laughter as they saw the funny side of it all. Trust Syd to tear them out of it, to get the laughter going, good old Syd!

'Hey Syd, give us a song,' called someone.

'Nah, fuck that, not today,' he responded and they left it at that.

And then Kevin suddenly realized that his black mood, his depression, the dark mood and gloomy thoughts had lifted, the shelling had ripped him the fuck out of it, right out of the doldrums and back into the light; bang, just like that!

And he was alive, oh man, he was alive.

They were all alive, miraculously they were all alive!

They got back to Cela and debussed next to the little church. Mark went off to report the day's happenings and after about an hour he returned. He looked happy, jovial almost.

'Gents, pull in,' he said, beckoning them closer.

'Sit!' he commanded and they sat on the grass, eyes turned upwards.

'Ferdie has made it, guys, he is going to live!'

There was a stunned silence and then all hell broke loose. The crew began to whoop and shout out their joy. Kevin did a full backward roll, his legs flopping about like strings of spaghetti.

The Noddy car crews were just as happy, grinning from ear to ear. Mark continued, 'The doc told me that he has never seen such a terrible wound and the guy still surviving. He took shrapnel through and through, in one side and out the other. It went through his lung cavity, spleen and liver. He had a hole, the size of a damn tennis ball right through his liver.

The doc says it cannot be described as nothing other than a miracle!' Mark finished.

Kevin felt euphoric, they were all alive. Miraculously they were all alive! Then Mark came up with the icing on the cake, 'Naatie is confirmed OK and they've found Malcolm as well, so guys, all's well that ends well, as they say!'

Kevin felt embarrassed by the last week's black mood and turning to Andy he confessed,

'Prew, sorry for being such a fucking girl over the last week, seriously, I was being a real prick!'

Andy looked at him and grinning, gave him a punch on the leg, so hard that it left a lump on his thigh. It hurt like hell!

Jungle justice!

'So here's the story!' continued Mark, 'today's balls-up in a nutshell.'

They fell silent and waited for him to continue.

'Nobody informed the gunners of our little excursion and so no one realized that we were in the area.'

'Remember the mountain to our right?' he asked.

They all nodded.

'Well, they told me that they had an OP placed on the side of it, overlooking the bridge for obvious reasons. As you will all remember there was a lot of mist about so they couldn't see us clearly, supposedly they had no idea we were there until the sappers starting drilling,' he paused.

They could all see that he was relatively pissed off. Then with just a touch of vehemence he added, 'They weren't too bothered until Andy and KD there,' he paused wagging his finger at the pair of them, 'started with their little fishing expedition!'

He gave Kevin and Andy a dirty look; not a bad dirty look, noticed Kevin, just an annoyed dirty look. Kevin wanted to remind them all that Mark gave them permission to do it but wisely kept his maw shut.

Mark continued, 'When the OP heard the explosions caused by Messer's Prew and Vos, they thought it was Cubans trying to blow up the bridge. So they brought down a marker shot and as the bridge blew, the marker landed on the pigs. They thought they were spot on target and called in a salvo, miraculously gents, miraculously!' he repeated, pausing for effect, 'they thought the bridge blowing up was a shell hit!'

'Only when the salvo came in did they realize that they were off target. We are one lucky bunch of bastards' boys, let me tell you that!' he finished. Kevin could see it in Mark's eyes, the acknowledgement of a miracle, that he was awed by the "luckiness" of it all.

His depression over, Kevin took to life with renewed vigour.

He knew in his heart, that there had to be something up there looking after him, all of them perhaps? All of the close shaves, all of the terrifying times when death reached out with his bony hand to claim them, only to have it stayed somehow.

Gents, there has to be a God!

Chapter Twenty Two: **Boys, we're going home!**

Times have changed and times are strange
Here I come, but I ain't the same
Mama, I'm coming home

Ozzy Osbourne

The sun was up and the countryside was bathed in its warm light. It had been another wet night but luckily they had spent the hours of darkness in a small church and had stayed dry.

They were supposed to have completed their military service months ago, but the "powers that be" had kept them on longer, conscripted national service extended by the stroke of some arsehole's pen!

Mark gathered them together that morning and gave them the good news. 'Gents, we are all going home!' he paused for effect. There was a silence as if they hadn't heard him, his words falling off incredulous, deaf ears.

'Guys, did you hear me?' he asked slightly bemused at their lack of response.

'We…Are…Going…Home,' he repeated, each word said with a pause between them.

'The whole task force, everyone, the whole lot of us, going home,' he expanded.

'We leave in two days, the bridge blowing escapade, well that was part of it.

They have been blowing bridges up on all access roads over the last few weeks, so that we can have a head start if they try and chase us,' he ended.

Kevin raised his hand, asked, 'Lieutenant, but why are the whole lot of us leaving?

I mean, I know we should have been home months ago, but why everyone?'

'Politics, Vos, politics. Gerald Ford, the US president, wants to stand for re-election.

He can't afford a political scandal, if word leaks that we are here because of American CIA backing he won't stand a chance of being re-elected.'

'What a fucking wanker!' they heard someone exclaim. 'All of this effort and now just like that; flick of a finger and we all fuck off home, fukken wankers!' Kevin had mixed feelings. He seriously wanted to go home. Yet in the same instant he saw the waste of it all; all of the trauma, the shit, blood and guts and all for nothing.

His eighteen-year old mind darkened forever by what he had experienced.

Fuck! But nonetheless he just wanted to go home now. It was time to go home.

Thanks for the drink, brigadier.

The entire battle group, with the exception of a few elements were spread out across the airfield. It was an impressive sight and for the first time in the entire campaign, Kevin had a sense of the scope of the whole thing. It had been big, well for Africa at least.

The city of Sa Da Bandera had reinvigorated itself. Some of the Portuguese inhabitants had returned and had begun to eke out a living in the shattered city. Well, at least the hardier souls had come back. The rest had left Angola forever and by then were back in their motherland.

It was late afternoon and they saw a Porra man in a small beat-up truck, moving slowly from one group of soldiers to another. He arrived at their position and it was then that they saw what he was up to. He was selling beer and *pão*, hard floured Portuguese bread rolls. They had been baked in an oval baking tin and were the size of a large man's fist.

When he had left, Kevin and Andy had bought four rolls and two beers each; it was the maximum number of beers he was allowed sell to each soldier. And no amount of cajoling, even by the very persuasive, expressive-faced Andy, could get him to change his mind. He just shook his head and moved on, muttering in Portuguese. He didn't want to break the rules and stuff up a good thing and you could hardly blame him, mused Kevin.

'Jeez, Prew!' exclaimed Kevin, his mouth full of bread. 'Now I know why it's called the staff of life, this bread, it's absolutely, bloody marvellous!'

It was the first time they had tasted bread in close to six months and Kevin's guts lurched with anticipation as he swallowed the carbohydrates, each delicious mouthful followed by a suck on his beer, more carbohydrates.

'Mmmphow,' replied Andy, the word muffled by a mouth full of bread.

That evening they sat watching the city lights in the distance.

A simple equation began to string itself out in Andy's head; city lights equals people, equals party time.

'KD, let's sneak off tonight and check what's potting in the city,' suggested Andy.

Kevin lay on his side, thinking, running Andy's suggestion through his mind.

'Maybe it's a plan,' offered Kevin, somewhat hesitantly. The last thing he needed was to get into some form of shit when they were on their way home.

'Maybe it's a bad idea,' responded Kevin after mulling it over a bit. 'You never know what could happen, my boet, on our way home and the next thing we're up to our neck in shit. There was a short silence.

Kevin continued, 'The convoy moves out tomorrow early and knowing the two of us we will get drunk, we will talk too much shit to the wrong fucking people, one thing will lead to another and we will probably end up in the shit!'

'Maybe you're right, KD,' agreed Andy after a few moments of deep reflection.

'But I'm fucking bored man, fukkit!'

'Prew, you're a hyperactive little shit!' was Kevin's retort. He continued,

'I heard a rumour that there is a brigadier who's got his bivvie up on the airport control tower,' and before he could carry on, Andy interrupted him.

'So, big fucking deal, KD, a brigadier on a fucking tower, KD!'

'Let me finish, for fucksakes!' snarled Kevin. There was a pregnant pause, the result of neither wanting to kick off the next part of the conversation.

'Well, if you don't want to hear what I'm about to say, well then, fuck you!' snapped a peeved Kevin.

'Stop being a girl and tell me what you want to tell me then,' returned Andy, his voice filled with irritation.

Kevin paused for effect, then stretched it out, just to make a point.

'Well?' prompted Andy.

'I have it from a reliable source,' Kevin paused for effect, 'that said brigadier has a very impressive selection of hooch which he has acquired over the last few months.

And I'm talking about some really good shit!' he finished with a flourish.

'Who told you that?' asked a sceptical Andy.

'I heard some officers talking about it when I went for a piss earlier,' was Kevin's response.

Andy sat up and looked at the control tower.

'Reminds me of a lit up *aapkas*,' he commented.

Kevin could sense the wheels turning in Andy's head. He waited for a few seconds, just to allow Andy to warm to the idea. Just before he started cooling to the notion and timing it perfectly, Kevin then suggested, 'I tell you what, let's sidle over there, climb up the stairs and check it out.

What's the worst case scenario, boet? If they stop us we just say we're curious, tell them we're sorry and fuck off!'

Ever the schemer, Andy responded in typical Prew fashion. 'KD, I'm not going up there and coming back empty handed. That brigadier or whoever the hell he is, is going to be wide awake and we will never get close, we must come up with a plan.

And so it was agreed, Andy would do the talking and Kevin the thieving. They reasoned that there was bound to be a guard left by the brigadier, especially if he wasn't there and even more likely, if the stash was as valuable as Kevin had overheard. Also the chances were pretty high that he was busy pissing it up and shagging his lungs out in the city, Kevin offered. And of course Prew had something up his sleeve.

'KD, I'll go with you on one condition!'

'What's that?' asked Kevin.

'We go to town afterwards,' was the response, Andy had him by the balls, Kevin realised, and he had to concede,

'Okay, Prew, it's a fucking deal!'

And so it was that an hour later they were walking silently up the stairs, rifles slung over their shoulders. The stairs were well lit so there was no point in sneaking up.

'Prew, when we get near the top we must act casual, you know, talk loudly and stuff. That way, if there is someone up there they'll think that we are just two curious Bats, checking the scene out,' reasoned Kevin.

'That's the plan KD, that the plan, my booyy!' He emphasised the booyy. Prew was having fun. So, as they neared the top of the stairs they began to chat, talking loudly as innocent explorers would do. They heard someone call, 'who goes there!'

As per the plan it was Andy who responded, 'Just two of us bud, checking things out.' They reached the landing at the top of the stairs, to be greeted by a sight for sore eyes; a newbie, steel helmet, rifle and boots, the lot, standing guard as they did back at the battalion. It was ridiculous and Kevin had to stifle a laugh. The newbie looked at the pair of them. There was awe in his eyes. They looked like madmen, unshaven, long hair and wearing cast-off cammo; bits and pieces of uniform and kit accumulated along the fast-tracked journey to manhood. And to add to it, Kevin was wearing a stinky, greasy looking cammo cap and Andy was bedecked with a white chef's hat, almost like a Turk's fez, perched on the top of his head at a jaunty angle. Each had their rifle slung over their shoulders, muzzle pointed downward. To add to the weirdness of it all, while Andy was wearing shorts and a shirt, Kevin was wearing a long filthy coat almost stretching down to his ankles. Once grey, it now had a dirty dark oily sheen to it. Most importantly it had pockets and lots of them. Big deep pockets!

Andy began to weave his magic.

'Shit man, so how long have you been up here?' he began, his voice laced with false, keen interest.

'Got here in January,' was the response.

The newbie asked Andy, open admiration in his eyes, 'So who are you guys?'

'We're mercenaries,' was the response.

Technically they were mercenaries, way past their actual demob date and being on record as being mercenaries throughout the campaign; fighting in Angola in makeshift vehicles, carrying makeshift weapons and cast off uniforms, having signed secrecy documents, covering the powers that be in a CIA backed operation. Fuck it, they were mercenaries, it could well be considered to be the truth!

Andy the spin doctor carried on, talking and laughing, drawing the guard into conversation, joking and laughing some more while Kevin, silently, edged his way onto the brigadier's little luxury apartment.

Bloody hell, Kevin almost blurted it out, he's got a proper fold-up cot, mattress, pillows the lot! And there it was, in a box, neatly packed the rumoured stash of hooch. Except that this was no rumour, it was there in front of his eyes. It was like finding the Holy Grail! Kevin quietly began to load the bottles into the recesses of his foul coat, all those lovely pockets conveniently sewn in all over the place. He moved back silently to where he had been standing and gave Andy a wink, job done, me old son!

'Boet, we getter get back,' suggested Kevin and began to walk out slowly. He heard a distinct clink, clink in his coat and his heart almost stood still. Amazingly the newbie didn't seem to pick up on it. Kevin was half way down the stairs when he heard Andy bidding the guard farewell. Together they walked back across the runway, giggling like girls and being accompanied by the happy sounds of clink, clink, clink as they walked along.

The bottles were expensive; a magnum of single malt whiskey, liqueurs and a bottle of port almost two hundred years old; all collected by the discerning brigadier, based on quality, age and collectability, and they disposed of it like pigs at a trough.

A few more of the crew pitched up and a small party developed, handing the bottles around from mouth to mouth, glugging it down as if it were bottles of cheap wine.

'Where the fuck did you guys get this shit'? Asked an impressed Syd. 'Up there,' responded a thoroughly inebriated Andy, pointing towards the lit up control tower.

'Fuck off!' was the collective, incredulous response followed by roars of laughter. 'You fukken mortarists are as bad as Poote and the guys,' piped up Lappies, taking a long swig of the very rare and undoubtedly expensive Port.

'No, wait, hang on guys you can't compare us to that caper,' Kevin was quick to respond. 'What those guys got up to was legendary!'

'You're right,' was the response. 'Fuck that was amazing. Being left to guard the bank right here in Sa Da Bandera and then robbing the fukken thing. Escudos, genuine fucking escudos. I'm sure that if those guys manage to smuggle that lot out they'd be as rich as fuck, jeez!'

There was a murmur of agreement, as they reflected on the deed. Kevin began to laugh, fuelled by the alcohol and the whole ludicrous concept of it all. Paratroopers left to guard a bank earlier in the campaign while Zulu was still advancing; and then they promptly go ahead and rob it.

'Hey guys', slurred Kevin. 'Remember that day on the parade ground, when commandant Olkers gave us his goodbye speech, the day before A Company left for the border?'

'Yes!' laughed Pete, his hand clasped firmly around the single malt whiskey. 'He told us that we were by far the worst bunch of retarded misfits he had ever had the misfortune of training.'

'Yep,' concurred Syd, 'I remember him asking us to please not shag the nannie girls.' There was a roar of laughter as Lappies mimicked the commandant,

'*Julle moet net nie die donderse meide steek nie, want julle is 'n klomp donderse krimineele*.' 'You must just not fuck the black women up there because you are nothing other than a bunch of bloody criminals!'

Syd burst out in song and they all followed suite, in a glorious out of tune sing-along.

Ground Control to Major Tom

Ground Control to Major Tom

Take your protein pills

and put your helmet on

Ground Control to Major Tom

Commencing countdown,

engines on

Check ignition

and may God's love be with you

Ten, Nine, Eight, Seven, Six, Five, Four, Three, Two, One, Lift-off

This is Ground Control to Major Tom

You've really made the grade

And the papers want to know whose shirts you wear

Now it's time to leave the capsule if you dare

This is Major Tom to Ground Control

I'm stepping through the door

And I'm floating in a most peculiar way

And the stars look very different today

For here am I sitting in a tin can
Far above the world
Planet Earth is blue
And there's nothing I can do
Though I'm past one hundred thousand miles
I'm feeling very still
And I think my spaceship knows which way to go
Tell my wife I love her very much
she knows
Ground Control to Major Tom
Your circuit's dead,
there's something wrong
Can you hear me, Major Tom?
Can you hear me, Major Tom?
Can you hear me, Major Tom?
Can you..Here am I floating
round my tin can
Far above the Moon
Planet Earth is blue
And there's nothing I can do.

How wrong he was, the commandant, thought Kevin. They had proved him to be very, very wrong. 'The commandant was wrong!' Kevin blurted out, just as he keeled over and passed out.

They were two days out when the tail end of the column went into a defensive position. A small vehicle had been spotted following them, sporting a large white flag being held out of a window and being waved madly from side to side. Two Noddy cars straddled the road, guns aimed at the little vehicle as it slowed to a crawl, the flag flapping frantically from side to side.

It stopped just short of the Noddy cars and Kevin saw that it was a small beat-up Fiat. Steam was coming from the bonnet and it had just made the column before the engine conked out.

Out climbed seven men, hands held high and the way they were dressed showed that they weren't newbies, but old campaigners.

How the hell all seven of them had endured the journey, let alone fit in that little car! It turned out that they had gone out partying and whoring in Sa Da Bandera the night before the column had left.

They had woken up the next morning and realizing that they were left behind, hijacked a car at gunpoint. They had just made it to the column before the engine died.

The paras watched in amusement as the seven stood rigidly at attention, while their sergeant screamed abuse at them.

They were damn lucky that they were alive!

As they headed south Kevin began to feel a sense of excitement at the prospect of going home, going back to Civvie Street and back to civilization.

During a stop break Mark called them together.

'Guys, listen up. I've been ordered to tell you that there will be no contraband allowed into South West Africa. I suggest that when we cross the Cunene river, you *bliksem* whatever you have into it.

It's not worth it, guys, trust me!' he finished, his voice serious.

'What about pictures, bayonets and souvenirs like that?' asked one of them.

'Gents, don't be stupid. Especially photographs. You guys know full well that this is a secret operation, doesn't matter what the pictures are, the knives, the bayonets, get rid of them!'

He paused, his eyes casting about. 'Listen, if they catch you with any of the shit you might have collected and MIGHT think is harmless, you will be charged.' Pausing for effect he continued.

'You have been through a long campaign, guys. You've been through shit that many men won't see in their entire lifetimes and you are going home. Keep the memories and nothing else, got it?'

'I'd rather not have some of the memories thanks very much,' murmured Kevin.

Mark looked at him and said nothing. Kevin knew that Mark agreed with him, too many memories for such young minds!

There was a collective grumble as the men dispersed, but they all knew and Mark too, that the lot of them would take a chance.

And so they continued south, the column grinding its way along homeward. 'Prew,' said Kevin later on. 'I've got an AK bayonet, a pistol and my diamond.

I don't mind the rest but the diamond stays with me!'

Prew looked at him, his eyebrows askew, one up and the other down; standard Prew look, the ever-sceptical Prew.

'KD, you're dreaming, that's no diamond it's nothing but a shiny rock. You might as well toss into the Cunene, its shit man. You might as well tape to your forehead, nobody will notice or give a shit if they do!'

'All they'll ask is, "Who's that cunt with a shiny stone strapped to his stupid forehead?" Keep the bayonet', Andy continued, 'but the pistol, that's looking for big shit.'

'So, what are you going to do with your shit?' Kevin asked.

'I'm keeping the lot!' was Andy's emphatic response.

Kevin laughed. Yep that's the para way!

When they reached the Cunene the column slowed as it crossed the river. Not a single thing was tossed into the river, Kevin noticed, not a thing. It was the first sign from all of these men, that they had done their bit and the powers that be can go and fuck themselves! Citizen force soldiers were manning the guard posts at the bridge and Kevin could see that they were older, they weren't youngsters.

For the first time they came across citizen force soldiers, men who had begun the first of many call-ups which was to become their burden for the next ten years. It didn't cross their young minds that, like the soldiers guarding the bridge, they too were being set up for the same crap. Years ahead of them, of being called up to serve the Nationalist Party in the guise of fighting the communist scourge.

Vir volk en vaderland, for the people and the fatherland!

It was only when they reached Pereira De Eca that the scope of the call-up hit Kevin. The force was big and it was obvious that the South African government had decided that this was as far as they were going to pull back. And it made sense. The town's large airfield could easily become an air base for Soviet planes to attack South West Africa.

Andy looked at the tents spread before them in and on the outskirts of the town and said, 'KD, check all of the hundreds of campers here. Think about it, these guys have got jobs and families. Just think what this is doing to the economy?'

'What, are you going to study economics or what?' responded Kevin sarcastically.

Andy kept quiet and Kevin felt like an idiot.

'Prew, I'm going to get rid of this pistol,' announced Kevin emphatically a while later. He had spied a field kitchen, jumped off the truck and headed that way. The aroma coming from the kitchen was more like a smell. Nothing palatable about it, it was a combination of boiled vegetables, oily fried "something" with just a hint of rotting garbage to give it the zest required of good cooking.

Fuck, what a heady combination, thought Kevin, as he cast his eyes about, looking for the bloke in charge.

A sergeant came up to him and gave Kevin the eye. The sergeant looked at the apparition before him and decided that to show just a little respect would be the wise thing to do. He could see that Kevin was a veteran; the respect came from what the sergeant could see. It was something in Kevin's eyes which made him uneasy. It's in the eyes, Kevin would be told over and over again when he got home.

'Your eyes, Kevin,' his mother would say when he got home weeks later. 'I don't like what I see in your eyes! Must I get the minister to talk to you?'

'Fuck the minister, mom!' as he watched the alarm grow in her eyes.

'Can I help you, man?' asked the sergeant.

'Yep,' Kevin responded. 'I want to swop something I have here,' he said patting his dirty jacket,' for something you might have in there,' he finished pointing into the steamy, smelly field kitchen.

The sergeant's eyes took on a sceptical look. 'What have you got there?' he asked jutting his chin in the direction of Kevin's jacket.

Kevin opened it just enough for the Tokarov grip to be seen. Kevin noted with some amusement as the look on the sergeant's face changed. It was almost like a film clip running on slow motion, frame by frame, the scene changing from scepticism to alarm to recognition until finally, the reel stuck on greedy interest.

'Come,' he said and walked to the back of the kitchen. And so Kevin completed the transaction, a Tokarov pistol in almost mint condition for a gigantic, caterer sized tin of yellow cling peaches.

That night Kevin and Andy went to sleep on a sugar high!

The next morning they left the shattered town of Pereira De Eca and as they departed Kevin felt a sense of foreboding. The feeling was overpowering and he had a strong sense, almost a conviction that he would be back there again. As mad as it sounded with the war being over, he just knew that he would be back again.

It was bloody depressing!

He looked on, morosely, as the last tiled roof disappeared from view. Many hours later they passed through the bullet-riddled town of Santa Clara and soon after that, they crossed the border into South West Africa.

Kevin had a sense of déjà vu as they crossed and then suddenly he knew why.

Right there in front of him he could see the trees under the water tower, where Dreyer had mocked his Okapi penknife.

It seemed a lifetime ago and in a sense it was!

Chapter Twenty Three: **Betrayal**

"If you're going to kick authority in the teeth, you might as well use two feet."

Keith Richards: In His Own Words

The deurgangskamp, or processing camp, at Grootfontein was horrible. A dusty sea of tents, pitched in the stinking heat. It felt as if they were in the Namib Desert, it was so hot!

'What a cunt farm, a *poes plaas*' groaned Kevin as he looked at the camp. Mark had told them that were only going to spend a couple of days there, to be processed before boarding a train back to Bloemfontein.

'It does, it looks like a total shithole,' added Andy as they all stood looking at the tents, row upon row of them pitched in the dust and searing heat. Each having two fire-buckets, one filled with sand and the other optimistically meant for water. The buckets looked like rows of red soldier ants standing at attention waiting for inspection.

'Well, at least it's only for a couple of days,' added Lappies rather optimistically. Turned out that Lappies was being very optimistic, in fact he and the rest of them were living in a fool's paradise!

Each morning they would get up and fall in for roll call, and somehow the whole thing seemed to be a charade. Each morning they expected news as to when they would be leaving, each morning they were told the trains would leave tomorrow.

Kevin gave the poor corporal who had the unenviable task of telling them the same thing over and over again, the nickname of "tomorrow".

'Check here comes Tomorrow, going to tell us that we're going to leave tomorrow!' he would chirp to a ripple of laughter.

Things started coming to a head pretty soon. On the fourth day they were all living the charade when poor old Tomorrow said it again, 'Sorry guys, no concrete news, perhaps we leave tomorrow. Go back to your tents. I'll call you if I hear anything.' This time they stayed. Not a man moved.

'Men, come, I said go back to your tents,' instructed a slightly worried corporal Tomorrow.

No one moved.

The corporal shook his head and walked off and as he did so the whole lot of them sat down in the sandy dust, or a better description would have been the dusty sand.

About twenty minutes later the leader group arrived en masse, striding purposefully through the rows of tents, kicking up the dust in little poofs at each step.

'Right lads, what the fuck is going on here?' asked the lieutenant, who had had the porridge stuck to his nose all that time ago. Kevin still had the image of him in his head, shaking the dirt off his parachute "sleeping bag", standing on the side of a mountain, exposed and behind Cuban lines; only five of them so far away from backup and here he was risking all of their lives. And then when Kevin corrected him he had told Kevin to fuck off!

Kevin had looked at him and out of earshot of the others had said, 'Do that again, lieutenant, and I will shoot you in the fucking head!'

But here he was, an officer back in an army camp strutting his stuff and back in his element. There was silence; nobody was quite prepared to defy military authority to its face; the training and resultant respect for authority had been ingrained into them.

'Well?' he repeated, his legs now astride, hands on his hips. He lifted his head up,

Il Duce style, chin jutting forward.

It was the chin that was the final straw; the straw which broke the camel's back, or in this case got Lappies pissed off!

'We're GATVOL!' stated Lappies, the gatvol leaving his lips as a shout. There was a murmur of agreement from amongst the group sitting in the sand.

'We've been fucked around for days, sitting here in this shithole, day in and day out. Always the same story, tomorrow, tomorrow; and tomorrow never fukken comes!'

he finished angrily.

'STAND UP WHEN YOU TALK TO ME TROOPER!' screamed Lieutenant Porridge-Nose.

Lappies stood up and as he did so, the rest of them did the same, to a man. They stood up as one, facing the Lieutenant. And the anger being exuded from them was palpable.

Porridge-Nose looked as if someone had slapped him in the face. Over the months of combat something different had developed between the men and their leaders. While authority was always respected, the men were true veterans and that authority had matured and morphed into something very different.

It was called mutual respect.

Someone, very clearly and quite audibly said, 'Go and fuck yourself, twat!'

Porridge-Nose went pale, white around the lips. He opened his mouth to say something and then shut it. For a moment he was dumbstruck. He opened his mouth again and before he could say anything, Mark stepped forward.

'Gents, this is bullshit and if I didn't know better I'd say it's a bloody mutiny,' he stated, his voice serious. With just the right balance of authority in his voice he said,

'Get back to your tents. This is out of our control. I will give you constructive feedback today,' he paused, his eyes making contact with every one of them, moving from man to man.

'I will personally establish what is going on and I will get back to you as soon as I know. Now go!'

Someone lifted his arm for attention, and when Mark looked at him, he asked the question which had been festering in their minds for days.

'Lieutenant, where is the money we were promised?'

They had all been promised money[16], mercenary pay, not just ordinary army pay.

Mercenary fucking pay-to go into Angola in what transpired to be a CIA-backed operation. It was a top secret operation, so secret that even the toothpaste tubes they were carrying had been scraped clean of any markings. The tins of food in the ration packs were the same, unmarked making dinner a bloody lottery.

'Guys, I can't answer that now. I know we were all promised mercenary pay and I really don't know.' He continued, 'The Minister of Defence is going to be here sometime and I believe that he will give us clarity on this, but guys, I really don't have a clue.'

'It was a signed deal, lieutenant, we have been promised money, a lot of it and we hear nothing!' added Lappies.

'Guys, like I said about our departure date, I will try and determine what is going on about the money as well. I will get back to you as soon as I know. Now guys, please, go!' He finished, with just a hint of impatience in his voice.

'Yes, lieutenant!' responded Lappies and Mark's men turned and began walking back to their tents. Kevin looked over his shoulder and saw that the rest were following. Porridge-Nose was still standing there, rigid and frozen like a pillar of salt.

'You *Doos*!' said someone out loudly as they walked away and they all knew he didn't mean Mark.

That night Kevin and Andy went on a walkabout out of pure boredom, and lo and

---

16.The Bats of Jan '75 intake were declared the fittest infantry company in SA and for that the PFs were to get a bonus and we were to get a month off our service – meaning clearing out 1st of December '75. Then we were informed that we have to stay on during December and towards middle December that we got a month's extended service.

behold, before them lay an oasis. They had stumbled upon a tent pitched near a mess hall, with a bar counter and all. Soft lights, cammo-net ceiling, pictures on the wall of armoured cars and soldiers running through the bush; they had a whole military theme going, shit they had gone the whole nine yards. There were even optics behind the bar fully charged with an assortment of spirits, rum, brandy and whiskey. There was even a large fridge stacked with beers and cold drinks behind the counter; a veritable jewel in the middle of the shithole that was the *deurgangskamp*.

The unit of engineers, who had pitched the sea of tents and built the toilets and showers, had also put their own pub together. They were campers, citizen force guys who had been called up and so they were a mature and relaxed bunch, far more relaxed than your average national serviceman.

They welcomed the two paras with open arms and soon it turned into a total piss-up! Kevin got drunk, very quickly and as a matter of fact, far too quickly. Apart from the pineapple beer and the drunken binge at Sa Da Bandera - compliments of the kind and probably still pissed-off brigadier - they had not had any other alcohol past their lips in months. So their tolerance for alcohol was virtually zero.

'Fuck me, I'm drunk Prew,' Kevin mumbled, looking at Andy. Andy's eyes looked like they had crossed over into a squint.

'I shink I'm shmunggs,' returned Andy incoherently, his prominent nose a nice shade of red. Kevin thought Andy looked like one of Father Christmas's gnomes or dwarves, or whatever. He began to laugh out loud, as a drunk man would at something only a drunk man would find funny. Suddenly, as drunk people sometimes do, Kevin decided it was time to leave. Just like that, he reached a drunkard's decision, got up and high-stepped out of the little bar and headed back towards his tent, leaving the rest of them partying away merrily.

Soon he was lost and after walking about aimlessly for what seemed an eternity, he staggered into a familiar looking tent. And as he did so someone shoved him in the face, hard.

'Wrong tent, twat!' he heard another voice yell, followed by a roar of laughter as he was shoved hard in the back, hitting the dirt hard.

Realising that he was far too pissed to do anything about it, he left amid the jeers of the back-shoving tent dwellers.

So he staggered off and lo and behold there before him he found a little pub packed with drinking men.

'Bloody hell, another pub,' thought Kevin as he happily wandered in. He wasn't quite sure where he was, until he heard Andy yell above the racket, 'Hey KD where've you been, man?'

He had gone full circle and had ended up where he had started. Soon more Bats arrived. The word had got out and soon most of the crew were partying away merrily. And so it went on, and on; and then they went on some more until the good engineers' had, had quite enough, closed shop and called it a night. They all left together singing drunkenly as they headed towards their tents. Luckily someone had a fair sense of direction and soon they reached familiar ground. They rounded a corner and there in the middle of a concrete slab they saw Poote, on his knees being punched and kicked by a group of men from 2 SAI (2 South African Infantry Battalion). It was as if something pulled a trigger, launching the paras into the group of fighting men, through them and into a group of spectators.

Kevin lost his footing fell and getting up, saw that the fight had become a spectacular one in mere seconds. Drunken paras smashing sober infantrymen, gunners, and whoever the hell else got in their way.

As he stood there, trying to make up his mind on whether it would be a good thing to get involved or just stand there and watch, he sensed someone standing next to him. Before he could turn to see who it was, he heard Mark ask him, 'So why aren't you in there helping them, Vossie?',

'Do you think they need my help, lieutenant?' responded Kevin, amazed at how lucid he had suddenly become.

There was a brief pause before Mark replied, 'Nah, I don't' think so.' And so the officer and the private stood together, watching the fight until it finally petered out.

'You guys look like shit, seems you lost the fight last night,' chirped Mark the next morning after breakfast.

He was right, half of the crew looked like they had been steamrolled into submission. Kevin felt a bit like a wart on a dog's arse standing there, his face unmarked. He felt guilty.

Parabats generally fought for the hell of it and Kevin was the rare exception this time. He looked at Andy standing next to him and made a mental note, he too was totally unmarked.

Mark continued, 'As I told you guys yesterday, the Minister of Defence is going to be here later this morning, wants to have a few words.'

'What about? Does he want to ask if he can fly us back with him?' chirped Pete, his voice laced with sarcasm.

Mark grinned before responding in equal vein, 'Okay, Pete I'll ask him for you. Maybe he'll fit you into his bloody luggage!'

The oblique reference to Peter's short stature was not lost on them and it brought a few chuckles to the group.

'OK guys you can go and *ballasbak*, until we call you,' he finished, walking away.

'Hey, Vossie?' chirped Lappies, nodding his head towards Andy.

'How come you and that other *soutie* look like you just came back from a beauty parlour, not a mark on your face, all pretty and all?'

'Why fight when you dumb Dutchmen are doing it for us?' snapped Andy in response. 'In any case I ended drinking with a bunch of the armour boys, so I was nowhere near,' he ended, scowling.

'And you, Vossie?' asked Jan, 'where were you?'

'Mark and I found a comfy spot to park off and we watched you cunts carrying on like a bunch of fucking hooligans,' responded Kevin testily. 'But in any case!' continued Kevin, 'It was only six weeks ago and we were all fighting the Cubans together as one. We would have died for some of those guys and them for us. A few fukken drinks too many and here we are fucking each other up! It's a bloody disgrace, I've had enough of all of this shit and right now, the army, you lot, yes everyone can come and suck my dick!' snarled Kevin.

There was a silence, and Kevin could see that Jan was uncomfortable; he had hit a raw nerve. The rest who had climbed onto the bandwagon had shut their traps and there was an uncomfortable silence as they drifted off towards the rows of khaki depression the army called tents.

It was a couple of hours later when they were summoned to the front of the *deurgangskamp*, the same spot where the mini rebellion had taken place. The engineers had rigged a temporary platform, complete with PA system, so that the good minister could be clearly heard.

The area was packed full of soldiers, almost all of the men who had taken part in Savannah stood there in silence, waiting.

The Minister of Defence[17], PW Botha, arrived and climbing the stairs he stood on the platform and looked at them. Mark's crew were close to the platform and Kevin could see that the Minister was beaming. He was in his element, addressing all of these veterans, these Aryan makers of war.

'Look at that twat,' Kevin heard Syd whisper. 'Fucking black suit, black shoes and that stupid, fucking black hat, goddam Dutch fuck. He and his national party mates should be ashamed, dressed up like a bunch of fucking dirty scarecrows!'

Kevin sniggered. 'Shut it Syd, the *doos* is going to hear us.' Kevin admonished. 'Well fuck him and the horse he rode into town on,' finished Syd with a snort. The Minister leaned towards the microphone and began to address them, remarkably in

---

17. We had lost confidence in the Government. We were constantly tuned in to the SABC's news flashes via B25s e.g.

English. It was as if he were part of the whole CIA thing, speak only English while you are in Angola, never in Afrikaans.

'Manne, men, it is a pleasurre to be standing heerre beforrre you all,' he started, rolling his RRR's in a heavy Afrikaans accent.

He stepped back and looked over his shoulder, slightly annoyed, until an officer quickly stepped forward and adjusted the microphone to suit the minister's height.

The staffer's whole body language was of subservience as he scraped and grovelled before the minister while he did so.

'Check that grovelling twat,' Kevin heard Syd mutter, followed by one or two suppressed chuckling snorts coming from those within earshot.

And so PW continued, switching between English and Afrikaans, waxing lyrically about the exploits and fantastic victories of the campaign. And then he made a mistake, a big one, underestimating the psyche of the conscripted soldier.

'The South Afrrrican defence forrrrce can stand prrroud and strrrong in the worrrld theatrrrrre with men like you as perrrrmananet memberrrrs of ourrrrr arrrrmy. I, as Ministerrrr of Defence invite all of you, each prrroud and strrrong soldierrr, to join up as perrrmanent memberrrs of this fantastic arrrmy of ourrrrs!' He finished, pausing, waiting for the expected, rapturous response from the young veterans standing before him.

There was silence.

He continued with his speech, unfazed by the stony response to what he obviously considered to be a fair invitation for these men to become servants of the glorious republic.

And then he made his second mistake.

'You arrre all young men who don't know how to handle money. If we give you the money all you will do is spend it all so therrre is no point to it,' he announced.

'As a show of ourrr grrratitudde we are issuing all of with a commemorrrrative, pen. It is a lovely pen, a genuine Parkerrr pen…

Someone laughed out aloud, very loud. And for once it wasn't a Parabat. The laughter spread rapidly, like a bushfire in a searing hot day running through tinder dry brush. It tore through the hundreds of men standing there, until it became a derision-filled roar. The Minister stood there like a stranded fish gasping for air amid the sea of roaring laughter. He had reneged on the deal which had been made months ago.

The expectation had been created, they had been promised money and they had earned it the hard way. Every one of them, standing in the heat before their Minister of Defence was being betrayed.

Kevin didn't know what to do; he wasn't laughing. He felt embarrassed for the Minister, his upbringing didn't allow him to show such disrespect, and it was foreign to him.

While he hated the racist policies of the Nationalist Party Government, even hating the way they dressed in black suits and hats; mirroring the *verkrampte* attitudes of a fucked up, racist regime, he just couldn't stand there and mock a man of his stature.

Then suddenly, like the last bit of a wave as it creeps up the beach, the water erasing footprints in the sand, so too were Kevin's final reservations erased. The men broke out into shouts, 'fuck him and fuck his mother!'

A chant developed which they all joined, 'Fuck you, fuck your mother, fuck you, fuck your mother, fuck you, fuck your mother!'

It carried on for almost a minute.

Kevin was among the first to turn their backs on PW and walk away and as the rest followed they kept on laughing and laughing and laughing.

As they walked away, Kevin remembered having to stand guard over the Minister and his wife once in Bloemfontein. There were two of them, Paratroopers, standing through the night armed with rifles and live ammunition.

They had been told to wake the couple up at 05h30 in the morning which Kevin dutifully did. The other had guy simply refused to go in and wake them up so Kevin had to do it. Botha had been friendly and passed a few pleasantries, the young soldier feeling slightly out of his depth standing the presence of a senior member of government.

'I should have shot the piece of shit then,' he said out loud.

None asked what he meant.

Chapter Twenty four: **Bye, bye soldier**

But thanks for your time, then you can thank me for mine
And after that's said Forget it.

- Rodriguez

The next morning only the Bats were called together on the same patch of dirt, where only the day before they had been given the "fuck you" by the government. No-one, not even their own officers knew why they had summoned there.

After hanging about for about twenty minutes, two trucks ground to a dusty halt a short distance away from them. The lead truck was full of military policemen, MP's or meat pies as they were derisively referred to by most of the army.

They debussed and formed a skirmish line in front of the unarmed paratroopers. 'Prew, check those idiots are all armed with Uzi's,' observed Kevin loudly. Kevin's eyes travelled across the line of MP's noting that they were all fully armed.

'This is a balls-up,' remarked Andy in return.

The back flap of the second truck was dropped and out climbed about fifteen bandaged and crippled infantrymen. Some were on crutches, some wore slings and others were carrying an assortment of bandages and patches attached to various parts of their bodies. A meat pie officer stepped forward and raised a megaphone to his face.

'Those of you who were involved in the fight with these men the night before last, step forward!' he ordered.

No one budged.

'I repeat, step forward!'

No movement!'

'If the culprits do not own up then we will be forced to detain all of you!' This time his voice had become a little less confident.

Pete stepped forward, and immediately every last one of them stepped forward as well. Pete stepped forward again, the rest followed. Kevin watched with some amusement as the meat pies began to look uncomfortable.

The meat pie officer looked across at Mark and the other officers, almost as if he was asking for help. Kevin saw one of them simply shrug a clear message to the meat pies,

'You're on your own, my mate!'

Meat pie lifted the megaphone and then stopped the movement halfway, before lowering slowly to his side.

Pete had stepped forward again, and the rest did the same, as one man.

The skirmish line cracked and with meat pie shouting incoherent commands, the whole lot of them got back onto their trucks and left to the sound of laughing parabats.

'Check here comes Tomorrow again,' someone chirped at roll call the next morning.

Oddly Tomorrow had a happy look on his face.

'Fuckin hell, check he's got a smile on his dial,' someone chirped as he strode up to them.

'Go fetch your kit, guys, we're leaving this cunt farm,' he said, grinning from ear to ear.

'Hey corporal, can I give you a hug?' Pete chirped as he slapped Lappies hard on his back.

'Tomorrow's grin widened to the extent that if it weren't for his ears, the top of his head would have been cut off. It was then that Kevin had a sense of what pressure the poor bloke had been under, being the bearer of shitty news each day.

He felt sorry for him … well just a little bit!

There was a collective shout of joy at the news as the men left to fetch their kit.

Kevin looked for Andy, he was gone. His kit was gone and the short shit was nowhere to be seen. Little did Kevin realise that he would only see Andy years later. Ever the operator, he had convinced the loading crew of a "Flossie" to allow him aboard for a direct flight to Bloemfontein!

Soon they found themselves at a railway station. A troop train was standing there waiting next to the platform, a large diesel locomotive its powerful engine throbbing at the head of it.

Kevin wanted to cry at the sound of it. 'I think I'm going to hug that fucking loco,' he said, 'it's taking us home!'

They were channelled through a gate and onto the station platform. Kevin noted with mild concern that both edges of the platform were lined with armed meat pies. There was nowhere to go so they simply had no choice but to stand there.

'Empty your kit out onto the ground!' commanded an officer and they had to oblige.

Kevin watched in a cold rage as the meat pies went through their kit, all he could think of was his diamond, stashed away he hoped beyond their reach. All he had apart from that was an AK bayonet, nicely strapped to his inner thigh.

He felt anger at the disrespect the Minister of Defence had shown them and now this further insult to injury made his blood boil.

They didn't find much, just petty stuff. They boys were far too clever for them. Kevin heard muttering, loud enough so that the men going through their kit could just hear them. 'So, have you found anything, fuck-face?'

'Very brave standing there with your Uzi, put it down let's see what you're made of, c'mon, be a big boy!'

There was no reaction none of the MP's took the bait and Kevin in a strange way was relieved. He had had enough of all of this shit! When they were finished and without a word, the meat pies left the station; leaving them to clean up the mess.

The train pulled out of the station and they watched the rows of tents disappeared along the tracks into the distance.

That night Kevin discovered that the diamond was missing.

The permanent force members at the battalion were all smiles. The guys had arrived from Angola and had acquitted themselves well.

The battalion received them with open arms and the respect shown was a revelation. From zeros to heroes and Kevin couldn't help thinking of the irony of it all.

There was a new commandant, Commandant Hills who gave them a stirring welcome, informing them that they had done their unit proud. He pointed out, that miraculously none of them had been killed with only a few wounded and that, that was testimony to the excellent training that they had received; and to the fact that they were excellent soldiers!

 Kevin stood there and somewhat reluctantly, felt proud.

Later on Kevin reminded them, 'Hey, guys, do you remember Commandant Olkers telling us what a bunch of useless fucks we were before we left for the border?

From zeros to heroes hey, guys, from zeros to fucking heroes!'

There was a last ditch attempt at convincing them to stay on and join the army permanently, but with the exception of one man none of them did. That one man rose to become the RSM of Parachute Battalion, his name is SS Baard.

And so they were set loose into the wide and wonderful world with some money and a train ticket which Kevin crumpled up and thrust into his pocket as he stood next to the freeway with his thumb out, hitching a ride back home.

No debriefing, no analysis of their states of mind. No help for those of them who had festering demons creeping around in their brains.

'Here's you train ticket soldier, thank you and now you can fuck off!'

Epilogue

I got home to Kilprivier in the Transvaal around March 1976, the exact date I cannot remember. I remember getting home to the stunned look on my mother's face, carrying my *ballsak* and striding into the yard with it on my shoulder, it felt as light as a feather. I had left home as a boy, the last time they had seen me was while I was still in training whenever I went home on the odd weekend pass.

Now I was told that I looked different.

I had changed and everyone commented on my eyes, they were different. My mom told me that they made her afraid.

My mom asked me to pick my sister and brother up after school and they were happy to see me, yet on the drive home they became strangely reserved. Was I no longer their brother?

My father and I got on for exactly one week, before he threatened to kick my head in. He challenged me to a fight outside which I declined and I laughed at him in mockery which I regret to this day.

My mother called me aside and reprimanded me like she would a child.

I was not a child, so very far from it.

My brother was a big, strong guy and one afternoon after he came back from school, we went fishing down at the river below our house. I wore jeans tucked into my boots, with an AK bayonet stuck into the outside of my right boot.

Weird that I had to dress like that!

We had been fishing for about an hour and my brother had crossed the rapids and was fishing on the opposite bank, when I heard a noise in the bushes. Placing my fishing rod on the ground I went to investigate.

I found a black woman lying on the ground, she was semi naked and her clothes were in tatters. A black man was standing over her. He was holding both her wrists and pulling her arms tightly towards him while he had his foot on her throat.

She was making rasping sounds while he was busy throttling her. I came in from behind him and hit him hard with the edge of my hand, connecting him on the neck below his right ear. As he started to collapse I caught him around the neck with my left arm, pulled the bayonet out of my boot and as I brought it up to his throat my brother tackled me.

He had crossed the river and caught me just in time and when I realised what I had almost done, I started to shake.

The next morning I left home and hitchhiked down to Durban.

It was the school holidays and my brother came down with me. I remember us getting a lift with a maniac who drove like a demon, getting us down to Durban in record time. He took stupid risks and I was exhilarated, whooping loudly as if he and I had a death wish.

I loved it, my brother was scared shitless and perhaps this experience changed him? He would later become a hell-bent, motorbike-thrashing Joburg Hell's Angel.

Arriving on the outskirts of Durban, we walked all the way through the city to the beachfront. It was a long walk and my brother struggled to keep up. I had to slow down every so often so that he could keep up in spite of him being a strong, fit boy.

He was certainly no wimp! I just walked and walked, a super fit man, and I could have walked forever. After all I had covered hundreds of kilometres in Angola on foot!

I was a paratrooper and no mean soldier!

We visited old friends, staying with different people and each time I could see that they were uncomfortable. They loved my brother but all of them, without exception, were reserved with me, distant, as if they did not trust this strange man or were perhaps afraid of him?

Two weeks later I put my brother on the train to Durban with a connecting ticket back to Johannesburg station, said goodbye and hitchhiked to Blythdale Beach.

For the next two months I lived off the sea, between the Umvoti and Tugela River mouths; every now and again going to the nearest town if I needed anything.

I had money in the bank and I used some of it. I would eat mussels, shellfish and catch fish, the little black-tail fish were easy to catch and they became my staple diet. Every now and again I got lucky with the odd rock cod.

The roar of the sea, the salt air in my lungs, watching the sand crabs running up and down following the waves washing up on the beach as if playing chicken; watching the Umvoti River pour into the Indian Ocean, spreading a brown stain into the blue sea; sitting at night with a small fire burning, watching the phosphorous in the waves.

All these things were medicine for the mind, cleansing me from within, pushing the demons back into a little dark corner of my mind. I would learn later that they would always be there, drooling and skulking in a small spot of my mind, like a dark cloud as dense as a black hole; just sitting there.

I know that they will always be there, waiting ...

And suddenly, one morning I woke up in a Natal drizzle, the sand in every nook and cranny of my body and I decided that I was ready. I knew that I was ready to move on.

It was as simple as that.

I knocked on a door at a house in Gledhow and Mr Dobbin opened it. I had stayed with him, his wife and sons Jimmy and Dennis, as a school boarder for over a year; just two and a half years before.

He looked at me, startled and almost closed the door on me until I told him who I was. His response was, 'Kevin, you have always been the damn sponger!' And then he let me in.

The first thing Mrs Dobbin did was make me shower and clean myself up and they allowed me to stay there for as long as I wanted to.

I will never forget their kindness, both long gone to a better place, they are still gentle on my mind. To this day Jimmy Dobbin and I are the best of mates!

A week later I went home.

It wasn't easy being back, not because of anything bad or wrong about my family. It was just that I didn't fit in. I didn't fit in with anyone or anywhere.

My mother told me later in life how she used to see me through the French doors into my room, lying on my back staring at the ceiling for hours. I bought myself a second-hand Volkswagen Beetle and I used to drive to Hillbrow, spending hours there, sitting on the pavement outside the Fontana Café, eating roast chicken and people-watching; just viewing the thin, fat, tall, pretty and ugly wander past.

I think I was trying to understand them and once again become one of them. Once I went into the German club, a place where Hitler's birthday was celebrated, and almost got into a fight. I left unscathed and after trying different places I discovered the Ambassador Hotel. A band played there most nights, their lead singer had a hunchback and he sang like an angel. He put the lead singer of Uriah Heap to shame, he was that good.

I moved from my room in the house into the servant's room, where I could be alone. I remember writing a Shakespearean verse on my wall with a black marker which became my philosophy for life, for the rest of my life;

> *This above all: to thine own self be true,*
> *and it must follow, as the night the day,*
> *Thou canst not then be false to any man.*

One day my dad called me aside and told me that he had a job for me at the company where he worked. I started working exactly a year after we had first entered Angola,

I had started my next adventure, life!

Appendix

Savannah – Parabats as experienced by Johan Marais

1 Para Bn, A Coy's border journey in Aug '75 to Feb '76

After solid and strenuous training we arrived in Rundu via train towards the latter part of August '75 to relieve Platoon 1 of A coy. I remember clearly that Northern Transvaal was playing Free State in the Currie Cup final - Pierre Spies scored the winning try in the final minute! It was rather relaxed and the Platoon 1 guys, who we were to replace, informed us that not much was happening – "for about 150 km across the border you will be lucky if you encounter any SWAPO".

We did the normal stuff: PT on the runway to get acclimatized, the odd patrol close by around Rundu - basic and boring stuff like this. However, we went on a trip in Southern Angola via Unimogs as SWAPO were apparently spotted. What stands out about these ops is that we never had any contact and that we were extremely hungry and THIRSTY. I can recall that Portuguese soldiers were with us (I think) and I suppose the rookie border element also played its role. We started drinking the drips during the evening and then Des MacGeer shot a magnificent Sable (Swartwitpens) – we all agreed that it was OK as we were starving - we had a feast that evening!

2. Operation Savannah

3. Cela

We worked quite a lot with the Recces at some stage and I particularly did most of these ops with SM FC van Zyl (what a soldier whilst being a true gentleman as well) and Cpl Cecil Eayres (who was an instructor at 1 Para Bn when we were rowers, then went for Recce selection and we met at Cela again). It was a true honour to work with both of them. SM FC did not get enough recognition with all his achievements, not that he would have wanted any of it. May these great soldiers RIP!

But a lot of guys were gatvol and many factors contributed:

1.   The Beatle episode is just an example of how we were treated by some of the brass.
2.   Our clothes and tekkies/vellies were pathetic to say the least.

I can honestly say that we were a tough bunch, but the leadership like Major G felt nothing for us. It was rather a situation where "I will show you bats who is in charge here", forget what is right of wrong, whilst us and the troops on the ground worked well together.

With this in mind, some guys asked me to approach Lt Blaauw to ask him to put pressure on the brass to send us home. He told me that it will never work and those who insist, will be court martialed. Luckily we received orders during that time that we have to withdraw and our leader said to me to inform all and to forget about it.

OP Beatle Map and descriptions

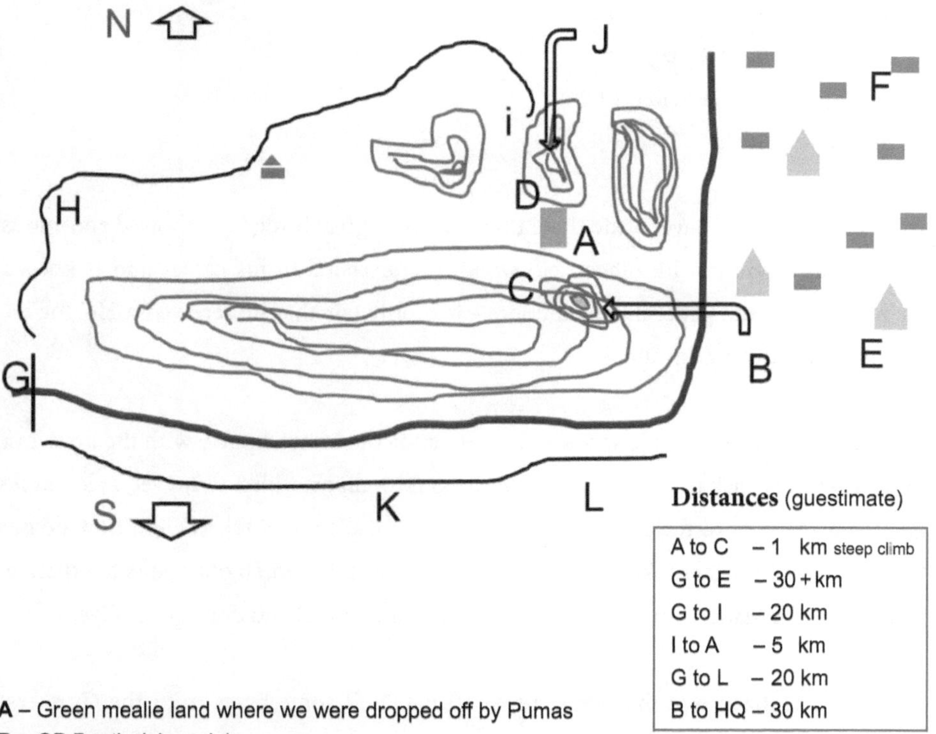

A – Green mealie land where we were dropped off by Pumas

B – OP Beatle (pinnacle)

C – Where Cubans & MPLA dug in for the ambush on our guys

D – Mountains that at least one Puma flew into

E – Cuban and plaaslike bevolking Kraals (and added tents)

F – Red Eyes that were parked into dug outs and fired from there – semi permanent positions

G – Pond where we camped and the river – crossed the river there

H – Road that we followed to evacuate our guys after the ambush
    also grey hut that was shot to pieces (Mike Coppen?)

I – Where convoy stopped and from there we went on foot to get our guys next to the mealie land

J – Place where I almost got killed through the boulders on our way back

K – Road that was used to drop us off in another convoy

L –Place where we were actually dropped off

Leadership

I want to add something about the leadership. In recent FB posts I have seen that many guys were talking about the pathetic PF leaders. I agree partly but it is a massive generalization. My view is that some of the leaders that we worked with were great:

Col Breytenbach (Bruinman)

SM FC van Zyl (Recce)

Cpl/Sgt Cecil Eares (Recce)

And many more

Closer to home I have to add that Lt Blaauw was a great leader and showed enormous maturity as a one pip PF officer. No wonder he excelled in his career and is known for his bravery and general contribution – it is only fair that he received a HC for his achievements during Savannah.

Also, Cpl Aubrey Cronje was always there and could have a party with the boys, but tomorrow all is back to normal and nobody could walk over him. However, at least one guy from the Bats (a fucking Candidate Officer nogal!) was a joke(r) and how he got there was even a bigger joke. This just proves my point that when one wants to criticize, in this case the leadership, be specific about each individual and don't generalize.

What I realized was that we were +- 60 Bats and some brass from the Gunners, Panzers and SAI units treated us like shit towards the end. I agree that we looked like bush pigs, but we had a job to do.

Many more stories to tell about the withdrawal, but more important when we got to Grootfontein and most of our kit were gone. I did not have boots, my private stuff got stolen and most of us got back looking like hooligans.

At a personal level:

I thought long and hard whether I should share the following and decided that I have to:

When I got back home, my father chatted to me shortly after my return and asked me, somehow embarrassed, whether anything happened to me on the 23rd of December. Reason for him asking was that my Mom, a bank manageress, could not get out of bed that morning as she was very ill with a fever etc. She insisted to go to work, but he got a call from the bank early morning asking whether he could come and fetch her as she was unable to drive her car. He brought her home and they made an appointment with the Doctor for later that afternoon. He informed me that he thought she was going to pass out at any moment – she was really in bad shape.

When I told him that I was nearly killed on the 23rd, that was when I walked into the Cuban, he started shaking and said he knew she was somehow in contact with me as by 14h00 her fever broke and she was instantly ok. He took her back to the bank and she completed her day and drove back home all by herself. By the way, we got back to the Pont just after lunch!!

Just something to think about…

Some names, not all, have been changed in this book

Many things are not as they seem: The worst things in life never are.

- Jim Butcher, White Night